68.14469 (10.10.68)

CARL LEIDEN is Associate Professor of Government
in The Middle East Center at The University of Texas.
He has lived and traveled extensively
in the Middle East.

KARL M. SCHMITT, Professor of Government
at The University of Texas,
is the author of several publications, including
Communism in Mexico: A Study in Political Frustration,
and co-author of *Evolution or Chaos:
Dynamics of Latin American Government and Politics.*

THE POLITICS
OF VIOLENCE

Revolution
in the
Modern World

EDITED BY
Carl Leiden AND *Karl M. Schmitt*

Prentice-Hall, Inc. Englewood Cliffs, N.J.

To
Jesse Stuart
and
G. B. S.
&
K. E. B. W. M.

Preface

This volume is not an attempt to break new theoretical ground. It is intended primarily for university students; it offers a summary of the literature on the theory and analysis of revolutionary causation and development. Additionally we have chosen out of our special areas of interest—Latin America and the Middle East—four case studies of twentieth-century revolution and have examined them from the perspectives developed in the earlier chapters.

A very great deal remains to be written about revolution as a political phenomenon. Individual revolutions are difficult to study in detail. Data about them appear only after the passage of many years or not at all. Often the data that we do have about revolutions do not answer the kinds of questions that interest us most as political scientists. At the present time we do not know enough to generalize in other than tentative terms. It is hoped that the readers of this book will remember that this is a tentative effort to view revolutions not as unique events but as processes. There is much that can be learned about the genus revolution; this volume is an attempt to connect theory with practice and to point out some of the promising avenues of research.

The completion of this work was aided by grants from the Institute of Latin American Studies, the Middle East Center, the University Research Institute (all of The University of Texas), and the Relm Foundation. Of course, none of these institutions necessarily endorses the views or conclusions of this work. A number of individuals have contributed, in one way or another, to making it a better book than it otherwise might have been. We are particularly grateful to Richard Adams, David Burks, David Edwards, Elizabeth and Robert Fernea, William Goetzman, Donald Hancock, Murray Havens, Gary Mounce, Charles Parrish, Ramón Ruiz, Philip Stoddard, and William Ritchie, who read various parts of the manuscript and gave us the benefit of their criticism. Ivo and Rosalind Feierabend were generous in sharing some of their research with us. We would also like to thank Kathryn Gunderson, Richard Kateley, and Bruce Mayfield for research assistance. William Livingston has been a colleague who has supported and encouraged this project in innumerable ways, for which we are most appreciative.

We are well aware that errors may remain. It seems appropriate to quote Ibn Khaldun, the fourteenth-century Arab historian who said, "I confess my inability to penetrate so difficult a subject. I wish that men of scholarly competence and wide knowledge would look at the book with a critical, rather than a complacent eye, and silently correct and overlook the mistakes they come upon. The capital of knowledge that an individual scholar has to offer is small. Admission (of one's shortcomings) saves from censure. Kindness from colleagues is hoped for." [1] The authors, of course, assume sole and full responsibility for fact and interpretation in this volume.

Carl Leiden
Karl M. Schmitt

Austin, Texas
1 January 1968

[1] Ibn Khaldun, *The Muqaddimah. An Introduction to History,* trans. Franz Rosenthal (New York: Pantheon Books, Inc., 1958), I, 14.

Contents

PART II
Case Studies in Revolution

CHAPTER 10

The Cuban Revolution 183

CHAPTER 11

Modern Revolutions:
Comparisons and Prospects 205

THE POLITICS
OF VIOLENCE

Revolution
in the
Modern World

I

THE THEORY OF REVOLUTION

1

The Pattern of Revolution

Force and violence are not isolated phenomena to be examined as something extraordinary in the life of a political community. Their omnipresence suggests a vital connection with the contemporary political process. Violence, particularly political violence, represents a disturbance to the political equilibrium of a state, a breakdown of its political system. Although political violence assumes many forms and associations, it is those related to revolution that interest us here. Since 1775, when the War for American Independence began, the world has suffered many hundreds of upheavals. To be sure, most of these have been unimportant to the larger scene, some have been short-lived, and many have been failures; yet the effects and repercussions of the French and Russian revolutions alone have been almost beyond measure. Moreover, violent revolution remains very much a current phenomenon. In the last decade alone there have been numerous social and political convulsions, notably in Cuba (1960), Algeria (1962), and Indonesia (1965).

What Is Revolution?

To the question of what a revolution is, it is not possible to give a conceptually precise answer, acceptable to all who study revolutions. To some it represents a wide range of activities that result in illegal changes in government. To others, revolution refers only to deep-seated social change, reflected invariably by alterations in the political fabric of society, often consummated through violence, and ultimately accompanied by the production of ideology. Such change involves much more than alterations in the political elite, the generation of new slogans, or the attachment to constitutional innovations. But

3

such change can hardly be rationalized outside the political process; it is for this reason that even social revolution is so often described in political terms. Furthermore, while structural social changes tend to undermine the political system, governments are naturally inclined to resist change. Just as naturally the final overt pressures of discontent and frustration generated by such resistance are directed at the political system. So revolution invariably involves the political system, although it is not always restricted to political change.

Given time enough, a resilient political system can often absorb underlying social changes without the necessity of revolution. Apparently the old regime of France was not able to absorb such changes, although, paradoxically, Louis XVI was a reforming monarch. The Russia of Nicholas II was totally incapable of adjusting to the enormous alterations of life and society bubbling up from below. The result in such cases is *violence* or the threat of violence, which for many characterizes all revolutions.

Because violence seems so often to be connected with revolution, we tend to transfer its transient character to revolution itself. We are impressed by the sudden, orgiastic nature of violence and conclude that revolution has the same nature. Thus we think of the French Revolution as somehow being centered around the events of July 1789, when the Bastille was stormed. Yet revolution is not just the abrupt, sudden violent upheaval of a society; it can, like the French Revolution, run its course over many years. An obvious modern example is the Chinese Revolution.

Whatever it is, revolution is certainly change and conflict. Students of revolutions, however, disagree fundamentally about the nature of the changes and conflicts that can properly be dubbed *revolution*. It is possible to approach the problem of definition of revolution by an examination of its historical development. Sigmund Neumann points out that the term was used originally to describe the rotation of celestial bodies following natural, inexorable laws.[1] Hannah Arendt in a similar context says that revolution implied irresistible change, but change that was lawful, and not new, not violent. During the Renaissance the word came to mean the interference of superhuman, uncontrollable forces in world events. Only in the seventeenth century was it finally used as a political term. As a political term, revolution was at first "reactionary," that is, it referred to a revolving return to some pre-established point, and by implication to some preordained order. The restoration of the English monarchy in 1660 was a revolution, the

---

[1] Sigmund Neumann, "The International Civil War," *World Politics*, Vol. 1 (1949), pp. 335-336.

upheavals of the 1640's, a rebellion.[2] Neumann points out that the
term took on new meaning in the eighteenth century in the writings
of such men as Condorcet. Here the "revolutionary" romantic hero
appears, the individual whose actions can alter the course of history.[3]
Machiavelli in an earlier age had thought of change as renewal or
renovation. His idea of revolt and rebellion contained no implications
of liberation or freedom so common to revolutionary ideology of the
eighteenth and nineteenth centuries. Arendt argues: "Only where this
pathos of novelty is present and where novelty is connected with the
idea of freedom are we entitled to speak of revolution."[4] She further
insists that revolutions are more than successful insurrections, that not
every coup is a revolution, and that a revolution is not present in
every civil war. Both Neumann and Arendt work the concept of social
change into modern revolutions. The former, particularly, emphasizes
the social factor, regarding revolution as a sweeping, fundamental
change not only in political organization, but also in the social structure, economic property control, and the predominant myth of the
social order. Unlike Arendt, however, Neumann does not insist that
freedom constitute a necessary ingredient in revolution. In fact, he
sees modern revolution as basically totalitarian, with discipline as the
password and no place for the individual hero or the romantic deed.

Other scholars understand revolution simply as "the acceptance of
violence in order to bring about change,"[5] or as "the wide range of
circumstances—from mere threats of force to major civil wars—in
which illegitimate violence is employed within a country to effect political change."[6] Alfred Meyer defines revolution in terms of three distinct processes: the destruction of an *ancien régime*, a period of chaotic
disorder, and the creation of a new order or political system.[7] It has
also been defined simply as "an extra-legal method of replacing one
government by another. . . ."[8] By some definitions revolution does
not necessarily imply violent convulsion of society or of the state. In

[2] Hannah Arendt, *On Revolution* (New York: The Viking Press, Inc., 1963), pp. 35-36.
[3] Neumann, *op. cit.*, p. 336.
[4] Arendt, *op. cit.*, p. 27.
[5] Chalmers Johnson, *Revolution and the Social System,* Hoover Institution Studies, No. 3 (Stanford: Hoover Institution, 1964), p. 10.
[6] Cyril E. Black, "Revolution, Modernization, and Communism," in Cyril E.
Black and Thomas P. Thornton (eds.), *Communism and Revolution: The Strategic
Uses of Political Violence* (Princeton: Princeton University Press, 1964), p. 4.
[7] Alfred G. Meyer, "The Functions of Ideology in the Soviet Political System,"
Soviet Studies, Vol. 17 (1966), p. 275.
[8] R. A. Humphreys, "Latin America: The Caudillo Tradition," in Michael
Howard (ed.), *Soldiers and Governments: Nine Studies in Civil-Military Rela-
tions* (Bloomington: Indiana University Press, 1959), p. 153.

fact, the term is used quite commonly today to denote industrial, managerial, colonial, cultural, scientific, technological, and other kinds of changes that constitute not sudden, violent upheavals but rather long-range processes with far-reaching results. The term is also applied at times to denote an evolutionary but fundamental shift in the political system.[9] In general, however, the term is used to describe the political change that occurs because of the presence of or at least a threat of force or violence.

One of the simplest models is that of Peter Amann.[10] Amann defines revolution as "a breakdown, momentary or prolonged, of the state's monopoly of power, usually accompanied by a lessening of the habit of obedience." He emphasizes the *power* relationship—"revolution prevails when the state's monopoly of power is effectively challenged and persists until a monopoly of power is re-established"[11]—but he is not unaware of the importance of what he calls the "habit of obedience" that supports power. In this he does not depart very fundamentally from Charles Ellwood's argument, a half century ago, that "revolutions are disturbances in the social order due to the sudden breakdown of social habits under conditions which make difficult the reconstruction of those habits. . . ."[12] By defining revolution in this way, Amann eliminates certain plaguing problems, notably the task of distinguishing between revolution and *coup d'état*. The chief value of the scheme, other than the ease of identifying the existence of revolution, which becomes very commonplace in his terminology, lies in its shift of "attention from the study of one power monopoly, the sovereign state, to two or more competing power blocs."[13] To Amann, revolution is simply a breakdown of the "habit of obedience" resulting in a "dispersal of power." What then becomes important is the study of these power fragments.

In recent years the Princeton University Center of International Studies has carried on research relating to revolution. Those involved have preferred to use the term *internal war* by which they mean "attempts to change by violence, or threat of violence, a government's policies, rulers, or organization."[14] One advantage of this terminological innovation is that there is less need to distinguish between

[9] Neumann, *op. cit.*, pp. 333-334, n. 1.

[10] Peter Amann, "Revolution: A Redefinition," *Political Science Quarterly,* Vol. 77 (1962), pp. 36-53.

[11] *Ibid.*, pp. 38-39.

[12] Charles A. Ellwood, "A Psychological Theory of Revolutions," *The American Journal of Sociology,* Vol. 11 (1905-1906), p. 51.

[13] Amann, *op. cit.*, p. 42.

[14] Harry Eckstein (ed.), *Internal War* (New York; The Free Press, 1964), p. 1., n.

revolution and counterrevolution; indeed, many different types of revolution tend to blend homogeneously into an internal war, subject to analysis. There is considerable emphasis given to violence in this analytical scheme; and as one observer has critically commented, it views "all forms of violent conflict . . . [as] anomalies, to be treated alike as pathological disorders of a similar species." [15]

More elaborately, Feliks Gross distinguishes between two kinds of forced change in government: the transfer of political power from "above" constituting a coup, and the fundamental social changes carried out from "below" that constitute social revolution. He points out that political revolutions are often but not always social, but that all social revolutions are political. He sees the peasant revolutions of the past, which, without ideology or organization, were easily suppressed, as variants of social revolutions, and civil wars as variants of either type.[16]

James Rosenau identifies three types of civil strife (or revolution). "Personnel" conflicts he defines as struggles over current roles in the existing structures with no aspirations to change major policies or the structure of society. Latin American *coups d'état* fall into this category. "Authority" wars are conflicts over the arrangement as well as over the occupancy of the roles in the political structure and, as in personnel conflicts, with no aspirations to change major policies or the structure of society. Colonial struggles for independence or conflicts to replace authoritarian governments with more representative forms furnish examples of "authority" wars. Finally, "structural" strife includes not only conflict over personnel and the structure of political authority, but also over major policies and the structure of society itself. Communist insurrections, agrarian revolts, and urban-based mass uprisings characterize this third form of civil strife, or "social revolution," as Gross would call it.[17]

Of those who define "revolution" in broad terms, Chalmers Johnson offers the most elaborate scheme of approach. He uses four criteria for distinguishing types of revolution: (1) the targets of revolution, whether the regime, the form of government, or the community; (2) the identity of the revolutionaries, whether elites, masses, or elite-led masses; (3) goals or ideology; and (4) timing, whether spontaneous

[15] Lawrence Stone, "Theories of Revolution," *World Politics*, Vol. 18 (1966), p. 161.

[16] Feliks Gross, *The Seizure of Political Power in a Century of Revolutions* (New York: The Philosophical Library, 1958), pp. xx-xxi, 39, 51.

[17] James N. Rosenau, "Internal War as an International Event," in James N. Rosenau (ed.), *International Aspects of Civil Strife* (Princeton: Princeton University Press, 1964), pp. 63-64.

or calculated. On the basis of these criteria, Johnson identifies six types of revolution: (1) the Jacquerie (the mass peasant uprising); (2) the Millenarian Rebellion (the Jacquerie plus charismatic leadership); (3) the Anarchistic Rebellion (the attempt to restore an already shattered society as in the Vendée Rebellion, 1793-1796); (4) the Jacobin-Communist Revolution (spontaneous social revolution as in France or Russia); (5) the Conspiratorial *Coup d'État;* and (6) the Militarized Mass Insurrection (calculated nationalist and social revolution utilizing guerrilla warfare as in China 1937-1949, Algeria 1954-1962, and North Vietnam, 1945-1954).[18]

There are many, however, who argue that revolution necessarily embodies more than violent attacks on some part or parts of the social structure, that is, it is something deep seated and relatively permanent. "The real revolution," Dale Yoder maintains, "is the change in the social attitudes and values basic to the traditional institutional order." [19] Rex Hopper says that revolutionary change is "that kind of social change which occurs when the basic institutional (i.e., legally enforced) values of a social order are rejected and new values accepted." [20] Godfrey Elton, too, limits the use of the term "revolution" to broad and sweeping changes in society. In fact, he denies the distinction between political and social revolution, holding that all revolutions are social revolutions. "But at the end of the 18th century," he admits, "more than ever before or since men believed that social evils could be healed by political formulae." He sees the French Revolution not as encompassing all the events between 1789 and 1814 but as "the French people's deep and instinctive sense of the need of certain changes, and their efforts, beneath certain easily distinguishable distractions, to accomplish them." [21] Along the same line of thought, William Stokes insists that up to 1952 Latin America had experienced only one revolution, that in Mexico in 1910. And he holds this position because he defines revolution as "fundamental change in the nature of the state, the functions of government, the principles of economic production and distribution, the relationship of the social classes, particularly as regards the control of government. . . ." In addition to "real" revolutions and coups, Stokes lists two other forms of violent action used in Latin America to obtain or to retain power:

[18] Johnson, *op. cit.,* pp. 27-28.

[19] Dale Yoder, "Current Definitions of Revolution," *The American Journal of Sociology,* Vol. 32 (1926), p. 441.

[20] Rex O. Hopper, "The Revolutionary Process: A Frame of Reference for the Study of Revolutionary Movements," *Social Forces,* Vol. 28 (1950), p. 271.

[21] Godfrey Elton, *The Revolutionary Idea in France, 1789-1871* (New York: Longmans, Green & Co., Inc., 1923), pp. iv, 4.

the barracks revolt and *machetismo* (the mobilization of violence by a local strong man or charismatic leader).[22]

We shall attempt no new definition of revolution in this work. We are content to leave the question open-ended. For our purposes the simple language of Peter Calvert seems adequate: Revolutions are "forcible interventions, either to replace governments, or to change the processes of government." [23]

The Revolutionary Tradition

"The modern concept of revolution . . ." states Hannah Arendt, "was unknown prior to the two great revolutions at the end of the eighteenth century." [24] Yet Dennis Brogan assures us that as "a concept, as a reality, revolution is one of the oldest political institutions of our western civilization." [25] Arendt is, of course, concerned with the struggle for freedom, which she is convinced is *modern;* Brogan simply notes that something, both violent and exceptional, temptingly termed *revolution,* has occurred for a very long time. It should not be astonishing that in the long sweep of world history there have been many social and political upheavals, many usurpations of power, many violent dynastic alterations, and many anomic and chaotic dislocations of political power.

If one approaches the study of revolutions by examining the degree to which they have influenced or have been related to one another, it becomes quickly evident that most of those in earlier times are isolated from one another and from those that followed. From the eighteenth century on they seem to cluster together in the sense of participating in a kindred revolutionary spirit (or tradition) to which they all have contributed. Since then change and reform have been in the wind, given acceleration by the impact of modern technology, of urban concentration, and of increased literacy. People are now much more aware of what others have and what they do not have. They find it easier to communicate their discontent to one another and to organize

[22] William S. Stokes, "Violence as a Power Factor in Latin American Politics," *The Western Political Quarterly,* Vol. 5 (1952), pp. 445, 447, 451, 456, 461. He also postulates four methods of indirect action, including elections, that are outwardly peaceful but rest on a foundation of force.

[23] Peter A. R. Calvert, "Revolution: The Politics of Violence," *Political Studies,* Vol. 15 (1967), p. 1.

[24] Arendt, *op. cit.,* p. 21.

[25] Dennis Brogan, *The Price of Revolution* (New York: Harper & Row, Publishers, 1951), p. 1.

and articulate their protests. The impact of all that we term modern—the technology, the knowledge, the spirit of freedom perhaps—has facilitated revolution.

It is interesting to trace the threads of this revolutionary spirit or tradition in time. No one can really deny that the English upheavals in 1649 and 1688 were related to the modern revolutionary movement, although they preceded by a century the revolutionary surge that interests us most. The Glorious Revolution (1688) had its articulate philosopher as well, John Locke. In his defense of that revolution he produced one of the masterpieces in the history of political thought, his *Two Treatises of Government*, published in 1690. He attacked the divine right of kings and defended natural rights; his was the phrase, "lives, liberties, and . . . property," which became in Thomas Jefferson's paraphrase, "life, liberty and the pursuit of happiness." Locke and the English system impressed imaginative people everywhere, on the continent and in America, and it is hardly surprising that when Americans had to justify their revolution in 1775, they leaned heavily on Locke and his contemporaries.

The French also knew Locke, but they had as well the eloquent agitations of Voltaire and not least of all the catalytic literature of Jean-Jacques Rousseau. Louis XVI, not nearly as ignorant and stupid as popular history has made him out to be, was fascinated throughout his life with the story of Charles I, whose fate he ultimately shared. (We do not know whether the last of the Romanovs, Nicholas II, spent much time, in captivity in Ekaterinburg, thinking of either Charles I or Louis XVI. But Lenin did! He said of the execution of Nicholas, "In England and France they executed their kings several centuries ago; it was only we who were late with our tsar. . . .") [26]

The American Revolution had little direct effect or influence on other revolutions; yet it ushered in the age of revolution. The French crown heavily committed itself to the aid of the American colonies in their struggle with England, with acute financial embarrassment the result. Undoubtedly this contributed to revolutionary discontent in France. France was, moreover, captivated by American "revolutionaries," notably Benjamin Franklin and Thomas Jefferson, by the "philosopher," Tom Paine, and by her own contribution to the American cause, Lafayette. Yet for all this captivation the influence of the American Revolution on the later revolutions in Europe was negligible.

Rather it was the French Revolution that shattered forever the political stability of Europe. It is true that the French Revolution was

[26] V. I. Lenin, *Collected Works* (Moscow: Progress Publishers, 1965), Vol. 28, pp. 172-173.

a traumatic experience, which the American Revolution was not. Some have even argued that the American Revolution was no revolution at all because it did not seriously disrupt the fabric of society; it made no radical alterations in the ruling elite; it instituted no terror and produced no charisma.

In 1789 France was one of the most powerful countries in the world and her monarchy was stable and respected. Her nobility was a burden but not desperately so; her taxes were heavy, yet were less crushing than in much of the rest of Europe; her armies had not been defeated anywhere, and there was no national disgrace to bear. Yet it was in powerful, sophisticated France that the most terrible revolution of the (then) modern world was unloosed. If revolution could happen in France, then there was hardly a cranny or crevice of Europe that might not bear the revolutionary burden. The French facilitated this infection. They produced the famous Declaration of the Rights of Man (and its supplementary ideology), which infested the minds of men everywhere; French armies, at first defending *la patrie* and then carrying victory in virtually every direction, continued to disseminate the revolutionary message.

We need note only briefly how widespread the recipients of this message were. There was the Belgian Revolution (1789) against the Austrians, and the Dutch rebellion against William of Orange in 1794. There was the Polish revolution, which finally collapsed under the weight of the Russians in 1794. Eastern Europe in general was aflame, at least ideologically; where violence was absent, incipient conspiracy was feared. This was especially true in Austria, Hungary, and in Russia herself, where Catherine the Great seemed obsessed with the danger of revolution.

> In the spring of 1792 St. Petersburg was gripped by the fear of an international revolutionary plot against all nobility and all monarchs, a plot in which Jacobins, Freemasons, Martinists, and devotees of occult societies everywhere were said to be involved, and of which the recent deaths of Gustavus III [in Sweden] and Leopold II [of Austria], the continuing revolution in Poland, and the French declaration of war upon Austria were supposed to be evidence. It was reported also that a Frenchman was heading for St. Petersburg with designs on the "health" of the empress.[27]

Revolution splashed among the political fragments of Italy, pushed across the Alps into Switzerland, confounded the Germans, and misled the Irish in 1798 into unfortunate adventures. Across the seas it pro-

---

[27] R. R. Palmer, *The Age of the Democratic Revolution: The Struggle* (Princeton: Princeton University Press, 1964), p. 145.

12   The Theory of Revolution

duced Citizen Genet and, as R. R. Palmer has suggested, contributed
to the two-party system in America.[28] And, in remote South Africa,
Dutch farmers, infuriated by Bantu cattle raiding and the impotence
of their government, rebelled against the Dutch East India Company
in 1795. In doing so they "donned tricolor cockades similar to those
worn by the French Revolutionary armies . . . [and] talked of
Jacobinism and 'Liberty, Equality, Fraternity'. . . ."[29]

The revolutionary spirit gained momentum in the early nineteenth
century. Within a handful of years after Napoleon's fall, there were
revolutions in Spain (1820) and Greece (1821). The events in Europe
inspired and provoked revolution in Latin America—led by such men
as Simón Bolívar and José de San Martín—while those in Greece
presaged the destruction of the Turkish empire in Europe, the final
consummation of which took nearly a century. In December 1825—
hence "The Decembrists"—a coup was attempted against the new
Tsar Nicholas I; it proved abortive but added an important element
to the Russian revolutionary tradition.

Charles X was overthrown in France in 1830; the same year saw the
Belgians achieve a constitution along with national independence.
Much of Europe responded to the revolutionary periodicity, which
had been given its impetus by the events of 1789. And in England the
reforms effected by the great Reform Act of 1832 anticipated some of
the revolutionary changes in Europe. In Latin America, hardly had
independence been won when strife began between Liberals and Conservatives, reflecting to some degree the ideological conflicts of Europe.
And then 1848!

Almost simultaneously revolution broke out and (temporarily) won in
France, the whole of Italy, the German States, most of the Hapsburg
Empire and Switzerland (1847). In a less acute form the unrest also
affected Spain, Denmark and Rumania, in a sporadic form Ireland,
Greece and Britain. There has never been anything closer to the world-
revolution of which the insurrectionaries of the period dreamed than
this spontaneous and general conflagration. . . . What had been in
1789 the rising of a single nation was now, it seemed, "the springtime
of peoples" of an entire continent.[30]

But the flood of revolutions did not end in 1848. The British suffered
the Indian Mutiny in 1857, and at home forestalled the revolutionary

[28] Ibid.
[29] Donald L. Wiedner, A History of Africa South of the Sahara (New York:
Vintage Books, 1962), p. 126.
[30] E. J. Hobsbawm, The Age of Revolution, 1789-1848 (Cleveland: The World
Publishing Company, 1962), p. 112.

spirit with the Reform Act of 1867. There was the Sudanese Mahdist rebellion in the 1880's involving General Gordon; it was to be put down only by General Kitchener in 1898. The Boer War began in September 1899, but it is better to view it as a revolution against British rule. The American Civil War was also a revolution in many ways—much more so indeed in its effects than was the revolution declared in 1776. Shortly after its end the Mexicans under Juárez succeeded in overthrowing the emperor Maximilian and establishing a "liberal regime." The Chinese Taiping rebellion (1848-1865) failed in spite of bloodshed and travail. In 1875-1876 a bloodless revolt in Turkey established the first period of Ottoman constitutionalism; it was to be short-lived. In 1867, a reforming Japanese nobility overthrew the Shogunate, exalted the emperor as a symbol of nationalism, and set the country on the road toward a modern, industrial state; these transitional alterations in Japan came to be called the Meiji Revolution. In France the Second Republic slipped into the Second Empire of Louis Napoleon, which collapsed in 1870. From the debris was born the Third Republic but only after much revolutionary agony, including the life and death of the famous Paris Commune.

The first decade of the twentieth century was filled with revolution and revolutionaries. There was the Russian Revolution of 1905; three years later Ottoman rule was altered by the rising of the Young Turks; the same years saw revolution in Iran. In Mexico, 1910 was the year of what was to become a major revolution; in this same year the monarchy was overthrown in Portugal. In China Sun Yat-sen was named provisional president of the republic in 1911.

The First World War produced revolutions in its wake, of which the Russian Revolution in 1917 was merely the most successful and spectacular. The Arabs "revolted" in 1916; the Afghans won their "independence" in 1919. A plethora of new states emerged in central and eastern Europe as a result of the collapse of the German, Austrian, and Russian empires. By 1922 the Fascists (and Mussolini) had marched on Rome, and Kemal Atatürk had pushed the burgeoning Turkish revolution into high gear. Hitler tried his *Putsch* in Munich in 1923 but it failed. In the same year General Miguel Primo de Rivera established his dictatorship in Spain; the king himself fell and the republic was proclaimed in 1931. Five years later the Spanish Civil War had begun. Latin America continued to generate a rash of palace revolutions, *coups d'état,* and alterations in its power structures.

Amid such events the Second World War began. War and revolution are inextricably entwined; many political systems could not survive this second round of international violence in the twentieth century. Colonialism was *passé* and increasing numbers of territories and peoples sought and found their way to independence. Indonesia, India, Burma, Israel, and Syria, among others, won their independence at the close of the war; a decade later literally all of French Africa and the better part of British Africa had become independent. It is not appropriate to speak of all these events as revolutionary—the Ivory Coast achieved her independence in 1960 quite peacefully, but Algeria was forced to struggle for hers—but they are all almost certainly the products of the revolutionary tradition.

Revolution is endemic in the modern world, and there is by now a large body of revolutionary precedent and example, and of revolutionary need that continues to move people to action.

The Classic Examples of Revolution

Both the French and Russian revolutions represented fundamental alterations in social, political, and economic structures. Both revolutions presaged the spread of revolutionary propaganda and the revolutionary spirit beyond their frontiers. Both revolutions were viewed with horror by their contemporaries, who sought to nullify their ends even by war. Both events were rich in revolutionary characteristics; both offered a mass of comparative detail, undeveloped or missing in many other revolutions. Together they represent a possible model of revolution.

In both France and Russia there was an *ancien régime*. The monarchy was absolutist in both countries, but it no longer possessed much strength. The court was the center of all things, and about the monarch there thronged the large mass of political aspirants and hangers-on, almost all of whom came from the privileged classes. The nobility, numerous as they were, monopolized privilege but neither wealth nor power. Both monarchs were weak individuals, easily led by others, and Nicholas added to this, it seems, simple-mindedness. Both had strong-willed wives, who were not loved by their subjects, and who played significant roles in the collapse of their regimes.

Although the truth of the matter is hardly so simple, it is customary to say that France was brought to her revolution by bankruptcy; Louis XVI had no choice but to call together the almost forgotten Estates-General, which had not met for 174 years, to resolve his financial crisis. Revolution was facilitated in Russia by the disaster of the First World War.

And in both France and Russia a critical moment came when troops refused to support their monarch; for Louis XVI on July 15, 1789— the Bastille had fallen the day before—when the unreliability of his

troops forced him to dismiss them and to abandon Paris to the popular
mob; for Nicholas, the moment might well have been March 9, 1917,
when the Cossacks refused to break up the revolutionary throngs.
"The collapse of the Romanov autocracy in March 1917 was one of
the most leaderless, spontaneous, anonymous revolutions of all time." [31]
Both Louis XVI and Nicholas II responded weakly to the forces confronting them. Both abdicated, both were arrested, and both were
executed.

Power quickly fled to those who could hold it. In France this meant
the Convention, and in the Convention final power was fought over by
the Girondins and the Jacobins (the Mountain); and after the victory
of the Mountain, the struggle was continued by cliques within itself.
In 1793 the Convention abdicated its powers to the Committee of
Public Safety, which was eventually dominated by Robespierre.

In Russia the March Revolution had caught many by surprise—of
the ultimate Bolshevik leaders, Lenin was in Geneva, Trotsky in New
York, and Stalin in Siberia—and almost no one wanted the symbols of
authority. Authority without power was taken by a short series of
weak governments, the best known of which was that of Kerensky, and
by October it was possible for the Bolsheviks almost by a *coup de
baguette* to "steal" the revolution, and along with it final power and
authority.

Both revolutions had a terror, in which many thousands of individuals were slaughtered. The French terror was an unplanned,
chaotic thing; but there was more purpose in the terror in Russia—
to frighten the masses of people into returning to habits of obedience.
The decision to murder the Tsar and his family, apparently made by
Lenin, was probably motivated by nothing more than the desire to
demonstrate that the Bolshevik government "meant business."

Robespierre fell on 9 Thermidor (in the revolutionary calendar) in
1794; most revolutions, including the Russian, seem to have their
thermidors. Crane Brinton, in his *The Anatomy of Revolution*, has defined thermidor as "a convalescence from the fever of revolution." [32]
In France, thermidor ushered in a period of drifting, stagnation, and
ultimately reaction, to be ended only with Napoleon's *coup d'état* on
18 Brumaire (1799). Perhaps the inauguration of the New Economic
Policy in 1921 marks thermidor in Russia,[33] ultimately to be stabilized
by Stalin's consolidation of power in the 1930's.

[31] William Henry Chamberlain, *The Russian Revolution, 1917-1921* (New York:
The Macmillan Company, 1957), Vol. 1, p. 73.
[32] Crane Brinton, *The Anatomy of Revolution* (New York: Vintage Books, 1956),
p. 215.
[33] This is Brinton's view (*ibid.*, p. 217).

French revolutionary armies fought everywhere on the continent, defending the revolution and disseminating its ideas. Civil war, with several epicenters, struck Russia in 1918 followed by a reckless revolutionary war in Poland. Strong armies, fed with successes, spawn their "men on horseback." Thus Napoleon in France. In the Soviet Union the military hero was Marshal M. N. Tukhachevskii, who was executed along with seven other generals—the vanguard of many thousands of other officers, similarly liquidated—by Stalin in June 1937. He was charged with treason and shot without trial; his real offense, in Stalin's later words, was Bonapartism.

In both revolutionary France and revolutionary Russia there was an initial frenzied effort to overhaul the whole fabric of society. In France whole classes of people were tormented or exiled, property rights overhauled and wealth redistributed, the church and priests reduced to impotence and for a brief moment a new Supreme Deity created. In Russia, virtually nothing was left untouched; land tenure, peasant agriculture, the old orthography, religion, these were but a few of the things that were to be overturned. To justify these changes the ideologues were busy in both France and Russia. Both revolutions spewed up enormous amounts of doctrine and ideology that have proved to be politically infectious in many another atmosphere.

Each of these revolutions had a tremendous effect on world opinion and events. They are remarkable in their similarity and in their tangential impacts. It is difficult not to compare other revolutions with these examples, even to the extent of judging the true character of a revolution by the degree of similarity uncovered. Yet revolution has many facets and takes many forms.

Our probings of the literature have not been exhaustive, but enough to indicate the many ramifications that revolution has thrown up. No really satisfactory analytical framework of revolution has been produced; those we have are of only fragmentary benefit. We will not create an elaborate model of revolution, yet any comparative effort to study revolutions results surely in a "model" of sorts. Our model, which will be quite unsophisticated, consists of nothing more than a compendium of those *aspects* of revolution that we think significant and worthy of special emphasis and study. These will be the perspectives from which revolutions can be most usefully examined. Not all revolutions will possess these (or other) aspects to identical degree; some may not possess one or more of them at all. But data about revolutions can be collected around these aspects as focal points for comparative study.

These aspects are treated in the following chapters of Part I. We will want to know what relation violence bears to revolution and in what other phenomena it may participate. We shall be concerned with the preconditions of revolution and the revolutionary environment. We will want to know, if possible, when revolution begins and, hopefully, when it ends. This suggests that there are stages in revolution. We will want to isolate the leaders and followers of revolution: the participants. Finally, we will be concerned with the role of ideology. In Part II we offer four case studies of modern revolutions. But these revolutions differ widely, and their analysis will support the fact that there is no single model of revolution.

2

Violence, Terror, and the *Coup d'État*

Violence as an Aspect of Revolution

Violence is common to many revolutions because, after all, *changes* are being sought by extralegal means; time and the normal channels of political influence are being short-circuited. To do this requires force or its threat; governments generally, but not always, resist. The resultant clash of forces generates the destruction and loss of life that so many associate with revolution. Violence begets violence; where effort is needed to consummate change, greater effort is generated to counteract it. (Governments, however, can sometimes be toppled by only a little push—as when the Russian Constituent Assembly was dispersed in January 1918 by a sailor who announced that the guard was tired and simply had the lights turned off—and when this happens there is often very little reactive violence.) For this reason, we must examine the role of violence in society, particularly in time of political stress.

As an instrument of political power, as opposed to its private use, violence may be said to fall into three categories. It may arise, though rarely, from "spontaneous" causes, from a chance concatenation of events. It may also develop because the process of law enforcement has broken down. Finally, it may be the deliberate result of organization, either by government or by lesser groups or individuals. It is apparent that violence has wide variability in the world with respect to intensity, duration, spontaneity, the vagaries of law enforcement, and the inclinations of governments to utilize it. In turn this variability is the product of diverse histories, cultures, and political and economic development.

There is a certain modicum of "spontaneous" violence in every

19

society. H. L. Nieburg says: "No system can hope to survive unless it can live with and adjust itself to the multitudinous threats of violence which are the basis of social change." [1] Although specific anomic acts are seldom predictable, the general conditions under which they erupt are well known. They are more likely in an atmosphere of uncertainty and discontent. An immediate context of frustration and disappointment in which the participants are emotionally involved may well set off a paroxysm of violent acts. The existence of the ingredients of violent action—for example, crowds drawn together for other reasons —facilitates the drift to normless action. Individuals have "flash points" at which they react in anger—manifested in different ways—to events that in themselves may be of little significance. Such individual reactions may catalyze a crowd to chaotic behavior. The degree of spontaneity in such behavior may be very high; but to the degree that it is, the activity itself is directionless, irrational, and short-lived. Still, a chain-reaction of influence may serve to prolong its tangible effects. The societal context is also important. General political conditions may deteriorate, and, even where there are traditions of discipline, public order may break down. The chaotic conditions throughout Europe immediately after the First World War are illustrative of the kind of context in which spontaneous violence is apt to occur.

The maintenance of public order everywhere requires the constant intervention of law enforcement agencies; their absence or neutralization even in the well-ordered society is conducive to violence and mob action. The Boston police strike of 1919 is surely an example. Violence and criminal acts that would never have occurred otherwise took place when the likelihood of apprehension and punishment diminished. Moreover, political turmoil makes it even more difficult for the police to perform their functions. The police are usually organized to cope with the criminal activity of a fraction of the population; they hardly can face the opposition of large groups of people, normally nonviolent. Moreover, the police may often have an empathy with the very people who are rioting; they have been known to waver in their loyalties at critical moments. It would be impossible to expect the police to function effectively in the atmosphere of revolutionary Russia in 1917 or in Saigon in 1964-1967.

The contemporary civil rights agitation in the United States aptly demonstrates the consequences of the breakdown of law enforcement. Very seldom has a riot developed that could not have been put down by police officials, in adequate numbers and properly organized. Some-

---

[1] H. L. Nieburg, "The Threat of Violence and Social Change," *The American Political Science Review,* Vol. 56 (1962), p. 873.

times these officials have been hamstrung by the political intervention of others; probably this was the case in Little Rock. In other cases, a clash of authorities—county vs. city, police vs. troops—has produced vacua in which violence could occur with impunity. In still other cases, the police have permitted activity with which they sympathized. Probably few lynchings in the past took place without some connivance with law enforcement officers. Finally, the police are sometimes actively involved in fomenting violence. The alleged participation of county police officials in the killing of three civil rights workers in Neshoba County, Mississippi, in June 1964 is a case in point.

The presence of violence in a community does not of itself mean that revolution becomes necessarily more likely, but it does suggest that revolution, if it does appear, will be accompanied by violence in generous quantities.[2] For example, the United States contains a great deal of criminal and delinquent violence, and certainly there has been violence at the polls. Fortunately our political process has not developed revolutionary pressures, but *if* we are a violent nation, then a revolution here would be violent. This conclusion is not absolute, yet the question it purports to answer is an interesting one: Does the degree of normal violence in a state serve as an indicator of the intensity of revolutionary violence? But then the question of measuring normal violence arises. Is there empirical evidence of large numbers of murders and criminal assaults, especially those with political overtones? Are riots and demonstrations, accompanied by loss of life and property damage, commonplace? Similarly, does the existence of police brutality, the *agent provocateur*, and the use of coercive force to achieve political ends add up to the modicum of normal violence that distinguishes one state from another? There is, after all, a great deal of violence in some areas and very little in others.

When revolution comes about, the degree of violence that will characterize it is only partly to be determined by its participants. Revolutionary leaders will have to determine what means to use in achieving their objectives; the legitimate authorities will have to come up with appropriate means to counteract their efforts. But beyond all these deliberations lies the stochastic qualities of every revolution. Mobs do not deliberate, and the momentary, seemingly trivial, decisions made by any number of individuals in a milieu of chaos can produce the violence and bloodshed that all might otherwise abhor. Perhaps the

---

[2] Ivo and Rosalind Feierabend have recently investigated the relationship between various aggressive behavior patterns and such things as political stability and international tension. See, for example, their article "Aggressive behavior within polities, 1948-1962: a cross-national study," *The Journal of Conflict Resolution*, Vol. 10 (1966), pp. 249-271.

major point to be made here is that where there already exist ingrained habits of violence, the more readily will the revolutionary power struggle splash over into incalculable, ungovernable, and destructive bursts of energy.

Revolution and the *Coup d'État*

There are many who hold that revolution occurs precisely at the moment when the political rulers have been overthrown. The qualities of the act accomplishing this, the suddenness, the violence, the chaos, are those that are most often associated with revolution. Usually, however, this act is termed the *coup d'état*.

A *coup d'état* is an unexpected, forceful substitution of one ruling group for another (or at the least any sudden *successful unconstitutional alteration* in government).[3] Although unexpected, its occurrence is seldom inconceivable. Coups occur, for example, with great frequency in Syria[4]—on the average, annually—or in Argentina,[5] but it is seldom that a successful coup is anticipated at the precise moment of its occurrence. Coups are consummated by the threat or use of force. Yet there need not be violence. Latin America offers many examples of bloodless, "palace revolutions."[6] The Egyptian *coup d'état* of July 22, 1952, involved no violence; neither, for that matter, did the Turkish coup of May 1960. The Bolshevik coup in 1917, the Boumédienne coup in Algeria in 1965, the Ghanaian coup in 1966, the Mobutu coup in the Congo in November 1965, Ayub Khan's coup in Pakistan in 1958, and Reza Khan's coup in Persia in 1921 were all essentially devoid of violence. On the other hand, the Sallal coup in Yemen in 1963 (which turned into civil war), the Iraqi coup in 1958 (and again in 1963), Chiang Kai-shek's coup in China in 1927, the coup that over-

---

[3] "In sum, the *coup d'état* is an unexpected, sudden, decisive, potentially violent, illegal act, dangerous for plotter as well as for intended victim, and needing great skill for execution" (David C. Rapoport, *"Coup d'état:* The View of the Men Firing Pistols," p. 60, in Carl J. Friedrich [ed.], *Revolution* [Nomos VIII] [New York: Atherton Press, 1966]). It is only fair to say that Rapoport considers this definition incomplete. The entire article is valuable.

[4] Carl Leiden, "Political Instability in Syria," *The Southwestern Social Science Quarterly,* Vol. 45 (1965), pp. 353-360.

[5] Some might prefer Venezuela as an historical example. *See* Rapoport, *op. cit.,* p. 73. It is his estimate that Venezuela has endured "eighty illegitimate successions in a century and probably four hundred and eighty unsuccessful attempts."

[6] *See* George I. Blanksten, "Revolutions" and Robert J. Alexander, "The Army in Politics," in Harold Eugene Davis (ed.), *Government and Politics in Latin America* (New York: The Ronald Press Company, 1958) for excellent discussions of revolution in Latin America.

threw Machado in Cuba in 1933, and the Nigerian coup in 1966 were all violent affairs.

Violence, of course, may ensue after the coup has taken place. It may take the form of isolated eliminations and executions or of public trials of whole groups of "traitors." Or it may become a general blood-bath. In other words, it may become *terror*. Benito Mussolini, Kemal Atatürk, Chiang Kai-shek, and Abdul Nasser, among others, contented themselves with sporadic elimination of opponents. Castro indulged in circuslike trials to eliminate hundreds of undesirables; so also did Mao Tse-tung in China, and Abdul Karim Kassem in Iraq. The blood-bath is also of not uncommon occurrence. The destruction of the Paris Commune in 1871, Hitler's destruction of the *Sturmabteilung* in 1934, Stalin's purges of the 1930's, and the massacre of the Communists in Indonesia in 1965-1966 are examples. Moreover, the coup, although successful, may not entirely eliminate other centers of power within the country with continuing violence the result.

A successful coup may actually involve very few people and have few repercussions on the general community. A mere substitution of one army junta or cabal for another, although it results in different leadership and conceivably different domestic or foreign policies, may be viewed with indifference by the general populace. In some states the coup has become almost institutionalized as a means for procuring new leadership. In such cases, it is axiomatic that the nation can hardly be expected to go repeatedly through the traumatic experience of treason trials and bloodbaths.

The *coup d'état* represents the seizure of a state's symbols of au-thority and its mechanisms for coercion, but this seizure does not in itself necessarily lead to social revolution. The successful conspirators in the coup may push on to more profound revolutionary measures; they may become charismatic leaders or inspire military adventures; or they may simply rest on their laurels and succumb ultimately to other conspirators more forceful. Invariably they try to legitimatize their seizure of power and to propagandize their retention of it. This results in the creation of doctrine and perhaps in all sorts of other peripheral political changes. Moreover, it may be expedient to refer to their deeds as revolutionary; the word is used loosely enough to accommodate most of these pretensions. Some argue that a coup must be distinguished from revolution. A coup is normally carried out by a small group of individuals whose deliberations and decisions have been secret and whose organization has been clandestine and con-spiratorial. But revolutions, it is argued, involve the masses. Major social and political change can take place only by committing large numbers of individuals and marshaling their opinions and support.

The modern systemic approach views a political system as the momentary resultant of many divergent forces. Any system, in a sense, is an equilibrium of tensions, but a system in revolutionary travail is likely to have many tensions, stresses, and strains. It would seem natural, therefore, to expect in any political system that there would be no lack of groups (politically aroused and frustrated) eager for governmental and elital alterations. From these would come the attempts at *coup d'état*. But there are at least two important preconditions. First of all, such a group must be prepared to overthrow a government by force rather than by other means. In many states political frustrations rarely produce such extreme commitments; moreover, there are few people in any society willing to take the risks, the opprobrium (which accompanies failure), and the stigma of "treason" that these actions suggest to many. Secondly, any rebellious group requires adequate coercive instruments in order to effect a coup. Without arms—guns, tanks, aircraft—and men skilled to use them, a rebellious group can often do nothing but wallow in its own frustrations. This is far more important today than it was in the past: modern weapons are so much more complicated, sophisticated, and difficult to come by. Surely this is a sufficient reason to explain the frequency of the army's involvement in modern coups.

In theory the *coup d'état*, if it accompanies social revolution at all, can occur at any time in the revolutionary life span. In reality, it more often occurs near the onset of a revolution. Thus the Egyptian revolution began with a coup, but the Bolshevik coup took place months after the beginning of revolutionary turmoil in Russia; in the France of the eighteenth century, there was in effect a series of coups beginning with the Tennis Court Oath (1789), when the Estates-General refused to accept its adjournment by Louis XVI. The Algerian revolution (culminating in independence in 1962) contained no coup at all, the Boumédienne coup being really postindependence and perhaps counterrevolutionary.

If a political system is beset by pressures for change, the coups these pressures produce are likely to become integral parts of a continuing revolution. There are also coups that are more the product of the fragmentation of the elite and the presence within the army of ambitious cliques. Such coups do not presage social change at all and may become, as in Syria, only a repetitive phenomenon.

In *The Conspirators*, Donald J. Goodspeed has made a persuasive case for the possibility of constructing a theory of the *coup d'état*. He suggests a strategy of coups, which must take into consideration "the sympathies of the nation's armed forces, the state of public opinion, and the international situation."[7] Failure to appreciate these "objective conditions" will often mean the failure of the coup. He argues that it is convenient to consider coups in three stages: *preparation, attack,* and *consolidation.* Of these, the first is the most hazardous. But all stages must be put together with tactical skill: the choice of leadership, the timing, the utilization of chance circumstance, the flexibility. Objectives of significance must be chosen—for example, leaders of opposition forces rather than bridges and power plants—if the coup is to be successful. Coups "are resorted to as a desperate remedy for a desperate disease, and in every case their outcome is unpredictable. In unsuccessful coups, even the execution of the rebels is not always enough to bring the episodes to a close, since the cause for which they died is often later victorious, but in a way they did not foresee or intend."[8] Goodspeed argues that this is largely true of coups that succeed as well as of those that fail. The *coup d'état* is a highly unpredictable, hazardous enterprise.

Violence, Revolutions, and the Armed Forces

The armed forces play a key role in any revolutionary movement. The modern instruments of violence and coercion are increasingly sophisticated and are precisely those that armies monopolize. Revolutions can no longer be mounted by sword and shield alone; they demand modern weaponry and organization, the very things that armies can provide. Any study of modern revolution must concern itself with the social role of the armed forces. Although the essential role of the army in revolution is conceded, it is obvious that armies cannot force through to completion every revolution they espouse. Moreover, the view (held by such writers as Gustave Le Bon[9] and Katherine C. Chorley[10]) that no revolution can be consummated without the army's support cannot be substantiated.

The existence of a loyal (and relatively powerful) army is a strong deterrent to armed insurrection. Such an army permits a regime to be more intransigent and unresponsive to the unrest that wells up within

[7] D. J. Goodspeed, *The Conspirators* (London: Macmillan and Co., Ltd., 1962), p. 210.

[8] *Ibid.*, p. 236.

[9] Gustave Le Bon, *The Psychology of Revolution* (New York: G. P. Putnam's Sons, 1913), p. 29.

[10] Katherine C. Chorley, *Armies and the Art of Revolution* (London: Faber & Faber, Ltd., 1943).

society; it may serve to encourage complacency within the ruling
elite. It may facilitate the substitution of coercion for political persuasion. In effect, such an army, while it acts as a deterrent to *coups
d'état,* may intensify the more deeply rooted social and political resentment that underlies revolutionary pressures.

An army can at times successfully combat armed insurgents; it is
hardly effective against the wellsprings of social change or its doctrinal concomitants; indeed, the army is often disaffected by the
propaganda of revolutionaries. An army can hardly combat the conditions that give rise to revolutionary pressures. Should it attempt to
do so the army inserts itself into politics and may establish a military
government. Yet even then there is no guarantee that it will prove to
be more perspicacious in divining the root causes of social unrest than
the civilian government it replaces. Armies can only be directed against
the violence that threatens the regime they support. They are probably
most effective against armed insurgency.

It is necessary to add that the success of guerrilla warfare in
Yugoslavia, China, Vietnam, and Cuba, among other places, seriously
weakens the claim that an army can always *cope* with its internal
enemies. Communist theoreticians continue to argue that a successful
revolutionary movement can be initiated by a very small number of
individuals. Che Guevara, for example, said, "Given suitable operating
terrain, land hunger, enemy injustices, etc., a hard core of thirty to
fifty men is, in my opinion, enough to initiate armed revolution in any
Latin American country." [11] The effective use of violence was demonstrated in both Palestine and Cyprus, where the British left rather
than undertake the military build-up necessary to maintain order;
even more striking is the example of Algeria, where a jerry-built
revolutionary movement succeeded in defeating a large, well-equipped
army.

Neither is the army a monolithic structure, loyal to its leaders and
speaking with but one voice. No army is immune to the forces that
spawn revolution; even the elitist guards, the *Schutzstaffel* of Hitler,
the Cossacks of the Tsar, or the Janissaries of the Ottoman Sultan
succumbed ultimately to the discontent underlying all successful
revolutions. All soldiers, after all, are related to the general population
by a multiplicity of contacts; they are not generically different from
other people; and they have stakes that are affected, along with those
of others, by revolution or its failure.

The army is not a homogeneous instrument, particularly in under-

[11] Che Guevara, *On Guerrilla Warfare* (New York: Frederick A. Praeger, Inc.,
1961), pp. 67-68.

developed areas. Its officers and men, drawn from different segments of the population, may display different attitudes and loyalties. Senior military leaders will usually have substantial stakes in preserving the status quo but this is less so for aspiring junior and middle-grade officers impatient for command and its rewards. These officers are also closer to their men and are much more likely to be accorded loyalty by these men in revolutionary situations. Indeed, most military *coups* are led by middle-grade officers, the critical rank apparently being the lieutenant-colonelcy. (It is often useful for them to have an older figurehead officer in their midst, however.)

Loyalty to a regime corrodes within a heterogeneous army at different rates. Senior officers are often intimately associated with a regime. They are likely to cut loose their moorings only in the face of disaster to the regime or as a result of serious military reverses (not necessarily in war) for which they are being forced to assume responsibility. The younger officer's target of loyalties is different. He is likely to be more idealistic than his senior colleagues; his personal ambitions have yet to run their course; and at any event he finds himself in a greater position of flexibility with respect to his loyalties than do many others. The rank and file are not necessarily blind in their loyalties, but they do have confused loyalty-obedience patterns. They expect to obey their superiors and generally do so; yet in the midst of revolution the common soldier, particularly the conscript, finds family, regional, and private loyalties affecting his behavior. Such soldiers' recompense for loyalty to a regime, personal and yet abstract, is never so immediately calculable as it is for their commanders. In the short-lived coup their loyalty to their officers can usually be counted upon; they may not even know that they are participating in a coup until it has been completed or repelled.

In practice all sorts of unique situations arise respecting the armed forces in revolution. One of the more interesting is illustrated by the role of the Lebanese army in the revolution in 1958. This revolution arose out of complicated issues involving communal politics, the alleged threat of international communism, and interference by other Arab states. Throughout the spring and summer of 1958, when violence first erupted, the army stood aloof. It neither defended the regime nor actively attacked it. The army's position was justified with the argument that the issues dividing the country were thoroughly reflected in the personnel of the army and had it intervened, the only result would have been the splintering of the army into warring factions. It is instructive that in the political settlement that followed, the only candidate for the presidency acceptable to all sides was General

Shihab, the army commander who had refused to commit his army.[12]

The Syrian army has also exhibited interesting characteristics in revolution. The army itself is drawn from all parts of a highly fragmented community, and *no wing of the army in revolt can ever command the support of all other wings.* Almost every *coup d'état,* whether successful or not, involves disputes among units of the army. And once stabilized around some commander the army quickly breeds within itself the roots of the next power struggle. The result in Syria is that army coups are generally *internal to the army;* the army struggles with itself rather than with "governments" and "regimes."

In Latin America, on the contrary, the military leaders do struggle with governments and regimes, and only to a lesser degree among themselves. The military forces seldom intervene in the political system unless they are unified on the major issues. Intramilitary fighting is most unusual even though some disagreements may exist. As a matter of fact, most military forces in Latin America are divided by factionalism, but these internal conflicts are seldom serious enough to breed open warfare. Competition, rather, is carried out by maneuver and persuasion, ending normally in some sort of compromise. Once in power, most military forces find themselves under considerable pressure to return the exercise of political authority to civilian hands, and these pressures in turn generate further unrest within the military on the questions of when and how to withdraw. Army leaders exercising political authority may be replaced by new military leaders or they may be forced to give way to civilians, but in either case a high degree of consensus is achieved within the military before such drastic actions will be attempted. Seldom if ever does such maneuvering lead to bloodshed or even the serious threat of armed conflict.

Much attention has been paid by students of revolution to the catalytic events that spur the revolutionary process to completion. Prominent among these events has been the concept of "national disgrace," which tends to loosen the bonds of loyalty to a regime and hasten the "need" for national rehabilitation. Very often national disgrace is a synonym for military reversal. Much is made of the fact that the Russian revolutions of 1905 and 1917 were given impetus by military disasters. Whenever national disgrace is in fact military disgrace, it is easy to understand the effect that this will have on the officer ranks. It seems likely that a coup will be spawned in order to discredit civilian government for the disaster. When the Confederates

[12] There is considerable literature on the Lebanese crisis of 1958. Of particular interest are Fahim I. Qubain *Crisis in Lebanon* (Washington: The Middle East Institute, 1961), and Leila M. T. Meo, *Lebanon: Improbable Nation* (Bloomington: Indiana University Press, 1965).

were threatening Washington in 1862 and army (and civilian) morale was low, there were many who urged General McClellan to mount a *coup d'état*. Yet in the case of Russia it was not the army command that rebelled in 1905 and 1917, and in 1917 it was the disintegration of the entire army that permitted the revolution to take the course it did. On the other hand, the disintegration of the Italian army after Caporetto in 1917 created similar conditions, but no revolutionary forces were able to exploit the situation.

In any case, successful *coups d'état* are more likely to arise from the army. It is true in many places that the officer corps has more contacts with the outside world and is thus more inclined to measure local inadequacies by external standards; it is often better educated and certainly has acquired administrative skills not always possessed by civilian colleagues; it has also the prestige that impels it to play the "guardian" role with respect to national destiny and welfare.[13] As has already been pointed out, the army has at its disposal modern war equipment that makes its power almost irresistible within the state should it strike with decision and accord. Chalmers Johnson has said, "officers' revolutions will always succeed when the officers are in fact commanding the army" [14] (or the major parts of it). This was true of the Turkish coup in 1960, the Iraqi coup in 1958, the Pakistani coup in 1958, and the Argentine coup in 1943 but *not*, however, of the Rastenburg conspiracy in 1944. In the latter case the high command of the army was unreliable and its commitments uncertain.

The military role in politics is, however, not a problem just for the emerging nation. It remains unresolved in even well-established and developed states.[15] To appreciate the dimensions of the problem we need only remind ourselves of Sir John French's campaign to bring down the British government during the First World War (or Lloyd George's frenzied fear that his generals would revolt), the massive interference of Marshal Pétain in the politics of interwar France, the machinations of Generals von Seeckt and von Schleicher (among others) in the Germany of the 1920's, the ambitions of Japan's

[13] See Morris Janowitz, *The Military in the Political Development of New Nations* (Chicago: University of Chicago Press, 1964), for a discussion of some of these points.

[14] Chalmers Johnson, *Revolution and the Social System,* Hoover Institution Studies, No. 3 (Stanford: Hoover Institution, 1964), p. 18.

[15] See the useful summary in Michael Howard (ed.), *Soldiers and Governments* (London: Eyre & Spottiswoode, Ltd., 1957). Samuel P. Huntington, *The Soldier and the State* (Cambridge: Harvard University Press, 1957) is a detailed analysis of the American scene. *See also* Harold D. Lasswell, "The Garrison-State Hypothesis Today," in Samuel P. Huntington (ed.), *Changing Patterns of Military Politics* (New York: The Free Press, 1962).

Kwantung Army leaders in 1931 (and the later rise of General Tojo), the careers of Generals Primo de Rivera, Emilio Mola, and Francisco Franco of Spain, and in the United States the tortured role of General Douglas MacArthur. And a distinguished American military commentator, General S. L. A. Marshall, indignant over *Dr. Strangelove* and similar motion pictures, could say in 1964, "The day could come when the officer corps—humiliated by its civilian superiors and held in public contempt—grows subversive, renounces honor and betrays its oath." [16] Out of such considerations the military coup is born.

The role of the armed forces in a revolutionary atmosphere is an ambiguous one. A strong, loyal army is a powerful deterrent to revolutionary violence although it is not impossible that violence will take place or that it will be successful. Moreover, because revolutionary pressures are themselves not proper targets for military action, armies do not always combat revolutions very effectively. *Coups d'état* may occur without or more likely with the army's blessing, and such violent overtures may well develop further revolutionary character. Increasingly, political coups either develop out of military circles or with their approbation. In social revolutions part or most of the army may be disaffected and will participate in revolutionary action. The delicate balance of civilian-military relationships everywhere, even in the most advanced, mature states suggests a continuing military involvement, whether reforming or chiliastic, in the quest for social and political change.

Terror as a Feature of Revolution

Terror has been defined as "a symbolic act designed to influence political behavior by extranormal means, entailing the use or threat of violence." [17] But terror can be conceptualized more broadly than this: it is the emanation of an atmosphere of fear and despair, generally accompanied by seemingly senseless and wanton threats to life and property, carried out in normless ways by the plural centers of power. Terror, as conceived here, is a congeries of acts, specifically all those contributing to such an atmosphere of despair: murder, assassination, sabotage and subversion, the destruction of public records, the spreading of rumor, the closing of churches, the sequestration of property, the breakdown of criminal law enforcement, the prostitution of the

[16] *The Saturday Evening Post*, September 5, 1964.
[17] Thomas Perry Thornton, "Terror as a Weapon of Political Agitation," in Harry Eckstein (ed.), *Internal War* (New York: The Free Press, 1964), p. 73. Italicized in original.

courts, the narcosis of the press—all these, as they contribute to a common end, constitute terror.

Revolution and terror often appear in conjunction with one another. In the consummation of revolution, habits of obedience are dissolved and the elements of power reapportioned. The old power centers must be attacked, the new consolidated and defended. Terror becomes a natural instrument to use, for it is quick and thorough and its effectiveness is wholesale. Terror often assumes the form of a paroxysm, an ecstatic purging of society in incalculable ways. It may be that terror is propelled into being by organized groups, government or insurrectionary, but it is often fed by the people, indeed at times by the victims themselves. Like a disease, terror is difficult to predict and its prognosis difficult to determine. It may die slowly with many convulsions, leaving in its wake a generation of people with atrophied values; it may simply vanish at the moment of its apogee.

We are here not interested in a general psychology of terror but rather in its importance in the revolutionary process. It is true that there are revolutions without terror, but it remains a common feature of revolution. It is possible to examine this terror from several perspectives. One author has suggested employing the terms *agitational terror* and *enforcement terror,* depending upon whether it is used by those aspiring to power or by those defending it.[18] We can also distinguish between the terror deliberately employed and that coming about from chance causes.

Terror is an atmosphere of despair. What value can such an atmosphere have? The answer lies, for both those who agitate and those who defend, in the effects that this atmosphere has on the mass and the elite, effects not readily attainable by normal means of persuasion and coercion. How do agitators persuade the traditional elite to step down and hand over their reins of power and authority? And how do these same agitators convince the mass to follow? And against such agitation how does the ruling elite consolidate and defend? None of these acts of "persuasion" can be normalized; they are all outside the "system." They have no moral or legal content; there is no other criterion except that of success: do they work? There are things that cannot be accomplished *within the system by the rules of the system;* only by some extraordinary, extralegal, extranormal process can they be effectuated. The creation of an atmosphere of despair breaks down the resistance of those who need to be persuaded; they are to be so shocked and numbed, so weakened and demoralized, and so pessimistic of hope that they become amenable to anything that promises re-

---

[18] *Ibid.,* p. 72.

lease from tension. It is possible for agitators to produce such despair
in the minds of the ruling elite or in those of the mass; it is also sometimes possible for a government to destroy an opposition by terror
rather than to mollify it by more normal political methods.[19]

It is by example that we see the point of these observations. In recent years, Algeria, Cyprus, and perhaps Hungary offer examples
of agitational terror, yet one of the most intriguing cases is that of the
Mau Mau movement in Kenya (circa 1952). Mau Mau grew out of
the frustrations of the Kikuyu tribe in Kenya, frustrations stemming
from land hunger, enforced urbanization, the disintegration of family
life, the continuing white exploitation, and perhaps not least of all
the vague stirrings of African nationalism. But how does a politically
unorganized and impotent tribal group force its views upon a government it rejects? There was literally no way within the British East
African system of the 1950's through which these protests could be
made effectively—except through terror. Yet the terror that ensued was
never organized in any rational coordinated sense. Not all Kikuyu
were involved; the leadership in any case was amorphous and uncertain; and the actual program of violence was never the result of rational
planning. But the result was an atmosphere of despair that "forced"
the British to kill some 10,000 Africans and imprison another 90,000
in the desperate struggle to stem the rebellion. The outbreak of violence
itself "almost broke down ordered government and its suppression
cost some sixty million pounds and a prolonged military effort with
the help of British troops." [20] And finally, it must be added, Mau Mau
hastened not only in Kenya but everywhere in Africa independence
from European colonial rule.

The Mau Mau instituted, although not altogether rationally, terror
in their struggle against white supremacy in Kenya. The settlers, in
addition to what organized government did, attempted to establish
their own counterterror to Mau Mau. The same emphasis on terror
can be found in the Ku Klux Klan, McCarthyism, and the various
organizations of French *Colons* in Algeria—to effect ends otherwise
unachievable.

Where governments are willing to adopt terror as a mechanism for

[19] *See* the theoretical sections on the growth of opposition parties in Robert A.
Dahl (ed.), *Political Oppositions in Western Democracies* (New Haven: Yale
University Press, 1966).

[20] Margery Perham's introduction to Josiah Mwangi Kariuki, *"Mau Mau" De-
tainee* (Baltimore: Penguin Books, Inc., 1964), p. 13. *See also* Fred Majdalany,
State of Emergency: The Full Story of Mau Mau (Boston: Houghton Mifflin
Company, 1963); Brian Crozier also treats Mau Mau in his excellent study of insurrections, *The Rebels* (London: Chatto & Windus, Ltd., 1960).

control, they can often maximize their chances of "success." Terror can be administered through the normal mechanisms: the courts, the political parties, the army. This combines the physical tools of coercion with an utterly ruthless and amoral willingness to employ them. The classic example of deliberate terror by a government remains the Stalinist period in the Soviet Union. Government (usually enforcement) terror is usually more effective than agitational terror, but this effectiveness depends upon a government's willingness to be ruthless. Where this willingness is incomplete, as was the case with the British in Ireland, Palestine, and Cyprus, the government will often lose its struggle. It is noteworthy that "nonviolence" as an agitational device has been successful only in India and the United States. But it must be added that government terror does not always work. The French failure in Algeria is perhaps the most dramatic recent example of such failure.

"Terrorism is a weapon of the weak," states Brian Crozier in his stimulating study of insurrections.[21] It is the natural weapon of insurgents. But it also is used by the desperate. In revolution, both the legitimate government and its revolutionary counterpart are often weak and desperate. In such situations the commitment to terroristic activity seems natural and inevitable.

Terror always has a variety of targets. For agitators, terror is often directed primarily against their own potential followers rather than against institutional enemies. Thus only about 30 Europeans were destroyed by the Mau Mau during the life of their movement, while some 1,700 Kikuyu tribesmen were killed.[22] The problem is that of mobilizing the mass. They can be forced to acquiesce with their more militant leaders by an appropriate touch of terroristic methods. The Grivas-Makarios struggle for union (*enosis*) in Cyprus offers an excellent example of how this develops. There had been unrest of sorts on the island for years—Cyprus with a large majority of Greeks and a minority of Turks, was governed by the British—but Archbishop Makarios III, who came to power in 1950, had found his political attempts to secure union of the island with Greece frustrating. By 1954 these frustrations had led him to turn to terror. Joined by a former Greek officer, Colonel George Grivas, he initiated a series of terroristic blows at both the British (and Turks) and the *Greek Cypriotes* themselves. The latter efforts were to eliminate opposition and "traitors *pour encourager les autres*," [23] to raise funds, and to demonstrate to

[21] Crozier, *op. cit.*, p. 159.
[22] Perham, *op. cit.*, p. 13.
[23] The phrase is Crozier's, *op. cit.*, p. 160.

all how personally futile and dangerous it would be to oppose, or perhaps to fail to respond positively to, the efforts of the Archbishop to
secure *enosis*. In the end it meant that more Greeks suffered from the
terror than did either British or Turks; but in the end the terror
succeeded.

The use of terror is not normally a characteristic of political conflict in Latin America. When on occasion it does appear, people react
with horror. Batista's desperate resort to terror in his last year probably
contributed more than Castro's charismatic qualities to his final down-
fall. In the traditional dictatorships of Latin America, terror has been
used sparingly. A few persons have reportedly suffered torture in
Paraguay, and numerous persons were subjected to cruel and unusual
punishments in the last years of Trujillo. Only in Haiti under "Papa
Doc" Duvalier has terror been utilized on a large scale to cow the
potential opposition. Whole families have been wiped out on the sus-
picion that some members, even distant relatives, have engaged in conspiracy or guerrilla actions. Present-day Haiti is as close to a terror
state as any that has ever arisen in Latin America. The more normal
mode of ridding a regime of its enemies is exile, even in revolutionary
regimes like Bolivia in the early 1950's or Cuba in the 1960's.

According to Crozier, terror "is generally a useful auxiliary weapon
rather than a decisive one." [24] Moreover, it is a weapon whose effects
are rarely predictable; violence and despair often get out of hand
with catastrophic consequences. It is a weapon naturally suited to the
struggle of colonial peoples against their foreign ruling elites or by
small conspiratorial groups *without* power bases. It is primarily an
agitational device; when government is inclined to institute terror,
and thus risk the chaos of a cumbersome and expensive weapon, it
does so because it views the threats confronting it as being so dangerous
that normal devices of coercion are likely to fail.

But this assumes that terror is always deliberately planned or deliberately instigated; it may sometimes develop utterly without intention and finally in the same way disappear without reason. Its
effects in every case may be haphazard. Yet one thing is quite clear: it
leaves behind chaos and bitterness, a legacy that makes final political
consolidation difficult and unrewarding.

There is no convenient index of terror to be applied to a revolutionary situation. It is tempting to record the numbers of deaths or im-
prisonments, the number of bombings and similar things. But no index
is entirely satisfactory. And in any event the figures we come up with
show surprising variation. In the French Revolution rough estimates

[24] *Ibid.*

of the Terror suggest perhaps 40,000 dead and some 300,000 arrested.[25] Of these only 8.5 percent were nobles and 6.5 percent clergy; the remainder came from the amorphous mass.[26] In Russia the actual November coup took place with but a handful of deaths; and even after the establishment of the Bolshevik government, there was relatively little enforcement terror. The *Cheka* was created in December 1917 and was responsible "officially," under the direction of Felix Dzerzhinsky, for some 6,300 executions in the next year.[27] Actually it was only with the attempt on Lenin's life in August 1918 that indiscriminate and wanton slaughter began. The Soviet Union was engaged in civil war, and it had been invaded from without; this fanned the already ignited flames of insecurity and weakness characterizing the government. The Soviet Union was to know terror in one or another form for more than a generation, but it is clear that the first phase of terror had run its course by the time of Lenin's death. It is difficult to estimate the extent of the holocaust, but it would certainly be of the order of hundreds of thousands of lives.

Beside these figures the results of the terror in Castro's Cuba or in Hungary are very modest indeed. Deaths from *consolidation* terror subsequent to coups in Africa and the Middle East generally run to less than one hundred. But it must be remembered that these are raw gross figures of only the dead, without regard to the size of the society, the extent of the struggle, and the amounts and kinds of the other aspects of terror: the exodus of refugees—for example, from Hungary, Cuba, Palestine—and the general deterioration of political rights.

Terror, the atmosphere of fear and despair brought about by threats or acts of violence, sabotage, or property spoliation, either deliberately or accidentally engendered, is a common ingredient in revolution. Terror can be mounted by those anxious to destroy the government or its institutions, or by those seeking to consolidate or defend it. Essentially it is a weapon of those for whom more normal means of coercion are closed, although there are few groups that do not indulge in terror if it seems advantageous to do so. Terror is rarely a rational weapon, and its effects are seldom predictable.

[25] Noted in George Lefebvre, *The French Revolution from 1793 to 1799* (New York: Columbia University Press, 1964), p. 120, based on the work of Donald Greer, *The Incidence of the Terror during the French Revolution* (Cambridge: Harvard University Press, 1935).

[26] *Ibid.*, p. 120.

[27] Quoted in Adam B. Ulam, *The Bolsheviks* (New York: The Macmillan Company, 1965), p. 421.

3

The Prerevolutionary Environment:
Causes of Revolution

Revolutions do not arise spontaneously; they spring from and are nurtured by human responses and reactions to changing political, cultural, social, and/or economic conditions of the environment. The environment, of course, encompasses not only the domestic, but the foreign scene considered as the total world conditions that affect particular revolutionary developments.

We are embarrassed by the wealth of the literature on causation in revolution. Beyond the attempt to understand the causes of specific revolutions, some scholars have tried to generalize about the causes of revolution. They have tried to find patterns in the prerevolutionary environment, and to predicate certain types of conditions and circumstances as the explanation of revolutions. Since revolutions are extremely complicated phenomena, virtually every effort to generalize about revolutionary causation has been criticized as faulty and unnecessarily restrictive. We intend in this work to examine the various theories of causation, to note some of their limitations, and in general to refrain from being very precise about the "causes" of revolution.

Several scholars have distinguished between long-term factors that contribute to discontent with the existing order of things, and immediate sources of irritation that lead to violent attempts to overthrow that order. Some writers refer to these different sets of factors as primary and secondary causes. Chalmers Johnson uses the terms "dysfunctions" and "accelerators." He defines "dysfunctions" as conditions that put a social system out of equilibrium. If the dysfunctions are severe and are not removed or softened "revolution will occur . . . unless the elite acts first and declares its bankruptcy by abdication,

resignation, or by otherwise terminating the old order non-violently." [1]
At the same time, Johnson warns, "dysfunctions," even when they are
coupled with a ruling elite stubbornly opposing change, do not of
themselves lead to revolution. The X factors necessary for an immediate
outbreak Johnson calls the "accelerators of dysfunctions," or triggers.
"Accelerators are occurrences that catalyze or throw into relief the
already existent revolutionary level of dysfunctions. They do not of
themselves cause revolution; but when they do occur in a system already bearing the necessary level of dysfunctions . . . , they will provide the sufficient cause of the immediately following revolution." [2]
Harry Eckstein somewhat more simply distinguishes between "preconditions" and "precipitants." By a precipitant he means an event that
actually initiates violence; by preconditions he means the circumstances
that make it possible for the precipitant to produce violence. "Clearly
no internal war can occur without precipitant events to set it off; and
clearly no precipitants can set off internal war unless the condition of
society makes it possible for them to do so." [3]

In this chapter we shall concern ourselves with the long-term developments, the preconditions, the dysfunctions—in other words, the underlying causes. The precipitants and accelerators we shall discuss at
some length in the chapter on the stages of revolutions. In both phases,
however, unrest and discontent seem to characterize the revolutionary
environment. Most people desire some conditions in society to be other
than they are, and many believe themselves incapable of instituting
change within the existing structures. When the frustrated become
severely discontented, grow large in numbers, and come to include
potential leaders, a revolutionary environment is created. On the other
hand, we have been unable to discover any formula to determine when,
where, or how these factors coalesce to create an upheaval in any given
society.

Foreign Control

The concept of "foreign control" embraces a broad spectrum of
political and economic relationships between the holders (or alleged
holders) of political power and economic resources and those dependent (or who believe themselves dependent) on them. Foreign control,

[1] Chalmers Johnson, *Revolution and the Social System*, Hoover Institution
Studies, No. 3 (Stanford: Hoover Institution, 1964), p. 8. *See also* Chalmers
Johnson, *Revolutionary Change* (Boston: Little, Brown & Co., 1966).
[2] Chalmers Johnson, *Revolution and the Social System*, p. 12.
[3] Harry Eckstein, "On the Etiology of Internal Wars," *History and Theory*,
Vol. 4 (1965), p. 140.

however, poses no revolutionary problems in a society until powerful sectors of "dependent" elements first of all conclude that they are dependent, secondly that the dependency is somehow unjust or improper, and thirdly that they can do something to change that relationship.

Foreign control may consist of nothing more than an alien dynasty of kings, and revolution the expulsion of such a dynasty by the indigenous aristocracy, as for example, in ancient Egypt at the time of the Hyksos. Or both control and revolution may be recognized in the shattering of an older political form (feudalism) in the wake of a new age (the coming of the nation-state), as for example in the expulsion of the English kings from their fiefs in France in the medieval period. In the modern and contemporary world, the motivating force behind opposition to foreign control has been nationalism of the type given political content during the French Revolution and economic content in the aftermath of the Second World War.

During the past 25 years, economically backward countries, independent in a formal political sense, have begun to realize that they can be controlled by rich, highly industrialized countries that lay no claims to direct political overlordship. The income from their prime products in world markets, the prices they pay for manufactures, the rates and direction of their economic growth, the size and sophistication of their armaments, and their very social and political structures can all be strongly influenced by the rich and powerful countries. The most open attempt at conscious restructuring through foreign pressures was embodied in the Alliance for Progress proposed by President Kennedy for Latin America.

Today few traditional types of political dependencies remain, and most subject peoples of former imperial states have gained their political freedom. The larger mandated or trusteed territories of the First and Second World Wars, nineteenth-century protectorates, crown colonies, multinational dynastic states such as Austria-Hungary, and overseas imperial domains such as India have all but disappeared. Some island territories in the Pacific have yet to join the community of nations, and a few restive people like the Slovaks and Croats may still conceivably cause internal turmoil for their dominant partners, the Czechs and Serbs. Foreign political control, where it exists in the latter half of the twentieth century, may be characterized as indirect even with respect to Soviet relations with East Europe and the United States' relations with countries of the Caribbean. Foreign economic control is more pervasive because of the great concentration of economic resources in the hands of the United States, the Soviet Union, and Western Europe. The conflicts between the "haves" and the "have-

nots" have never been more acute than at the present moment. In one
sense the whole underdeveloped world is "in revolt" against the great
economic powers, whether against the kind of immediate controls that
United States economic preponderance forced upon Cuba before Castro, or against the indirect efforts of Western technology in weakening
tribal structures as in Africa, or against the mere fact of a dependency
relationship as demonstrated in East Europe vis-à-vis the Soviet Union.

Yet why does not foreign control produce everywhere and at every
period of time the same unrest? The answer, of course, is not profound. Foreign control is not everywhere the same nor does it continue unaltered in time. The identical observations can be made of
the peoples who are controlled; they change in time and space as
they acquire wealth, education, and general articulateness; they also
become more politically oriented and involved as they are forced to
face traumatic issues in their relations with foreign ruling elites. Something of this process occurred in Hungary in the early 1950's. With
the revival of Western ideas and the increase of Western contacts
through trade and tourism, increasing resentment became not only
more intense but more vocal against the Hungarian Communist elite
and their subservience to Moscow. In typical fashion, writers, artists,
scholars, and students, the "spiritual *elite* of the country," aired their
grievances and elicited a growing response from large masses of
people.[4] Particularly unsettling had been the exaggerated promises of
Communist propaganda that the regime could not possibly fulfill.
Communist indoctrination, however, not only raised people's expectations, but provided them with standards by which they could measure
the regime's failures. More important, perhaps, than those material
shortcomings in creating discontent were the typical colonialist response to personal insecurity, affronts to individual dignity and self-
respect, and national humiliation.[5] By 1956 a revolutionary environment of unrest and frustration existed in Hungary, particularly in
Budapest. What was lacking until the fall of that year was Chalmers
Johnson's accelerator, and it was soon supplied by the agitation in
Poland.

Still another source of frustration in colonial areas Eric Hoffer attributes to the crumbling or weakening of communal solidarity and
ways of life among tribally organized peoples. He maintains that
much of the discontent is directed not primarily against exploitation
by domineering foreigners, but stems from a disorientation that results

    [4] Janós Mészáros, "On the Eve of a Revolution," *Journal of Central European Affairs,* Vol. 18 (1958), p. 66.
    [5] Paul E. Zinner, *Revolution in Hungary* (New York: Columbia University Press, 1962), pp. 359-360.

from the imposition of Western political, economic, and social structures upon more primitive native forms. "The nationalist movements in the colonial countries," he says, "are partly striving after group existence and an escape from Western individualism." [6]

Economic Conditions

Karl Marx and Alexis de Tocqueville, among the pioneer theorists on the relationship between economics and social revolution, differed almost diametrically in their interpretations. Marx believed that the strongest human motives for social change lay in the drive for improved productive conditions. For Marx, economics was an overriding issue. He saw the quest for material progress, however, obstructed by outmoded social and political structures that persisted beyond their usefulness, frustrating economic development, increasing human misery, and finally being destroyed by revolution.[7] Tocqueville, on the other hand, rather slighted economic phenomena in his study of the French Revolution. He did note, however, "that it was precisely the most prosperous parts of France that had most enthusiastically supported the Revolution." He theorized that revolution, rather than occurring when conditions are worsening, tends to come when an oppressive regime lightens the burdens and attempts some reform.[8]

Despite Marx's preoccupation with economics, and Tocqueville's relative unconcern, Tocqueville seems to have the better of the argument. Unrest and discontent may well follow generally deteriorating economic conditions. Wild inflation, large-scale unemployment, famine, the familiar cycles of boom and bust—all these contribute to discontent in large measure. Such discontent, however, does not necessarily mean revolution or even a *coup d'état*. People are remarkably resilient, or apathetic, or both. We know that people have lived for months, indeed generations, under the most squalid and unfortunate conditions without rebelling or even protesting. The failure to rebel does not mean contentment and satisfaction! Rebellion is not an automatic concomitant of discontent with one's material condition in life.

Economic unrest has been commonplace in the modern world. The worldwide economic distress of the 1930's produced a high degree of

[6] Eric Hoffer, *The True Believer: Thoughts on the Nature of Mass Movements* (New York: The New American Library, 1958), p. 42.

[7] Eduard Heimann, *History of Economic Doctrines: An Introduction to Economic Theory* (New York: Oxford University Press, 1945), p. 142.

[8] Melvin Richter, "Tocqueville's Contributions to the Theory of Revolution," in Carl J. Friedrich (ed.), *Revolution* (Nomos VIII) (New York: Atherton Press, 1966), pp. 118-120.

discontent, yet few coups and relatively little social revolution accompanied it. It might be argued that the rise of Hitler in Germany and Dollfus in Austria came about because of the Depression, but the really remarkable thing is that there were no revolutions in Great Britain, France, the United States, or Eastern Europe, or in Africa in the many colonial possessions, and that in Asia there were only a handful of revolutionary movements. Economic deterioration and decline alone do not result in revolution.

Commentators on the French Revolution never tire of pointing out that France was the most advanced country materially and culturally on the continent of Europe in 1789, that her economic growth rate for half a century and more had remained steady, that her peasantry was acquiring land, and that countries far below her attainments avoided revolution while the old regime in France collapsed. Students of the Russian Revolution have pointed out similar economic and social changes in nineteenth-century Russia: the industrial growth rate was impressive, serfs were not only freed but were coming into possession of land, the middle class was increasing and prospering.

What happened? Various theories have been offered. Godfrey Elton suggests that the French middle class, though prosperous, was constantly worried about its future well-being because of the inefficient bureaucracy that administered the country. He holds that "it was precisely this craving for an unhazardous prosperity which had made the middle classes the Revolutionaries of 1789." [9] Crane Brinton notes in the four revolutions that he studied (English, American, French, and Russian), that although the societies were all prosperous, the governments were in financial straits; and economic leaders believed that "prevailing conditions limit or hinder their economic activity." [10] In other words, revolution is not made by the oppressed of society but by the rising or already successful operators who believe that further advance is blocked by existing conditions. Amplifying this latter thesis, James Davies demonstrates with several case studies that "revolutions are most likely to occur when a prolonged period of objective economic and social development is followed by a short period of sharp reversal." [11] He believes further that the actual state of social and economic development is less important than the mental state of anxiety and frustration over future development. "It is the dissatisfied

[9] Godfrey Elton, *The Revolutionary Idea in France, 1789-1871* (New York: Longmans, Green & Co., Inc., 1923), p. 6.

[10] Crane Brinton, *The Anatomy of Revolution* (New York: Vintage Books, 1956), p. 34.

[11] James C. Davies, "Toward a Theory of Revolution," *American Sociological Review*, Vol. 27 (1962), p. 6.

state of mind rather than the tangible provision of 'adequate' or 'inadequate' supplies of food, equality, or liberty which produces the revolution."[12] Moreover, Davies continues, revolutions do *not* occur when a society is generally impoverished. Constant preoccupation with the necessities of life often results in withdrawal from any important kinds of activities unrelated to staying alive. "Far from making people into revolutionaries, enduring poverty makes for concern with one's solitary self or solitary family at best and resignation or mute despair at worst."[13] Most people, too, prefer to keep their bondage to losing their lives. It is only when the bonds are loosened and when expectations are high for preserving their lives that people can think seriously of the luxury of a rebellion. To develop in reality a revolutionary environment, the continued and habitual expectations of improved opportunities to satisfy basic needs must be faced with an unrelenting threat to the satisfaction of those needs. Economic development and the granting of reforms by the elite might well alleviate a developing revolutionary condition. As Davies says, "The crucial factor is the vague or specific fear that ground gained over a long period of time will be quickly lost."[14]

Other observers hold that rapid economic change in preindustrial societies causes social dislocation and possibly revolution. W. Arthur Lewis, in speaking of the emergent nations, particularly in Africa, sees the rise of new socioeconomic groups, the disturbance of old income patterns, the unevenness of economic growth, the creation of new wealth and new poverty side by side as contributions to frustration, discontent, and upheaval. Mancur Olson argues that revolution in economically developing societies may be spawned from both the new rich and new poor. The latter corresponds to the dislocated with whom Lewis is concerned: not only the unemployed but workers whose income has dropped or who find their livelihoods being squeezed out by new techniques or new demands.[15]

To sum up the various theories on the contribution of economic conditions to revolution, all major interpreters from Tocqueville to Davies, with the notable exception of Marx, have a common theme that runs through their many specific variations of economic situations. That theme holds that the actual state of material well-being (or ill-being) of people does not in itself produce revolutionary fervor, but rather that the attitudes of people toward their conditions constitute

[12] *Ibid.*
[13] *Ibid.*, p. 7.
[14] *Ibid.*, p. 8.
[15] Both Lewis and Olson are cited in Lawrence Stone, "Theories of Revolution," *World Politics*, Vol. 18 (1966), pp. 170-171.

a major factor. As Lawrence Stone says: "Human satisfaction is related not to existing conditions but to the condition of a social group
against which the individual measures his situation." [16]

Political Disputes

Unrest may come about because of political agitation and the appeal
of political slogans; it may result from ideological absorption; or it
may be the product of nothing more serious than a large excess of
political energy, left over from a strenuous campaign or a political
struggle over other issues. Perhaps there is something to be learned
from examining the rebellious flash points of a university campus, such
as that of Berkeley. A general restlessness on such a campus may be
produced by the individual need for recognition, by a desire to assert
maturity by rebelling. The most trivial thing may prompt mass support of individual rebellion. The result is campus revolution. There
is a great distance between campus rebellion in the United States
and political revolution, but the major point is that the triggering
elements that provoke violence are very likely the same in both instances. That campus protest or racial violence does not escalate into
political revolution lies in the fact that the "dysfunctions" in the
society are not numerous enough, sufficiently widespread among the
inhabitants, or essentially interconnected in the minds of the discontented. Where they have been, as in parts of Latin America, governments have fallen as a result of violence originally instigated by students.

Individual unrest must be transformed into *integrative* mass unrest
before it is likely that much political activity will take place. Integrative mass unrest means not only that large numbers of individuals
are aroused but that they are communicating their concern to each
other and beginning to articulate their feelings in conjunction with
one another. Individual unrest alone is hardly likely to produce revolution, although a variety of political activities may feed upon it. It is
the cumulative energy of the mass, when it is finally set in motion,
that can bring about revolutionary changes.

Most analysts of revolution and political upheaval point to the lack
of congruence between the social system on one side and the political
system on the other. Brinton emphasizes that in almost any modern
society one may find some degree of separation of economic power
from political power and social distinction. It is only when these

[16] Stone, *op. cit.*, p. 173.

attain a certain intensity and combine with other sources of discontent that a revolutionary situation is created.[17] Tocqueville pointed out, however, that the same conditions often prevail with political discontent as with economic dissatisfaction, that is, that a granting of political reforms or concessions followed by retreat or even a slowing down of the pace of reform may well provoke revolutionary disturbances.[18] Again it is the problem of expectations surpassing achievement. In the same way, the radical right in the United States apparently includes substantial numbers of persons who are economically well-off but insecure in social status and dissatisfied with the extent (or lack thereof) of their political influence.[19]

Political concessions seem easier to grant than social or economic reforms. A lesser degree of real sacrifice is required of elites to widen the suffrage, open government job opportunities, and ease the entry of new groups into political office than is required to guarantee minimum wages, provide schools and cultural centers, and decent health and housing facilities for the masses. Electoral changes enacted in 1912 in Argentina effectively released the steam from an already straining revolutionary engine. Prior to the new electoral law, a rising middle class of white-collar workers, small entrepreneurs, and sons of immigrants not only had organized a new political party, but had rioted and revolted, albeit unsuccessfully, in the two preceding decades. The reform itself was a political concession that basically left untouched the social and economic structures of the country, but it was sufficient to calm political passions for almost two decades.[20] Conversely, estrangement between a governing elite and its subjects in a premodern society may lead to revolution if the rulers adopt new social customs and mores that are alien to their people. A sense of profound separation alienates the governed and undermines the political position of the elite even though the latter grant concessions of a socioeconomic nature. Eckstein notes that the attack of the French revolutionaries "upon the refined and parasitic court nobility" was more severe than upon the less parasitic provincial nobility, who kept some contact with their peasants.[21] In modern societies this condition cannot become as severe as in preindustrial types, but Eckstein

---

[17] Brinton, *op. cit.*, pp. 28-36.

[18] Alexis de Tocqueville, *The Old Regime and the French Revolution* (Garden City: Doubleday & Company, Inc., 1955), pp. 138-211.

[19] Murray Clark Havens, "The Radical Right in the Southwest: Community Response to Shifting Socio-Economic Patterns," a paper delivered at the 1964 Annual Meeting of the American Political Science Association, Chicago.

[20] Arthur P. Whitaker, *Argentina* (Englewood Cliffs, N.J.: Prentice-Hall, Inc., 1964), pp. 48-49, 65-66, 83 ff.

[21] Eckstein, *op. cit.*, p. 146.

does note that the late nineteenth century, "the most prolonged period of civil unrest in American history," witnessed a conscious effort on the part of the American plutocracy to ape European manners. Says Eckstein: "At no other time in American history was the elite so profoundly estranged from American life." [22] On the other hand, the estrangements and conflicts at no time seriously approached revolutionary proportions in the United States.

Defects in the Regime

Some writers emphasize the *disorder* of the prerevolutionary environment. A weak government does not immediately produce disorder. People, obeying from habit governments that at one time were universally accepted as legitimate, will tolerate for a long period governmental structures that have lost their *raison d'être*. Nevertheless, the political entropy of a system, left to itself, will generally increase; thus, such a political system will become more and more disorderly. But a system is left to itself only when government is weak; where it is strong, disorder is controlled. Disorder then is dependent upon the weakness that government exhibits. On the other hand, some countries have experienced almost insurmountable obstacles in establishing governments that are accepted as legitimate by all important and articulate sectors of society. All but a handful of the Latin American countries have been so troubled, and so have virtually all of the new nations of Asia and Africa. As Eckstein points out, "internal wars can, and often do, become chronic." One act of violence follows another, "establishing a predisposition toward violence that is inculcated by the experience of violence itself." In these situations, Eckstein argues cogently, "internal wars" result not from any particular set of objective conditions or even from the loss of legitimacy of any particular regime, but "from a general lack of receptivity to legitimacy of any kind." [23]

It is sometimes argued that the most important prerevolutionary condition is the *weakening* of the old regime. Where the government displays energy and determination, where it is alive to the issues that move the mass, then revolution will rarely take place. Much is made of the fact that the old regimes in both France and Russia were decadent, impotent, and moribund. The same could be said of the Egyptian government prior to its revolution in 1952; certainly from the colonial point of view this was also the case with respect to the Dutch in Indo-

[22] *Ibid.*, pp. 146-147.
[23] *Ibid.*, pp. 150-151.

nesia and the Belgians in the Congo when independence movements swept them away. For that matter, De Gaulle's assumption of power in 1958 followed precisely such a weakening of an old government.

It is not so important here that a regime be *old* as that it be weak, that it be increasingly unable to solve or resolve the problems facing it. The prerevolutionary French government crept from financial crisis to financial crisis; the problems themselves do not seem immense in retrospect, but Louis XVI was unable to summon sufficient resources to cope with them. Similarly the Romanov regime was drifting in the early days of the twentieth century; it was devoid of both *élan* and imagination; it had assumed a weary air of defeatism, which was not disguised by the pomp and circumstance of its court or by the recklessness with which it went to war. Indeed, both the Russo-Japanese War and the First World War quickly dispelled the myth that Russia was a first-class power; those who nurtured visions of altering its power elite could not help but be encouraged.

The weakness of Japanese civilian government in the 1920's and 1930's encouraged military intransigence and finally intervention. Mussolini "marched" on Rome in 1922 because the Italian government had been paralyzed into inaction; Hitler was appointed chancellor by the senile President Paul von Hindenberg. The chronic weaknesses of Latin America governments have encouraged the palace revolution.

Even new, developing, nationalistic states exhibit weaknesses in their governments more often than would seem likely, and as a consequence have spawned a spate of *coups*. Typical examples have been the governments of U Nu in Burma, Sukarno in Indonesia, and Kasavubu in the Congo. The pattern is evident: a nationalist government assumes power from the colonial suzerain but the problems it faces are not entirely those that can be solved by applications of nationalist fervor. The economy typically stagnates; the bureaucracy wallows in traditional corruption, and the elite, other than in feathering its nests, busies itself in international intrigues and postures. Such characteristics are often "built in" by the colonial regime in its preparations (or lack of them) for the independence of its colonies.

But whatever the genesis of the difficulties, the results are the same: governments that cannot govern in an atmosphere of problems that do not go away. The weakness of such governments tempts potential power centers to challenge them for control. The rapidity with which loyalty to the old elite evaporates substantiates the fragility of the myth of its omnipotence. An interesting case is the attempted coup in Ethiopia in 1960. Haile Selassie, the emperor, was in Brazil on a state visit when units of the palace guard, members of his government, and even members of his own family attempted to depose him and bring about reforms in his administration. In this case there were miscalculations. Unexpected pockets of loyalty prevented the quick consummation of the coup and the emperor's prompt return galvanized his supporters into sufficient action to abort the coup. (Would a prompt return of Kwame Nkrumah to Ghana in February 1966 have had similar effects?) But undoubtedly the emperor was frightened by the suddenly revealed weaknesses of his regime. He could only hope to become the leader of the unleashed revolutionary forces himself.

As a government and its authority weaken, problems that governments should solve go untended with the development of distress; individuals and groups organize in order to protest, and at the same time the government is unable to control or stifle them. Weakness thus not only encourages but it permits the growth of dissident groups, spawning a plurality of loyalties and chaotic interactions.

A weak government is one in disrepute. It is one without respect and increasingly without support. All governments rest on the myth of their supremacy; weakness in government is an acid to that myth. As the myth declines so also does the base of loyalty upon which every government rests. The mythology of politics cannot be expressed as a simple model, and in any event it is not possible to treat the rise and fall of revolutions purely in terms of myth structure. Yet it is undoubtedly this factor that is the catalyst of the revolutionary process. Its importance can be seen in the attempt to answer the question: When does the mantle of *de jure* loyalty fall on an insurrectionary government? If, for example, the Southern Confederacy had been successful militarily, the result would have been a completed revolution directed against the previous government and its policies. But it was not; the revolution was aborted. The loyalty myth of the United States had already dissolved in the states of the Confederacy and in the border states, and in other areas, both North and South, there were many individuals who could possess only an ambivalent attachment to this myth; for them the question of loyalty remained a real and continuing one.

Some governments are not so much weak in their ability to carry out reform as they are trapped by the web of vested interests that support them, and by the concepts and ideas upon which they rest. In this sense the weaknesses lie in the very nature of the regimes themselves. In outbreaks against certain foreign regimes, Henry Mason finds in his case studies that underlying factors contributing to the outbreak "were beyond governmental manipulation, considering the quality of the governments involved." The Dutch chafed under Nazi rule in the 1940's, the Hungarians under Russian domination, and the Panamanians in the face of American might in the Canal Zone.[24] Although none of the dominant powers could have alleviated the basic discontent that led to violence without a complete and virtually impossible change in fundamental policies, in these cases they did have the brute strength to hold their basic positions. But also in France in 1789 and in Russia in 1917, the regimes could have done little to manipulate the underlying factors of discontent. These *anciens régimes* were held together by a system of hierarchies and privileges, the source of most of the discontent. The removal of these would have entailed "revolutionary" changes, but no one has suggested that such changes could have been enacted without violence and bloodshed.

Revolutionary success frequently depends upon the degree of efficiency of the old regime. For all its vaunted military training and equipment, the Batista armed forces in Cuba could never bring their full might to bear against Castro's rebellious force. Furthermore, inefficient police methods in repressing discontent may broaden disaffection and engender popular contempt for a regime, and if it does not cause a government to fall to its enemies, it may well cause it to fall to its friends who become fearful for their own interests. In the spring of 1966, for example, army elements overthrew a military junta in Ecuador in part because of the regime's ineffective handling of widespread discontent among leftist students.

Disruption of the Incumbent Power Structure

Another factor often noted in the prerevolutionary environment is the deterioration or disintegration of the ruling elite. This is, of course, connected with government weakness: where an elite has lost its vitality, the result is weakness or apathy. Trotsky believed elite decline, that is, internal dissension and loss of faith in itself, was a necessary element for revolution. Other observers, too, have seen the origins of revolutions as basically quarrels within the elite. Eckstein believes that the occurrence of at least some "internal wars" may be explained in elite characteristics alone. "A ruling elite may decay, may become torn by severe conflict, may be reluctant to use power, may come to lack vital political skills—and thus make it perfectly possible for a relatively weak, even disorganized, opposition of a sort that may exist in any political system to rise against it and destroy it." [25] Brinton

---

[24] Henry L. Mason, *Mass Demonstrations against Foreign Regimes*, Tulane Studies in Political Science, Vol. X (New Orleans: Tulane University, 1966), pp. 96-97.

[25] Eckstein, *op. cit.*, p. 146.

in his four case studies concludes that the ruling classes, defined
broadly, were divided and inept. A successful ruling class, he believes,
ought to combine a determination to use a moderate amount of force,
a respect for established ideas and mode of action, and a willingness to
compromise or even innovate. Conversely an elite loses its cohesion
and ability when numerous and important members begin to believe
that all men are equal, that they hold power unjustly, or that the ideas
of their society are "silly." [26] Eckstein states that "internal wars" are
almost always preceded by functional failures, particularly in financial
administration, on the part of the elite—"perhaps because finance
impinges on the ability of governments to perform all their functions." [27] The well-meaning but weak and ineffective Louis XVI and
the frivolous Marie Antoinette are favorite targets of historians attempting to demonstrate the decay of the old regime in France. More
important, however, was the attraction of large numbers of the nobility to the new philosophic concepts and the political critiques of
the eighteenth century. By 1789 many of the leading aristocrats believed that reforms had to be made and that their own status in society
could not be justified. In early twentieth-century Russia the aristocrats
customarily complained of the backwardness of their country. Many
believed that their privileged positions could not endure. "Even in
court," as Brinton points out, "it was quite the fashion by 1916 to ridi-
cule the Czar and his intimates." [28]

Stone also sees elital failure as a vital element in creating a revolutionary situation. He further believes that a combination of any two or
more features of that failure will prove dangerous: loss of manipulative
skill, military superiority, cohesion, or self-confidence; estrangement
from the non-elite; inability to cope with a financial crisis; incompe-
tence, weakness, brutality. "What is ultimately fatal, however, is the
compounding of its errors by intransigence. If it fails to anticipate the
need for reform, if it blocks all peaceful, constitutional means of social
adjustment, then it unites the various deprived elements in single-
minded opposition to it, and drives them down the narrow road to
violence." [29] At the same time Stone poses the paradox "that measures
designed to restore equilibrium in fact upset equilibrium," that is,
that reforms themselves often precipitate further change, even revolution, rather than restore stability. Brinton also strongly emphasizes the
role that attempted governmental reforms play in revolution. "Nothing

[26] Brinton, op. cit., pp. 53-54.
[27] Eckstein, op. cit., p. 148.
[28] Brinton, op. cit., p. 55.
[29] Stone, op. cit., p. 165.

can be more erroneous than the picture of the old regime as an un-
regenerate tyranny, sweeping to its end in a climax of despotic indifference to the clamor if its abused subjects." [30] Brinton admits that
the reforms were incomplete and sometimes nullified by sabotage on
the part of the privileged. The explanation probably lies again in the
weakness, division, and uncertainty on the part of the ruling elite: too
little and too late.

A vital element in the disintegration of an elite is the alienation of
large and important segments of the intellectual community of a
society. Eckstein points out that almost all students of revolution note
the desertion of important segments of the intellectuals from the ruling
group to the discontented. He believes that these shifts of allegiance
make "revolutionary momentum irreversible" because of the role of
intellectuals in shaping attitudes, in providing guidelines to behavior,
in educating adolescents and young people, and in developing political
"myths." [31] Brinton cautions, however, that in all societies at all times
some intellectuals are alienated, that almost all criticize some aspects
of their environment, and that they seldom, if ever, have consensus
among themselves.[32] The question of the intellectuals' alienation,
then, becomes one of quantity as well as of quality of their criticism.
Writers and scholars complained about various things in Victorian
England, but few felt any urgency about the need for revolutionary
change. Conversely, in Bourbon France, the carping was extremely bitter, the great majority of commentators were doctrinaire in their views,
and they expected the changes to be made in the political arena. Con-
cerning late-nineteenth- and early-twentieth-century Russia, says Brinton, "to write or teach in those days meant being against the government." [33]

One factor clearly emerges from these several examples, and that is
that intellectuals occupy a critical role in society owing to their access
to communications networks. Control of the media, whether primitive
or sophisticated, helps governments control revolutionaries (or would-
be revolutionaries), particularly in their myth-making activities. The
withdrawal or alienation of a substantial section of the intellectual
community destroys the regime's monoply of the media, gives revolutionary forces access to some outlets at least, and facilitates their creation of myths and unrest. In the process it assists the revolutionary
leadership in welding unity among its scattered followers and recruit-

[30] Brinton, *op. cit.*, p. 40.
[31] Eckstein, *op. cit.*, p. 150.
[32] Brinton, *op. cit.*, pp. 44-46.
[33] *Ibid.*, p. 47.

ing additional forces. Tom Paine's pamphlets and the literature of the
Committees of Correspondence performed these functions in the era
prior to the outbreak of the American Revolution.[34]

Conclusions

Certainly no one environmental model will elucidate the causes of
revolution. The contextual factors of space and time will provide a
general milieu in which a revolution must be examined. Conditions
associated with revolution in nineteenth-century Europe may have
little comparative relationship with conditions obtaining in mid-twen-
tieth-century Africa or Asia. It is always possible, *after the event*, to
describe the environmental pattern in persuasive and convincing terms
—that is, it is possible to demonstrate the fact that revolution did
occur and ought to have occurred where and when it did. The environmental conditions of a *specific* revolution can, of course, be described
in specific terms; these are far more persuasive than those couched
in generality. Or within a regional area it may often be possible to
specify factors that are generally absent elsewhere. Thus Merle Kling,
referring to Latin America, states that "chronic political instability
is a function of the contradiction between the realities of a colonial
economy and the political requirements of legal sovereignty among
the Latin American states." [35]

It is tempting to argue that revolution is somehow related to the
tensions produced by a heterogeneous population. The Indian population, for example, with its religious elements (Hindus, Muslims, and
Sikhs among others) and its language areas (the Telagu- and Marati-
speaking peoples) has been among the most restless. It is also tempting
to suggest that revolution is less likely to occur where economic development has taken place or where the general level of political "maturity" is high. Like all the other conditions discussed these are only partially convincing (where they are meaningful at all); certainly
generalizations can be made only tentatively. Discontent can take
many forms. Religious and racial discrimination and persecution certainly can result in considerable unrest, often punctuated by tremors
of violence. In most cases, however, such discrimination is the act of
a majority (and where it is not, as in South Africa, it is the act of an

[34] See Karl W. Deutsch, *The Nerves of Government* (New York: The Free Press
1963).
[35] Merle Kling, "Towards a Theory of Power and Political Instability in Latin
America," *The Western Political Quarterly*, Vol. 9 (1956), p. 34. Italicized in the
original.

extremely powerful minority); such unrest does not always presage revolution.

Questions certainly arise with respect to the disintegration of elites. This deterioration can be expressed rather tautologically: when those who govern lose their will or ability to do so, they are simply shoved aside by those who can govern. There is nothing profound about this observation.

Among the circumstances related to revolution may be a political elite that is increasingly unable to give direction or meaning to the political process or to give protection to its myths and symbols. What is interesting is not that this phenomenon exists in conjunction with revolution, for we would be astonished if it did not, but rather *how* and *why* an elite deteriorates to the point that it does. Revolution and elital deterioration are not causally connected; they both stem from more basic factors. The disintegration of an elite may often characterize revolution but it is probably not a fundamental cause. Furthermore, revolutions or at least *coups d'état* do occur where the political elite has deteriorated in only superficial ways, if at all. It is difficult to argue that Nkrumah and his cohorts had deteriorated in any major way when the Ghana coup took place in 1966. Similarly the Menderes-Bayar regime in Turkey, which was overthrown in 1960, was not a disintegrated elite in the ordinary sense of the term. Moreover, where an elite atrophies naturally, revolution is not an automatic and inevitable accompaniment. If Tsar Nicholas II and those associated with him came to nothing, as it were, in 1917, it is also safe to say that they never had a value, at least in any consequential terms. What was important was the political apprehension of the Tsar's weakness. An elite can deteriorate but revolutionaries must be aware of it, must be persuaded of it, and must act as if it were so.

4

The Stages of Revolution

The concept of revolution covers a whole range of acts in defiance of constituted authority, from palace revolts and *coups d'état*, to full-scale civil wars and mass uprisings. The beginnings of some revolts are rather easy to pinpoint; others are all but impossible to identify with precision. Godfrey Elton insists that there is no answer to the question of when the French Revolution began. Dates and outbreaks, he says, are the conventions and conveniences of history. He advances the thesis that this revolution was in being for many years prior to 1789. Actually, Elton sees in all revolutions a continuation of a gradual process, with roots deep in the past, and blames historians for creating the illusion of sharp breaks, by exaggerating certain events that were in essence part of an evolutionary process.[1] In a sense Elton is correct, if all that is meant by revolution is substantial change between one point and another in a "relatively short" time scale. But surely the process of social and political change in France differed from that in England from the late eighteenth century. The forceful overthrow of governments, the terror and the radical alternation of regimes in the former, were things entirely absent in England, where similar disputes and social pressures were, for various reasons, restricted to protests and demonstrations. Both countries "evolved" in time toward greater political democracy and toward a more egalitarian society, but the process was different. In contrast with England, France was wracked with political discontinuity. Moreover, the revolutionary upheavals in France can be outlined in rather clearly delineated stages, including births or beginnings.

[1] Godfrey Elton, *The Revolutionary Idea in France, 1789-1871* (New York: Longmans, Green & Co., Inc., 1923), pp. 1-3.

The Birth of Revolution

Rather than a single dramatic incident, the birth of a revolution may consist of a series of related events.[2] For example, it is difficult to hold the proposition that the Declaration of Independence marked the birth of the American Revolution. There were, after all, Lexington and Concord; and other acts of violence and defiance of authority (the tea affair in Boston) preceded it as well. Moreover, efforts to resolve the dispute short of independence followed these initial skirmishes. Had these last peace efforts succeeded, there would have been no revolution at all. The cataclysms in France and Russia offer similar problems about beginnings, seemingly insoluble. Insistence on precision in these cases can lead only to arbitrary and distorted conclusions. The difficulties presented have led some historians to dismiss the question as one of no importance. Elton, concerned more with long-term trends, is simply uninterested in the problem, while Crane Brinton, trying to evaluate events from the contemporaries' point of view, says that the first steps of revolution, particularly the transition from agitation to revolution, are not always clear to the revolutionists themselves. In his study Brinton prefers to note the chronological sequence of events without attempting to designate an exact beginning for his revolutions.[3]

No one can predict the outbreak of violence and defiance of authority. Most observers refer to "triggering elements" or "accelerators," but generally these are unpredictable and uncontrollable. Foreign wars, famine, or other natural catastrophes combined with agitators and political organizers who can articulate and mobilize discontent are at times the elements that trigger a revolution.[4] Other factors, particularly the response of the governing elite to opposition demands, are vitally significant, but the precise combination of factors and the intensity of human reactions that produce an outbreak have not yet been discovered.

To some degree violence is the midwife at every revolutionary birth. Incumbents may surrender to a mere threat of force if the regime is weak or if the insurgents are well prepared, "but if the threat is not

[2] Paul E. Zinner, *Revolution in Hungary* (New York: Columbia University Press, 1962), pp. 239, 360.

[3] Crane Brinton, *The Anatomy of Revolution* (New York: Vintage Books, 1956), pp. 72-73.

[4] Chalmers Johnson, *Revolution and the Social System,* Hoover Institution Studies, No. 3 (Stanford: Hoover Institution, 1964), pp. 34, 67.

effective violence breaks out." [5] Beyond this common denominator, there seem to be three basic modes or styles that have marked the initiation of revolutionary activity. One type is characterized by gradually intensifying disputes, frequently clothed in legal or constitutional terms, between large and powerful competing groups within the existing power structure. If the disputants cannot agree upon suitable compromises or palliatives, violence, leading to a sudden overthrow or to civil war, may ensue. Such conflicts as these have no precise starting points. To this genre belong the English Revolution of the seventeenth century, the American Revolution, and the French Revolution. More recently this style characterized the beginning of the revolution in Vietnam against the French.

A second type of revolutionary birth is the *coup d'état*. Perón's rise to power in Argentina in October 1945 is a classic example of a coup. In June 1943 the Argentine army overthrew a conservative land-based regime that it had been propping up since 1930. Among middle-grade officers, a certain Juan Domingo Perón received the Department of Labor, a position of low prestige. Recognizing the need of the military government for mass support, Perón began to favor labor unions and drew them under his personal control. His standing and influence in the government rose rapidly, but his enemies likewise increased. Finally, in early October 1945, his military opponents arrested him and packed him off to the naval prison on Martín García Island in the Plata Estuary. His captors, however, were divided among themselves as to their next steps, and while they hesitated, Perón's mistress, Eva Duarte, and his allied labor union bosses rallied the labor rank and file. On the morning of October 17, Peronist strong-arm squads swarmed through Buenos Aires, intimidated anti-Perón groups, and shouted for the restoration of their leader. The pro-Perón police sat by and watched. Late that evening the military gave way and restored Perón to his political offices. The coup was won with the leader in prison. [6] One should note the limited and controlled violence, the virtual absence of bloodshed, the coup-within-a-coup feature of the movement, and for the moment, the simple replacement of some personnel. In the aftermath, however, Perón had himself elected president, founded a political party that bore his name, established a virtual dictatorship, and, most important, based his strength in large part upon the urban laboring masses who previously had no share in political

[5] Cyril E. Black, "Revolution, Modernization, and Communism," in Cyril E. Black and Thomas P. Thornton (eds.), *Communism and Revolution: The Strategic Uses of Political Violence* (Princeton: Princeton University Press, 1964), p. 5.

[6] Arthur Whitaker, *Argentina* (Englewood Cliffs, N.J.: Prentice-Hall, Inc., 1964), pp. 118-119.

power. The social revolution was only partial, but it can never be undone, and its unsolved problems plague Argentina today.

Finally, revolution is sometimes the end product of hostilities, often begun in modest ways. The style has two major variants: the mass uprising from which leaders emerge, or the small guerrilla attack that hopes to attract mass support. This type of attack includes a variety of rebellions from a traditional jacquerie or millenarian outburst to a modern nationalist or socialist revolution. One thing all major participants have in common, however, is that virtually all are outside the power structure, and certainly outside the government. The social revolutions of Mexico (1910) and Bolivia (1952) belong in this category, and so does the Cuban Castro Revolution, although in this case the plans called for the overthrow of the Batista government by an urban coup at the moment of Castro's invasion. The French revolution in 1848 clearly belongs in this group, and so does the Hungarian uprising of 1956. In speaking of the latter, Paul Zinner pinpoints the outbreak of armed rebellion at some moment between 8:00 P.M. and 9:00 P.M. on October 23, in front of the central headquarters of the national broadcasting corporation. In what appeared to be a spontaneous mass action, people threw bricks, the police hurled tear gas, both sides fired shots, both sides suffered casualties. Unquestionably these mass demonstrations were inspired by the reforms just made in Poland, and in the beginning the mobs had little or no thought of bringing down the government. Well-considered concessions to the people of Budapest by the government might well have avoided the uprising. But the harsh and uncompromising stand of officialdom coupled with the bayonet charge of the police ignited the general conflagration. Within a matter of hours the rebels had control of the city, and as the news spread through the countryside, the Communist Party simply melted away while local groups assumed control with little violence. Only after the revolution had been won did its leaders, particularly Imre Nagy, assume command. As a mass uprising, almost leaderless in its initial attack, the Hungarian revolution was an astonishingly complete success. It was crushed only with the overwhelming weight of a foreign armed force.[7]

Types of Revolutionary Acts

Every political revolution begins with an act that uses or threatens violence. But not every such act necessarily leads to a revolution. A would-be revolutionary act may have no effect at all, or it may simply

[7] Zinner, *op. cit.*, pp. 239, 243, 360.

force a change in policy. On the other hand, one change in policy forced upon an incumbent administration may well weaken its resolve against further demands, increase the self-confidence of the opposition, and lead eventually to a thoroughgoing revolution. The Tennis Court Oath was in reality not very dramatic and not very revolutionary, but it led in rapid stages to the overthrow of the Bastille (another symbolic act), the virtual capture of the king, the overthrow of the monarchy, and the establishment of the First Republic. Zinner in his account of the Hungarian uprising of 1956 holds that the initial act of violence "has both actual significance as a test of strength between the forces opposing each other and symbolic meaning as a point of no return in resolving the differences between them." He admits, however, that "the mechanism involved in triggering a revolutionary outburst is less perfectly understood than the process that leads to a nuclear explosion." [8]

The warehouse of history is well stocked with a rich and varied store of successful revolutionary acts. Some are heroic, some are farcical; some border on the ridiculous, some are merely pathetic. Some are dull, some sordid, some are dramatic, some are almost routine. Mussolini's seizure of power in 1922 was preceded by three years of violence, conspiracy, bombast, and mounting national disorder. The actual victory, however, proved almost routine. The king invited Mussolini to come from Milan to form a government, well-wishers met him at the train stations along the way, and the mobs that had assembled in Rome on his call greeted him enthusiastically. There was a march through the streets of the capital, but it all went off smoothly and almost anticlimactically. Mussolini tried later to dramatize the March on Rome by claiming that 3,000 lives were lost in the Fascist revolution, but it did not really happen that way at all.[9]

The Argentine revolution of September 1930 offers an interesting example of how drab and even sordid a revolutionary act can be. Ill and senile, President Yrigoyen had lost all control over his government. Fellow members of his governing Radical Party were enriching themselves, their families, and their friends at national expense. Under normal conditions, these activities would have been sufficient to create a crisis; but in the depression year of 1930 they became intolerable to much of the population. Yrigoyen's popular following melted away rapidly, the military withdrew its support, and leading figures in public and private life urged him to resign. Only a few, however, appeared willing to take positive action against the old man. Among those few

[8] *Ibid.*, p. 239.
[9] D. J. Goodspeed, *The Conspirators* (London: Macmillan & Co., Ltd., 1962), p. 166.

was General José Félix Uriburu, a one-time Radical, now a reactionary, fascist-oriented, would-be dictator. With a few military cadets, a handful of regular troops, and very few officers, Uriburu marched into the capital and simply took over. The crowds of Buenos Aires cheered madly, sacked several hotels and restaurants where Radical Party leaders customarily met, and even invaded the humble private apartment of Yrigoyen, throwing his simple iron cot into the street. The military forces sat on their hands. Yrigoyen's few remaining friends, who put up virtually no resistance, bundled the old man, almost too sick to move, into an automobile and drove him away.[10] The revolutionary act was obviously the march into the city, but it was a weak effort and Uriburu himself was doubtful of the outcome. Any organized and determined resistance to Uriburu's forces at that moment would probably have been successful. The point is that opposition to the coup simply did not materialize; the government was tottering, about to fall from its own internal rot, yet the forces of Uriburu lacked cohesion and self-confidence. Nevertheless, what little strength the attackers had was sufficient to overthrow the government and the regime. The measure of Uriburu's basic weakness lies in his loss of power to a rival civil-military faction within a year of his own coup.

Abortive Revolutions

Not all revolutionary acts are successful in forcing policy changes, much less in overthrowing governments. Many never pass beyond the planning stage, some because they are prematurely betrayed to the authorities, and some because the conspirators lose heart, or conditions change that obviate the necessity of such drastic action. At times foreign wars or religious revivals, such as Methodism in eighteenth-century Great Britain, serve (unconsciously or as a matter of policy) to drain off potentially revolutionary unrest. And, of course, many revolts are simply suppressed. One of the most famous failures of a coup in modern times was the attempt by certain German army officers to overthrow the Nazi regime in July 1944. The plot hinged entirely on the assassination of Adolf Hitler (with a bomb) at his eastern-front headquarters at Rastenburg. Once Hitler was dead, the plans called for regular-army seizures of key internal points such as Berlin and Paris as well as the command of frontline forces. Although it can be demonstrated that many of the conspirators were inept and that the

---

[10] Ysabel F. Rennie, *The Argentine Republic* (New York: The Macmillan Company, 1945), pp. 222-224.

regime recovered quickly after the initial shock had passed, none-theless much credit for the failure of the rebellion must be assigned purely to chance. There were a number of major unforeseen events that contributed to the failure of the plot, but the primary factor was the failure of the bomb to kill Hitler—and that failure itself hinged on two entirely uncontrollable factors. First, the site of the daily briefing session at Rastenburg was moved unforeseeably in the early afternoon of July 20 from the customary meeting place, a thick, windowless con-crete bunker, to a wood and stone hut above the ground. Had the bomb exploded in the solidly constructed, enclosed bunker, the con-cussion would probably have killed or seriously maimed every member of the session. Instead, in the hut much of the force of the explosion escaped through the large open windows, Hitler himself receiving only comparatively minor wounds. Yet even with this change of site, the chief conspirator Colonel von Stauffenberg managed to place the bomb, enclosed in a briefcase, within six feet of Hitler. Colonel Brandt, one of the staff members at the briefing, felt the briefcase with his foot and moved it to a more convenient spot. Brandt was killed, Hitler escaped, and the conspirators were rounded up.[11]

Mass uprisings are also subject to failure, particularly jacqueries and millenarianist rebellions. These two types are doomed to almost cer-tain failure by their very nature. Jacqueries, mass rural revolts, are directed primarily to the removal of hated officials. These uprisings are not aimed at the overthrow of government, have little or no ideo-logical content, and no plans for general reforms. If a messiah with a salvationist remedy for social ills appears, and if he can obtain a jacquerie-like following, the consequence is termed revolutionary mil-lenarianism. The target of the rebellion is changed from an attack on bad government to an attack on the system itself. Not all such millen-arianism, however, is necessarily revolutionary, the primary doctrine consisting of an expectation of the millennium, that is, a world free of its present troubles.

Both jacqueries and millenarian revolts are easy targets for the exist-ing power structure. The jacquerie without a social program, with limited leadership capabilities, cannot exploit its initial victories won in the first wild upsurge of hatred and resentment. Victorious on the battlefield, its participants can only appeal to the king or potentate, as to a father figure, to set things right, to revert to the old, just ways of doing things. In these circumstances the incumbent power structure is able to regroup its forces and either smash the rebellion or disrupt it by capturing and executing its leaders. The millenarianists suffer

[11] Goodspeed, *op. cit.*, pp. 172-202.

from some of the same disabilities since they usually have no plans for the governing of society, expecting the solutions of problems to come about in some divine way. The millenarianists, however, do symbolize and articulate some deep-seated and fundamental social and economic problems of their society. While their rebellions generally fail in the short run, they are often harbingers of basic changes to come. Jacqueries usually are not, although governments may make some effort to alleviate the specific grievances that gave rise to the revolt.[12]

Modern mass insurrections, with ideology, trained cadres, and popular support are also subject to frustration. The Hungarian uprising in 1956, although successful as a spontaneous mass revolt, was crushed later by the Russian army, while the civil strife in South Vietnam is stalemated with outside forces fighting on both sides. The Paris Commune of 1871, on the contrary, was crushed by forces entirely indigenous.

The Period of Revolutionary Turmoil

Those who would mount a revolution must destroy the old system and hamstring the elite that give it life. They must eat away at traditional loyalties and ideologies. They must reject enough of the past to build the future on firm foundations. In short, they are first of all nihilists. But they must also build and reconstruct; they must institute in one form or another the political and social changes that originally motivated their revolutionary behavior. Those they attack are also forced into this destruction-reconstruction dichotomy. Any government is likely to defend itself. It seeks to destroy the forces of revolution when it can; and when it cannot, it attempts to placate and temporize. But in any event such a government must reconstruct, either from the wreckage of its successful defense against the revolutionary forces, or from the resultant ideological and structural position to which it has been forced by the unleashed revolutionary pressures.

Actual revolution then superimposes upon its environment the twin elements of destruction and reconstruction. Where the destruction has been deep and vast, the task of rebuilding becomes immense. A *great* revolution[13] involves such destruction-reconstruction in great measure.

The Chinese revolution, now more than a half-century old, exhibits

[12] Johnson, *op. cit.*, pp. 31-39.
[13] In the sense that Pettee uses the term. See George S. Pettee, *The Process of Revolution* (New York: Harper and Bros., 1938).

in many of its multistages this identical phenomenon. The Manchus "fell" to a temporizing regime of Yuan Shi-kai, which in turn succumbed to the Kuomintang, which was overrun by Mao and the Chinese Communists. In all these stages there was something to be destroyed, or compromised, or nullified. In some cases institutions were overthrown—the monarchy was abolished, for example—or the class structure altered (which was accomplished by executing the landlords and justified by the need to create a new political base). Family life and the social mores were attacked and the mechanism of military service used to uproot the individual from his traditional context. Essentially in each stage the dominant group attempted to destroy what could not be molded into acquiescence. These phases were cumulative; relatively little remains today of the Chinese political system of 1900. Ultimately several generations of destruction had to be balanced by ideological consolidation and political rehabilitation. This has been the task of Mao Tse-tung since at least 1949. Reconstruction has taken the form of the amelioration of material conditions, a regeneration of ideological justifications—the Red Guard purge—and a frenzied effort to rebuild for all of Asia.[14]

Perhaps nothing symbolizes this destruction-reconstruction dyad better than the ubiquitous treason trials held during or following virtually every revolution and the equally common attempts to create new constitutions. The former represents destruction: individuals are removed and punished. The act symbolizes the rejection of the past. Then a new beginning must be made. What better way is there than to go back to the *Grundnorm* and produce a new constitutional document that symbolizes the changes to come? It does not matter that the punishments meted out in typical treason trials may have nothing essentially to do with the traditional political system being rejected or that the new constitution, once it is enthusiastically adopted, has no relationship to the political system that evolves. All are symbols and all reflect the basic nature of the revolutionary process.

Those who mount revolutions must find big traitors to punish and important institutions to topple. Equally important, when revolution has been successful, it is necessary to put something grandiose in the place of the things that have been destroyed. Usually this is symbolic rather than material. Often there are few material changes that can be made that are big and dramatic enough to justify a revolution. What changes there are, are at the beginning almost entirely negative, that is to say, destructive. The more positive changes inevitably come more

[14] *See* Arthur A. Cohen, *The Communism of Mao Tse-tung* (Chicago: University of Chicago Press, 1964), particularly Chapter II, "Mao and Revolution."

slowly and are less effective. No revolutionary government can resolve its political problems overnight; it cannot immediately raise the
standard of living or alleviate some national disgrace. The search for
national dignity or a place in the sun requires time for its consummation as does the resolution of the chaotic forces unleashed by the revolution itself. Yet it is mandatory that the revolutionary government
(assuming that it has won) *demonstrate dramatic progress* toward the
consummation of its goals.

It is almost essential that in its immediate context this progress be
symbolic. It is tempting, first of all, to transsubstantiate the mass into
The People; the result has been a rash of people's republics and people's democracies. But we should realize "the fraudulence of . . . [the
revolutionary] claim to transfer power to 'the people.'" [15] The very
opposite is generally the case, as Tocqueville noted a century ago,
whether we label it thermidor or something else. "So clear," as Eugene
Kamenka has pointed out, "and so apparently inevitable, is the central-
izing, dictatorial trend of revolutions that for the first time in human
history we actually find revolution cynically used as a *means* for welding together a diffuse [and perhaps even a democratic!] society, for
creating centralized authority and power." [16]

The Marxian term for this revolutionary centralization is "dictatorship of the proletariat" and for its surcease, "the withering away of
the state." The mass is thus enjoined not to measure revolutionary
expectations against immediate achievements but rather against the
ultimate desideratum.

There is a host of other symbolic changes instituted by the revolutionary regime. The *king* is dead; long live the *president!* Titles are
abolished or altered and a variety of other names and labels under-
goes similar transmogrifications. Palaces and buildings of the old regime
may be plundered or abandoned—thus Amanullah Shah's palaces in
Kabul were left unoccupied for more than a generation after his deposition in 1929—or frantic efforts at eliminating flies or rats become
the index of revolutionary progress. Revolutionary Egypt (after 1952)
had as its symbolic dream the construction of an Aswan High Dam, for
which no sacrifice was too great. Similarly the nationalization of the
Suez Canal symbolized the achievements of the revolution. Where a
disparity of land ownership exists, as so very often is the case in much
of Asia and Latin America, then "land reform" becomes the symbolic
change that justifies revolutionary travail. It does not matter much,

---

[15] Eugene Kamenka, "The Concept of a Political Revolution," in Carl J.
Friedrich (ed.), *Revolution* (Nomos VIII) (New York: Atherton Press, 1966),
p. 131.
[16] *Ibid.*

of course, that this land reform may be incomplete or ineffective or that land productivity is unaltered or decreased by the reform; the symbol remains untarnished. Revolutionary leaders may go unshaved or without ties or wear uniforms to symbolize the continuing struggle to achieve that for which, ideologically at least, the revolution was originally mounted.

One of the most common of symbolic gestures of revolutionary achievement is the preparation of a new constitution. It seems only natural that the constitution of an overthrown and discredited regime should itself be replaced. The new constitution becomes a promise of the great things to come, the symbol of political reconstruction. Although it would not seem creditable that basic constitutional norms would need changing very often, in practice even the most trivial *coup d'état* is likely to presage a new constitutional document. But two things should be noted here: the process of producing a new constitution with its accompaniment of publicity and propaganda is really far more important than the document that is produced; and the final document rarely departs very much from its predecessor in terms of rights, goals, and guarantees. One needn't explore the rich constitutional pastures of Latin America or Asia to find examples of this constant constitutional justification of revolutionary (or pseudorevolutionary) change. French history since 1789 offers an incredible panorama of such changes. France, after all, is now in her *fifth* republic (not to count a congeries of restorations, empires, and a fascist interlude). Most of these required new constitutional documents.

The creation of a new revolutionary party to mobilize the mass is a commonplace of this reconstruction period. The Communist Party became this vehicle in the Soviet Union; the Kuomintang in China, the Republican People's Party in Turkey, and the Falange in Spain. Sometimes the party is elitist (as in the Soviet Union) but usually it is not, for after all its function is to channel the political energies of as many people as possible into support of the regime. This party (or whatever it is called) usually takes the place of all other parties. It performs a variety of subsidiary functions. It recruits new leadership, provides a mechanism for training and indoctrination, creates a new and enlightened culture, supervises education, stimulates the arts, and in general provides the impetus for regimenting life around the revolutionary standards.

It is sometimes argued that revolution carries in its wake a near complete rejection of the totality of the culture of the old regime, whatever this might have been, and that as a consequence the revolutionary environment is characterized by the rise of value-opposites, specifically of lawlessness, moral laxity, atheism, the destruction of property, the upsurge of patriotism, and a variety of similar attributes. It can be seen that this process, if it actually takes place, must be proportional to the *depth* of revolutionary fervor and energy. But many of these attributes are not comparable (for example, lawlessness and patriotism) and some of them cannot be noted unambiguously, for example, moral laxity. Lawlessness, if this is the proper term to employ, is simply the inevitable product of the confusion and chaos that accompanies revolution. It would be incredible to expect that in an atmosphere where so many of the *normal* operations of society have been compromised—the failure to provide food in the cities, to transport workers to their jobs and children to their schools, to inform people of the course of events, and not least of all to provide fire and police protection—that an increasing number of individuals would not act for themselves, careless of regulations and rules that no longer seem to obtain. They may need to do this in order simply to survive.

Where any part of the old system or its myth is challenged (and revolution is an enormous challenge), then all parts suffer from the weakening of the bonds of loyalty and respect. In such circumstances laws are less apt to be obeyed and the rules of social conduct less likely to be observed. In essence, it means that large numbers of people are cut adrift from their normal moorings. Their confused efforts to re-establish standards, in the midst of revolutionary travail, may be identified by some as moral laxity and lawlessness. In fact, individuals respond to revolutionary stimuli in such a variety of ways that it is enormously difficult to generalize very confidently. Some observers report, instead of moral laxity, a return to puritanism and a heightened sense of social responsibility.

The Postrevolutionary Stage

It is not an easy task to determine when a revolution has run its course. In any event, there may not be a sharp division between the environment of the revolution itself and that which follows. The destruction-reconstruction dichotomy is, of course, carried on into the postrevolutionary period. This is the period of "mopping-up" and consolidation. Destruction remains but it is generally different from the wild cataclysm of the revolution itself. The revolution, especially if it is prolonged, has exhausted the energies of the mass. The elite has undoubtedly suffered too; perhaps it has been purged or emasculated. There is likely to be widespread longing for a return to "normality," that is, for a suspension of excitement and a resumption of the daily lives of individual ambition so difficult to pursue in the midst of revolution.

The energies of a revolution may even be cyclical in that they spend themselves more than once, rebuilding on each occasion to a portion of their former strength. Whether a revolutionary upheaval subsides suddenly or in one long decline or whether it ends only after many starts and stops, the final results are much the same. The same revolutionary exhaustion is there, the same need for recuperation and rehabilitation.

It is possible that the life of the revolution will be interrupted by counterrevolution,[17] produced by hostile power centers (not necessarily representing the old regime). There are some students of revolution who believe that revolution inevitably produces counterrevolution, as a kind of natural action-reaction process, but this depends, of course, on the precise definition given to counterrevolution. Counterrevolution may be viewed as nothing more complicated than the weathering of revolutionary zeal. Or it may be thought of as any *obstructionary* force, any impediment to revolutionary fruition. It is tempting for the revolutionary to view it in this manner, but the identification is hardly very consequential for our purposes. Viewed as above, however, counterrevolution would be very commonplace. If the term is given more substance, if it is thought of as an additional revolutionary force whose direction-vector is noncoincident with the main revolutionary movement, then the phenomenon is not so common and certainly not inevitable.

Ultimately the main revolutionary (and counterrevolutionary) forces are spent or at least resolved, and the postrevolutionary environment is entered upon. Although this is the period of rebuilding and consolidation, there is apt to be considerable chaos for several years. Some of the political managers and actors will have changed along with many of their functions. Whatever changes will have occurred in the bureaucracy will merely exacerbate feelings of insecurity and uncertainty. The government on the highest level will also be characterized by uncertainty. Revolutionary leaders will now have become government leaders; they will have encountered problems unanticipated and acquired responsibilities unformulated. Ultimately order returns. But the chaotic uncertainties are not eliminated quickly. Years may be required to tranquilize the *great* revolution; even the *coup d'état* (or its attempt) will produce its reverberations of unsettlement.

[17] A recent volume of pertinence is James H. Meisel, *Counter-Revolution: How Revolutions Die* (New York: Atherton Press, 1966).

One prominent feature of this period of postrevolutionary troubles is the tendency to embrace all sorts of programs or adventures as aspects of revolutionary goals. This may be the innocuous land reform, or at any rate, some meddling with the agricultural and/or industrial marketplace. It may mean military adventures abroad. The enthusiasm and sincerity of government leaders for these widely varying programs may be quite real. They now own a government; the opportunity to do the many things long dreamed of is at hand, and it would be remarkable indeed if revolutionary leaders did not engage in a plethora of experimentation.

For some revolutionaries the success of *their* revolution merely presages the even more grand success of world revolution. In theory Marxism has always suggested world revolution; the great struggle between Trotsky and Stalin revolved (again in theory) about "permanent revolution" and "socialism in one country." [18] Hitler was eager to infect Europe with his own revolution. Revolutionary France and revolutionary Russia had messages for the world and were determined to disseminate these messages regardless of the agony involved. Castro has talked of "exporting" revolution to the remainder of Latin America.

Ultimately, it seems, most revolutions produce centralization of authority. This suggests to some that the almost inevitable product of revolution is dictatorship of some sort and, if not quite that to others, that "tyrants or a succession of tyrants are almost always the creation of revolutions." [19] But if dictatorship and some sort of tyranny are the results of revolution—of course, this is not always the case—then the postrevolutionary environment, as the early chaos is absorbed, becomes increasingly authoritarian and totalitarian. Does such an environmental change make further revolution more likely? Sometimes it does, especially if the faith in the new order deteriorates when revolutionary expectations are unrealized.

More important, the fact that a revolution has occurred can never quite be erased. Successful revolution often encourages future attempts to rebel; once the sanctity of the state myth has been shattered, every successive attempt at extraconstitutional political alteration becomes easier to achieve. The extreme is where *coups d'état* become institutionalized as methods of obtaining *any* political alteration in government. Thus revolutions often result in more authoritarian government, and at the same time in government more likely to succumb to future revolution.

[18] Of interest is Gunter Nollau, *International Communism and World Revolution* (London: Hollis and Carter, 1961).

[19] Calvin B. Hoover, "Revolutions and Tyranny," *The Virginia Quarterly Review,* Vol. 36 (1960), p. 183. Italics in original.

The External Environment[20]

Political events, including revolutions, do not occur in isolation. It may appear to us that a particular revolution is of wholly indigenous and even spontaneous origin, but the probability of such an occurrence must be very small indeed. Such a revolution would have to be led by men unsponsored, unaided, and uninspired by the extranational scene; its course would be totally unaffected by the world environment, and its final consummation and success utterly independent of foreign attitudes and actions. This is a fanciful picture that simply does not exist. Indeed if it is realized that the modern revolutionary impulse is to a very high degree the result of foreign agitation, of foreign assistance, and if not these, at least of foreign inspiration, then the sterility of a revolutionary model in isolation becomes apparent.

Americans need not be reminded of the vital role played in their own revolution by the French. The French Revolution in its turn cannot remotely be comprehended outside of the context of the European arena of the late eighteenth century. The Russian Revolution was not unrelated to its external environment. Indeed, it is virtually impossible to find an example of a successful revolution uninfluenced by the world community. Even the relatively spontaneous *coup d'état* in some obscure country carried out by a motley collection of even more obscure army officers may very well have—indeed is very likely to have— drawn its inspiration from events abroad. We can therefore lay down the general proposition that revolutions never occur in isolation; but the more interesting question of how the external environment affects the course of revolution remains to be answered. We keep searching, for example, for the effects of the external environment on the Hanoi government in North Vietnam. To what degree are its actions shaped by Soviet and/or Red Chinese advisors, and by American military efforts? The same situation obtains in most revolutions. It is difficult to quantify "aid and support," and it is almost impossible to be specific about inspiration.

The contemporary world is one characterized by a great deal of intercommunication and value exchange. Increasingly groups are led to conspiracy and insurrection by comparison of the benefits that they derive from their government with those other peoples have derived from theirs. In this case the external environment influences by simply existing. But there are also propaganda outlets in the world that

[20] James N. Rosenau (ed.), *International Aspects of Civil Strife* (Princeton: Princeton University Press, 1964) is a useful compilation on this general subject.

encourage revolution by extolling the virtues of change, and there
are governments actively engaged in fomenting revolution among their
neighbors. For example, an African Liberation Committee was formed
in 1963 from among the Black African states with the express purpose
to aid and abet the destruction of the current regimes in Portuguese
Africa and the Republic of South Africa.[21]

The foregoing represents an active environment, one in which revolution is fostered and encouraged. The twentieth-century world certainly has been such an environment. It is commonplace to observe
the clarion appeal of Communist revolution. Twentieth-century Americans have found themselves the inheritors of a revolutionary tradition
that is occasionally embarrassing to us. Subject peoples, or those in the
throes of revolution, often expect a great deal from us in sympathy
and aid *precisely because our national origin was revolutionary.* We
have, however, lost some of our revolutionary zeal, although we remember enough of our past to feel guilty about our lack of empathy
with present-day "colonial peoples" struggling for independence. On
the other hand, we are anxious to encourage revolution against Communist regimes. But the United States and the Soviet Union (as well
as Red China) are not the sole sources of revolutionary encouragement; indeed, it is not necessary to be a major power to serve as a
source of such disturbances. The energetic propaganda of an active
leader of a small state may generate results out of all proportion to
its base. Cuba is not a major state; it is certainly not powerful. But
Castro's revolutionary call in the early 1960's was still a heady message
that frightened political leaders all over the Americas. The same could
be said of the sometime African leaders, Ahmed Ben Bella and Kwame
Nkrumah, whose revolutionary messages found ready audiences in
Asia and Africa.

A state can propagandize revolution among its neighbors; it can also
aid and abet revolution by more material means. The American role
in the various Cuban revolutionary attempts to overthrow Castro—
culminating in the Bay of Pigs episode—is an appropriate example.
We did more than encourage the overthrow of Castro. We financed
expeditions against him, we trained and organized those who partici-
pated in such expeditions, and we designed a national policy to weaken
the Castro regime and make revolution against it more readily attainable. This leads often to outright *intervention,* which is perhaps the
extreme form that the external environment can take. We did not take
the final overt step of intervention in Cuba, although we did intervene

[21] Leonard M. Thompson, *Politics in the Republic of South Africa* (Boston:
Little, Brown & Co., 1966), p. 12.

in the Dominican Republic in 1965. It was the Russians who intervened in the Hungarian revolution in 1956.

With intervention the revolution is no longer quite an internal war; it can become the excuse for an international clash of force over issues transcending the revolution itself. The decision by the Russians to employ force in November 1956 against the Hungarian revolutionary government of Imre Nagy was hardly based on Russian sympathy with one Hungarian group or another or their views; it was dictated by Russian stakes in Europe and her prestige position in the world; moreover, it was facilitated by Western apathy plus involvement in Suez. As Zinner has remarked:

> The Soviet intervention in Hungary was as effective as it was brutal. Communists throughout Eastern Europe, including Tito, condoned it. The victory of the revolution would have threatened them all. More important, the successful Soviet intervention (and the corollary inactivity of the West) caused a definite reorientation in the thinking of the people. The Hungarian effort showed them the national and international limits of disruption of Communist control. Instead of nurturing further hopes of liberation against the wishes of Moscow, they came to recognize that any amelioration in their condition must be achieved through and with the consent of Moscow. Eastern Europe became pacified.[22]

Moreover, just as Soviet intervention in Hungary was necessitated by extra-Hungarian issues, so would American intervention or counter-intervention in Hungary in 1956 have been dictated by something else than an abstract attachment to the liberation of peoples subjected to Communist control.

There are many examples of intervention in the revolutionary affairs of other nations. Some political leaders are not above planting the seeds of revolution among their neighbors and then nurturing the young rebellious shoots until the destruction of a regime has been brought about. These activities generate considerable indignation and denunciation, but it is likely that such intervention will continue for a very long time to come.

We have, of course, "the requirement in international law that every unusual change in governmental arrangements, be it caused by a coup, revolt, or revolution, must be recognized by other members of the international community."[23] Recognition is a major element in the

[22] Zinner, *op. cit.*, p. 349.
[23] George Modelski, "International Settlement of Internal War," in Rosenau, *op. cit.*, p. 128.

influence that the external environment presses upon a revolution. A revolutionary government, in order to survive, must deal with other governments, negotiate agreements with them, and promote trade with their states. A government that fails to secure recognition from a great proportion of the international community is less likely to survive; it is because of this that some nations have had *recognition policies* designed to discourage the existence of governments of which they disapprove.

Thus the international community did not immediately recognize the Soviet government after the Russian revolution—the United States did not recognize the Soviet Union until 1933—nor does it completely recognize the Red Chinese government today. In the case of large nations such as these, nonrecognition has undoubtedly been inconvenient to the revolutionary regimes but not fatal to their survival. On the other hand, the lack of recognition spelled the extinction of Moise Tshombe's independent Katanga in 1963. "World opinion," whatever it may mean in detail, can be a compelling factor in some revolutionary situations. That is why military groups are so anxious to have prestigious front men to symbolize their coup. Such men will be more likely to generate enthusiasm abroad and to obtain recognition and support in the critical postrevolutionary period.

There is no doubt that the external environment can influence the life of a revolution or the coup that heralds its birth. The proper study of a revolution must include this environment as an integral part of the revolution itself. Theories of revolution are perforce incomplete that do not give attention to the many facets of this external environment; the inspiration to revolution by external propaganda and events; the covert and overt support given to revolutionaries by their doctrinal or sentimental compatriots abroad (which sometimes assumes the extreme form of intervention); finally the postrevolutionary recognition and support that can be given to or withheld from the revolutionary government.

Summary and Conclusions

Revolution is a phenomenon in space-time. It occurs within an environment that it simultaneously affects. It seems useful to speak of "stages" in the revolutionary process. If we restrict the definition of revolution to the application of force, or the threat of force, to overturn a government, or to force a government to make substantial changes in policies or personnel, then we can pinpoint the birth of revolution with some precision. It is the latter meaning that we have attached to the term.

All revolutions begin with violence, actual or implied. Despite the many types, purposes, and results that revolutions may have, their beginnings appear to be limited to three distinct formats: (1) the protracted political struggle between powerful elite factions, parties, and groups for dominance that leads eventually to armed conflict; (2) the sudden uprising by a small band of conspirators to seize immediate control of the state apparatus (the coup); and (3) an outburst of armed violence by either massed forces or a small group of guerrilla fighters.

Whichever of the three forms of initial action that the revolution may take, a triggering element is necessary to propel potential revolutionaries into motion. Obviously agitators, organizers, and other types of leaders are helpful, but sometimes catastrophes, natural or manmade, or even reforms and improvements initiated by the incumbent government can set off violent mass upheavals motivated by the desire for change and the belief that it is attainable by forceful action. A few uprisings, doomed to failure, are the responses of desperate men to intolerable situations. In modern times revolutionary parties have been instrumental in giving guidance and focus to the discontented, and in choosing the auspicious moment to attack the incumbents. At other times, the constituted authorities themselves have invited attacks by intransigence or stupidity in the face of popular demands.

Finally, whatever the reasons for revolutions, whatever the format of initial action, whatever the triggering elements, nothing is inevitable in the birth or the course of revolution. Concessions and reforms, if handled properly, can turn revolutionaries into conservatives under given circumstances; on the other hand, intransigence on the part of the incumbents, if accompanied by a judicious use of force, may well suppress a revolutionary outbreak. The revolutionaries themselves may well fail owing to a faulty estimate of their own strength in relation to the strength of their enemies. A successful outbreak depends much on the leadership available to both sides, and above all, chance can never be discounted. Revolutions are made and directed and opposed by men, men who are fallible, men who do not have complete control of their destinies.

The lifespan of revolutions is a variable thing. Some require years for their consummation; others mature within days or even hours. It seems reasonable to expect that such variability produces a heterogeneity of stages. But every revolution will possess the destruction-reconstruction dyad. To rebel is to destroy, in some measure, the features (or at the very least, to remove the personnel) of the incumbent regime. Yet it is obvious that no revolution can be restricted merely to destruction. It must be justified by what it does in refurbishing the political system.

Revolutions must be consolidated; there must ultimately be a return to stability and acceptance. The postrevolutionary environment will be characterized by the many ideological and practical efforts to justify and hypostatize the revolutionary fervor.

No revolution is immune to the world environment. Revolution may be fostered within a given area by other governments; it is certainly inspired by examples elsewhere. Reciprocally its success or failure will affect the chances of revolution in other places and times.

5

Revolutionary Leaders and Followers

Of Napoleon, Godfrey Elton has said that obscure forces in the French Revolution raised him up to satisfy their own needs, "and had there been no Napoleon to determine and consolidate the Revolution, the Revolution must have found some other to play his rôle." [1] On the other hand there is Eric Hoffer. He sees mass movements arising as the old order is discredited, but insists that "the discrediting is not an automatic result of the blunders and abuses of those in power." Rather, he argues, it is "the deliberate work of men of words with a grievance." Furthermore, "where men of words are absent, a regime may long continue despite abuses, where the regime has some merit but men of words damn it, it can be swept away." [2]

Revolutionary Leaders

Assuming that men of leadership ability have some degree of influence on revolutionary movements, what are their various roles and functions? For the initiation, organization, and success of mass movements, Hoffer posits three distinct categories of leadership: men of words to prepare the ground, fanatics to hatch the actual movement, and men of action to consolidate and carry it through. The function of the men of words is not only to discredit the prevailing myths and institutions and to alienate the people from them, but also to furnish new doctrines and slogans to give a new faith to the masses. At the

[1] Godfrey Elton, *The Revolutionary Idea in France, 1789-1871* (New York: Longmans, Green & Co., Inc., 1923), p. 87.
[2] Eric Hoffer, *The True Believer: Thoughts on the Nature of Mass Movements* (New York: The New American Library, 1958), p. 119.

same time, such men undermine the convictions of the ruling elites in order to weaken their will to resist the revolution when it comes. Even though the ground may thus be well prepared by the men of words, it is argued that a mass movement does not materialize without the second type of leader, the fanatic.

> It needs the iron will, daring and vision of an exceptional leader to concert and mobilize existing attitudes and impulses into the collective drive of a mass movement. The leader personifies the certitude of the creed and the defiance and grandeur of power. He articulates and justifies the resentment dammed up in the souls of the frustrated. He kindles the vision of a breathtaking future so as to justify the sacrifice of a transitory present. He stages the world of make believe so indispensable for the realization of self-sacrifice and united action. He evokes the enthusiasm of communion—the sense of liberation from a petty and meaningless individual existence.[3]

But, Hoffer warns, a leader "cannot conjure a movement out of the void." Mass discontent and dissatisfaction must first exist before leader and movement can appear. No matter how gifted the leader, no matter how cogent the cause, followers do not appear until conditions are ripe. Many leaders must wait for years before their hour comes. "Accidents and the activities of other men have to set the stage for them before they can enter and start their performance." [4]

Once the revolution is won, still a third type of leadership is necessary, that which can consolidate the revolutionary participants and mold them into a new order.[5] Rex Hopper divides these "men of action" into two subcategories, the statesmen and the administrative executives. The statesmen formulate the social policies promised in the period of ferment and upheaval; they are men particularly astute in estimating and evaluating the nature and direction of the prevailing social forces.[6] The administrators, on the other hand, are the technicians skilled in creating and manipulating institutional arrangements to carry out the policies enunciated by the statesmen. In the final consolidation of victory the technicians administer the policies formulated by the statesmen to satisfy demands voiced by prophets and reformers, in consequence of unrest generated by agitators.[7]

Harold Lasswell uses a model similar to Hoffer's. For the latter's men

---

[3] *Ibid.*, p. 105.
[4] *Ibid.*, pp. 103-104.
[5] *Ibid.*, p. 135.
[6] Rex D. Hopper, "The Revolutionary Process: A Frame of Reference for the Study of Revolutionary Movements," *Social Forces*, Vol. 28 (1950), p. 277.
[7] *Ibid.*, pp. 378-379.

of words Lasswell has manipulators of symbols; for fanatics, managers of violence; and for men of action, organizers. Lasswell points out, however, that the relative importance of these three types varies from revolution to revolution. In China, for example, the specialist on violence played a particularly large role while the specialist on symbols had a role substantially reduced. Administrators formed about half the revolutionary elite, the military one-third, and journalists and educators a very small percentage.[8]

In a study of riots and crowds George Rudé found that the role and function of leaders in preindustrial disturbances varied depending upon the type of disturbance, that is, whether the uprising was a food riot, wage strike, religious dispute, machinery-breaking binge, tenant-farmer outburst, or farm-laborer rebellion; whether it was urban or rural. Some leaders came from outside the group, some from within, but in all cases the leaders gave the crowds cohesion and unity, guided and directed their energies, and provided them with manifestoes and ideas if not always an ideology. Some "leaders" of rebellious groups have found themselves recruited to a role they did not want in a movement of which they disapproved—for example, Martin Luther and the peasant uprising in Germany. Other leaders have found their ideas adapted to purposes and means other than those they intended. Because of the frequent difference in social class between the followers and leaders, and because, therefore, of the lack of concordance in their social and political aspirations, leaders have also found themselves forced to accede to some of their followers' demands against their own inclinations. In the French Revolution, for example, the masses imposed price ceilings on basic commodities against prevailing Jacobin support of the free market.[9] In other words, at times leaders must also be followers if they wish to remain leaders.

In the performance of his role, the revolutionary leader today is frequently in direct contact with his followers or target groups. This was not always so. Prior to the mid-nineteenth century (the revolutions of 1848 and the Chartist Movement) direct communication between leaders and masses was rare. Robespierre talked in the National Assembly and in the Jacobin Clubs, while intermediaries took his words to the crowds. The press was used, manifestoes circulated, and

[8] Robert C. North and Ithiel de Sola Pool, "Kuomintang and Chinese Communist Elites," in Harold D. Lasswell and Daniel Lerner (eds.), *World Revolutionary Elites: Studies in Coercive Ideological Movements* (Cambridge: M.I.T. Press, 1965), pp. 386-387.

[9] George Rudé, *The Crowd in History: A Study of Popular Disturbances in France and England, 1730-1848* (New York: John Wiley and Sons, Inc. [c. 1964]), pp. 247-249.

word-of-mouth campaigns were conducted. The direct personal ha-
rangue by a leader of an audience does not become common until the
latter part of the nineteenth century.[10]

In contrast to the mass movement discussed above, the *coup d'état*
involving relatively few people calls for different kinds of leadership
roles. D. J. Goodspeed notes that basically two functions are called for:
strategy and tactics, and ideally a clear division of responsibility between the two is advisable. In a coup, strategy must be concerned
primarily with political considerations. Particularly if the regime has
some merit and some substantial support, the coup leaders must be
aware of potentially adverse reactions to an overthrow of government,
and plan adequate measures to counteract them. Goodspeed believes
that in a nation at any given time only a few men possess strategic or
political acumen. A flair for tactics is much more common, but even
the tactician must be concerned somewhat with political considerations. The political leaders of a coup—that is, the future government
leaders—must direct the overall strategy and timing, while the tactical
leaders must command the action squads. The political leaders must
be men who are able to win the allegiance of the army and the government bureaucracy, and it assists them immeasurably if they are known
and respected abroad. Tactical leaders must have courage and determination, but not too much intelligence or too much interest in politics,
or too much ambition. Discipline is always a problem within a revolutionary group, and unreliable types must be excluded if possible.
Seldom are both strategic and tactical leadership combined in the
same person.[11] Although both functions were performed by General
Uriburu in the Argentine revolution of 1930, his success resulted more
from the decay of the incumbent administration than from his own
abilities. His lack of political acumen was demonstrated repeatedly
during his period in power, until he was finally overthrown by more
able political leaders within the military and the civilian circles he
ostensibly led.[12]

Characteristics of Revolutionary Leaders

Is it possible to speak of a revolutionary type? Are certain personality traits necessary for revolutionary leadership? Are certain qualities
of character *sine qua non* to instill trust and confidence in subordinates

[10] *Ibid.*, p. 249.
[11] D. J. Goodspeed, *The Conspirators* (London: The Macmillan Co., 1962),
pp. 216-217.
[12] Ysabel F. Rennie, *The Argentine Republic* (New York: The Macmillan Co.,
1945), pp. 221-228.

and followers? Is age important? Are social class and economic status determinants of leadership involving violent action? Students of revolutions have not arrived at definitive conclusions, but in certain broad areas they demonstrate considerable agreement.

First, let us dispose of a myth or two. The bitter opponents of revolution, either in the abstract or concrete, have often portrayed revolutionists as wild-eyed, frequently bearded, and unkempt bomb-throwers and criminals who revel in violence for the sake of violence. No one denies that such characters have appeared in revolutionary movements. Many rebels, including underworld figures, have been attracted to revolution because of its violence, and emerge for a time into notoriety. Although they welcome revolution, they could never bring it about, and they relapse into obscurity as soon as order of any kind is restored. A model of this behavior is Nestor Makhno's career as a guerrilla leader in the Russia of 1917 to 1920. Crane Brinton says flatly that it is not possible "to isolate a revolutionary type labeled 'criminal,' 'degenerate,' and neatly conforming to some anthropometric standards. . . . Certainly there are many revolutionists who . . . behave as criminals behave in stable societies; but the proportion of such revolutionists does not seem extraordinarily high." [13] Another common myth holds that even if rebels are not criminal types, they are recruited primarily from the lowest rungs of society. Even a cursory look at a few leaders of several revolutions denies the truth of this. Robespierre and Lenin were provincial middle class, while Washington and Jefferson were colonial oligarchs, and Cromwell a country gentleman.

The varying roles and functions of leaders at different stages of the revolutionary movement obviously demand different leadership qualifications. Frequently, therefore, personnel changes occur as the revolutionary movement progresses, since rarely does the same individual possess all the traits necessary for the various roles. In France the *philosophes* gave way to the lawyers and bureaucrats, the moderates to the radicals, the democrats to the authoritarians, the civilians to the military. At times, however, a single leader can provide the original inspiration, the political organization, the road to victory, the consolidation of power, and finally even the destruction of a revolutionary mass movement, as did Hitler in Germany.

Rex Hopper has postulated two types of early agitators. Where the people are apathetic he sees him as "the calm, dignified type who stirs the people not by what he does, but by what he says." [14] Frequently such leaders are not recognized as progenitors of revolution until after

[13] Crane Brinton, *The Anatomy of Revolution* (New York: Vintage Books, 1956), p. 119.
[14] Hopper, *op. cit.*, p. 272.

80 The Theory of Revolution

the fact. The other type, which appears when the people are already aroused but too timid or ignorant to act, is "excitable, restless, and aggressive." [15] Then, when the movement proceeds beyond aimless unrest and focuses on specific problems, a second stage of revolutionary leadership emerges. Some agitators are like prophets—men who see themselves as set apart, who believe that they have special knowledge of the causes of unrest and discontent. They speak with authority and proclaim a new message, a new philosophy. Others are reformers attacking specific evils and developing clearly defined programs. Then come the men who attempt to change conditions. They are the men Hoffer calls fanatics.[16] Various authors have used the terms authoritarian, frustrated, inflexible, abnormal, and emotional to describe the revolutionary leader at this stage. Chalmers Johnson notes that in troubled societies some persons attack the system violently because they "feel" the need of change.[17] Goodspeed points out that the rebel leaders that he studied differed from ordinary men in "the determination and inflexibility with which they held their political opinions." [18] He says further that most "had highly emotional natures and had completely convinced themselves of the absolute rightness of their cause." [19] Johnson in his broader and more theoretical study supports this position by maintaining that coup conspirators always assume that a system is out of balance whether or not it is.

> They further believe that the masses are victimized by the unsatisfactory way in which the system functions, but they suppose that the masses themselves do not have a "complete" sense of dysfunction and do not understand precisely how the system ought to function. Therefore, the conspirators plan to seize power in the name of, and for the sake of, the masses but without the masses' active participation.[20]

So convinced of the rightness of their cause are most revolutionary leaders that they assume autocratic dictatorial control when their revolutions or coups are successful no matter what their previous public political philosophy may have been. Priscilla Robertson says that the greatest failure in the uprisings of 1848 was that the men who led the revolts never really trusted the people. Most became either mass hypnotists like Robert Blum or authoritarian improvers like Mazzini,

[15] *Ibid.*
[16] *Ibid.*, pp. 274-275.
[17] Chalmers Johnson, *Revolution and the Social System,* Hoover Institution Studies, No. 3 (Stanford: Hoover Institution, 1964), p. 51.
[18] Goodspeed, *op. cit.,* p. 233.
[19] *Ibid.*
[20] Johnson, *op. cit.,* pp. 52-53.

Blanc, and Kossuth, all of whom were democrats in theory.[21] It may well be, however, that only authoritarian personalities have the drive and the conviction to carry out revolutions successfully.

Brian Crozier says "it takes a rebel to rebel." By that he means "intolerable conditions" are an insufficient explanation for revolutions. Some men tolerate more than others. Millions in India are passive under conditions that would be "intolerable" in the United States or Western Europe. Or put another way, "hunger may spur a man to rebel, but not if it is hunger so acute and constant that he is robbed of energy and the will to fight." [22] Not only must a potential rebel leader believe that he can succeed and improve his condition, but he must also have the vital qualities of will, courage, and the ability to concentrate on essentials. To be born with these is not enough; the would-be rebel must cultivate these qualities during the long years of waiting for the right conditions to prevail for his leadership to be effective. In his concentration on essentials, the rebel leader must not only know what he is against, but also what he is for. The first is easier to develop than the second. Most of the African rebels knew they were against colonial rule, but were vague about what kind of an independent country they wanted, and hazier still about how to achieve a viable society. By contrast General Grivas in Cyprus fought against British rule and just as definitely for union with Greece.[23] In pursuing his aims the rebel leader must be tough, courageous, and intransigent. Most are uncompromising, and few worry much about the morality of revolution. In Goodspeed's studies only the anti-Nazi rebels of 1944 were men of deep religious convictions who struggled with their consciences over assassinations. Of the others, Goodspeed says: "Whatever their convictions, they held them with a pathological intensity. . . . Sane men do not carve women up with their swords or empty their revolvers into bodies already dead." [24]

All students of revolutionary leadership have pointed to the presence of fanaticism in most challengers to established orders, but none more so than Eric Hoffer. In his list of a dozen important characteristics for the top leader of a mass movement, he names four as primary: (1) audacity; (2) capacity for winning and holding the loyalty of a group of able lieutenants; (3) understanding that the greatest craving of his followers is for communion and unity; and (4) a fanatical con-

[21] Priscilla Robertson, *Revolutions of 1848: A Social History* (New York: Harper & Row, Publishers, 1960), pp. 418-419.
[22] Brian Crozier, *The Rebels: A Study of Post-War Insurrections* (London: Chatto & Windus, Ltd., 1960), p. 9.
[23] *Ibid.*, p. 10.
[24] Goodspeed, *op. cit.*, p. 234.

viction that he has the one and only truth. The others are iron will, joy in defiance, faith in his luck and destiny, capacity for passionate hatred, contempt for the present, a cunning estimate of human nature, a delight in spectacles and ceremonials, and an unbounded brazenness in his disregard of fairness and consistency. What the leader does not need is exceptional intelligence, noble character, or originality. In fact, Hoffer says, these are perhaps not even desirable. The quality of a leader's ideas seems to play a minor role in his success. The arrogant gesture, singlehanded defiance of the world, and disregard of other's opinions are far more effective in winning support.[25] "Charlatanism of some degree is indispensable to effective leadership. There can be no mass movement without some deliberate misrepresentation of facts."[26] Neither does the rebel leader need to be original. A realist in his understanding of human nature, he must talk the language of the visionary and the idealist. But in so doing he can borrow from both friend and foe, both past and contemporary.[27] Finally he must believe, and believe fanatically, in himself and in his cause. Hoffer insists that only a fanatic can hatch a genuine mass movement. Only he can direct the disaffection created by the men of words, only he can push reforms to basic structural changes. "When the old order begins to crack, he wades in with all his might and recklessness to blow the whole hated present to high heaven."[28] Action is essential to a successful rebel leader since not only he but the bulk of his followers are persons whose talents and temperament are suited for a life of action but are condemned by circumstances to idleness. Lenin, Trotsky, Mussolini, and Hitler were all endless talkers who suddenly sprang to action when the time was ripe. Unfortunately, the fanatic has difficulty settling down even after the victory is won and his new order begins to emerge. The true fanatic keeps groping for extremes, and if not brought under control tears his movement apart by creating dissension.[29]

One other major quality a successful revolutionary must have is the personal magnetism to attract able followers and to command blind obedience. "All mass movements rank obedience with the highest virtues and put it on a level with faith. . . ."[30] And with good reason, since a revolutionary mass movement depends for success on its solidarity and the necessity of great sacrifice, even of life, on the part of the followers. The would-be leader must attract not only an ignorant or

[25] Hoffer, *op. cit.*, pp. 105-106.
[26] *Ibid.*, p. 107.
[27] *Ibid.*, pp. 107-108.
[28] *Ibid.*, p. 131.
[29] *Ibid.*, p. 133.
[30] *Ibid.*, p. 108.

poorly informed rank and file but a large group of intelligent and fearless lieutenants who can organize and administer large-scale enterprises. These same lieutenants, however, must have limited political ambitions for themselves, and must "submit wholly to the will of the leader, draw their inspiration and driving force from him, and glory in this submission." [31]

The men of action who emerge after the revolutionary victory generally have personalities distinct from those of both the men of words and the fanatics. These men tend to be cool-headed, calculating, eclectic, and often ruthless. "The genuine man of action," says Eric Hoffer, "is not a man of faith but a man of law." [32] He tries to preserve an impressive façade of faith within the new order, continues to use propaganda, but relies mainly on force for compliance with his will. He spares no effort to present the new order as "the glorious consummation of the hopes and struggles of the early days," [33] but borrows from everywhere, even from the old order, to achieve permanence and stability. Dictatorship is a characteristic of this stage not only as a manifestation of a lust for power, but as the "deliberate employment of a device" to establish order. [34]

In some of the preindustrial food riots and wage strikes, there were no real leaders, but the police tended to arrest as such the more exuberant, the more daring, or those who were pushed forward as spokesmen for the rioters. The boisterous, brawling types seem to appear frequently in the more primitive and traditional kinds of political violence. [35] William Stokes points out that the old-fashioned provincial *caudillo* (leader) of Latin America frequently rose to his position of authority by an outstanding performance among local bosses in some combination of drinking, card-playing, carousing, and brawling. When this happened, public controversies were resolved quickly and relatively peaceably, but in a way entirely disassociated from the formal structure of government. When no one local boss could establish his personal authority, endemic violence, costly and time-consuming, could wreck a province or region of a country. [36]

One further question we must ask about our revolutionary leaders. Why did they choose to challenge the society in which they lived, to the point where they were willing to risk their lives and liberty? Many

[31] *Ibid.*, p. 106.
[32] *Ibid.*, p. 136.
[33] *Ibid.*, p. 137.
[34] *Ibid.*
[35] Rudé, *op. cit.*, pp. 250-251.
[36] William S. Stokes, "Violence as a Power Factor in Latin American Politics," *The Western Political Quarterly,* Vol. 5 (1952), pp. 448-449.

men have leadership qualities for innumerable kinds of enterprises, including politics. Why do some pursue the incredibly difficult and dangerous task of overturning their governments? There is perhaps one explanation that stands out beyond all others: frustration. Eric Hoffer's *The True Believer* is an almost unrelieved study in frustration, that is, "the inability to act." Crozier defines the term as "the inability to do something one badly wants to do, through circumstances beyond one's control." [37] He goes on to say that "the nature of their frustrations [and one can add their degree as well] varies enormously. . . ." Some slight changes in circumstances would probably have discouraged the Argentine coup of 1930, but nothing short of completely altered national and perhaps international conditions could have stopped Lenin, Hitler, or Mussolini. If this is true, then obviously the successful revolutionary leader is one who can overcome that inability, that sense of inadequacy, that frustration, by launching himself and his frustrated followers into action, "a cure for all that ails them." [38] Crozier agrees with Eric Hoffer's estimate by insisting that "[f]rustration is the one element common to all rebels, whatever their aims, political ideas or social backgrounds," [39] and that where conditions that create frustrations continue, rebellion is bound to occur. In an even more pessimistic vein, Crozier maintains that where the origins of the frustration are personal and psychological, the authorities can do virtually nothing to relieve the situation.[40]

But to offer frustration as the explanation of revolutionary leadership is incomplete. Of course, some people with enough courage, will, drive, or what have you, will fight and struggle and risk their lives to do or be something that they cannot when they want it badly enough. The contented and the well-adjusted are obviously not going to overturn that which contributes to their well-being and happiness. We must ask the further question: What creates the frustration? In a large sense we have already tried to answer this question with respect to mass movements in Chapter 3, but it might be well at this point to examine it somewhat more closely on the personal level. Of the leaders involved in his studies, Goodspeed holds that all but the German conspirators of 1944 were, if not insane, mentally unbalanced or unstable. Most, he says, had personality quirks. The Irish leaders of the Easter Rebellion were, "perhaps, mystics, dreamers, men exalted, but they were not completely sane. It is the same with the Bolsheviks. . . . Mussolini, of the bulging eyes and the timid disposition, was clearly

[37] Crozier, *op. cit.*, p. 16.
[38] Hoffer, *op. cit.*, p. 112.
[39] Crozier, *op. cit.*, p. 15.
[40] *Ibid.*

psychopathic." [41] He goes on to say that the use of secret societies, oaths, signs, code names, disguises, and posturing indicate that these rebels "lived perpetually in a realm of phantasy." [42] Goodspeed concludes that "these people were not merely men whose moral and emotional development was prematurely arrested. . . . These were children gone mad, who tragically found real guns to play with." [43]

Perhaps all of Goodspeed's examples were insane or mentally unbalanced (and even this is open to some dispute), but to offer "madness" as the compelling reason for revolutionary activity seems a gross oversimplification. Brinton offers a more sophisticated explanation of frustration than simple mental unbalance. More or less assuming that all revolutionary leaders are "frustrated," he does not deny that the criminal, the lunatic, the fanatic, the monster, have come to the fore in revolutionary movements, but he insists that their hour is a brief one. "Once the line of revolutionary orthodoxy is established—and though . . . it is a grim and rigid line, it is not a crazy and aberrant one—once this orthodoxy is established the lunatics, mild or serious, are pretty well kept down." [44] (One might argue with this in view of the German experience, 1933-1945.) On the other hand, argues Brinton, the disputatious, contentious, contrary-minded person, the nonconformist who likes to stand out from the crowd, is a more typical revolutionary type. Frequently, this kind of person is motivated by the highest ideals, however doctrinaire and fanatic he may become. In normal times such idealists do not occupy positions of power and responsibility, but revolutions present them with their chance.[45] Some "frustrated" revolutionary leaders come from the top or middle levels of the old regime; men who should be relatively satisfied with things as they are. Brinton suggests that Lafayette's awkwardness at court contributed to his sponsoring of reforms and changes, that Condorcet's sensitive nature and inherent kindness made him an idealist, and that Mirabeau's and Talleyrand's opportunism persuaded them to shift with the tides as they sensed the victory of the revolution, Napoleon, and finally the restoration.[46] Finally, Brinton postulates the revolutionary type whose talents were never fully utilized, appreciated, or given scope for development in normal times. Marat found an outlet for his talents (and his hatred and envy) in revolutionary journalism; Samuel Adams as a revolutionary propagandist and organizer; and

[41] Goodspeed, *op. cit.*, p. 234.
[42] *Ibid.*, pp. 234-235.
[43] *Ibid.*, p. 235.
[44] Brinton, *op. cit.*, p. 119.
[45] *Ibid.*, pp. 119-121.
[46] *Ibid.*, pp. 114-115.

Oliver Cromwell, a man of practical abilities and some accomplish-
ments, in military leadership. Cromwell would probably have remained
relatively obscure and undistinguished had it not been for the revolution.[47]

Revolutions are led by *comparatively* young men. The very young
and the very old do not figure importantly in revolutionary leadership.
In most revolutions the average age of the leaders tends to span the
range from the late twenties to the early forties. Only in times of upheaval does one find an elite this young, because "[i]n a stable society
political leadership is likely to be a function of achieved status." [48]
In ten Jacobin Clubs that Brinton studied, the average age came to
41.8 years.[49] The average age of the Bolshevik Politburo in 1917 was
39, but by 1957 this average had risen to 57.[50] In the revolt of the
Paris Commune in 1871 the average age of government ministers was
62, while that of the First Executive Committee of the Commune was
37, that of the Committee of Public Safety of the Commune was 40,
and that of the Company of the National Guard defending Fort
Montrouge was 32.5, 40 percent of whom were under 21. Frank
Jellinek maintains that the National Guard Company was representative of the rank and file Communards.[51] The Chinese Revolution of the
twentieth century demonstrates the same patterns. From 1921 to 1931
the average age of the Communist Politburo ranged between 27 and
33. Leaders of the Kuomintang were also young. Most of the revolutionaries, both Communists and Kuomintang, joined the movements in
their student years. Until 1945 no Kuomintang Central Executive Committee had an average age over 45, and no Politburo over 40. After that
the age levels rose steadily.[52] Some exceptions obviously exist: Perón
was 49 when he came to power in Argentina although he had partici-
pated in revolutions and conspiracies since his early thirties.

Just as revolutionary leadership is drawn from a rather broad middle
spectrum in terms of age, so it is similarly drawn in terms of social
origins. The lower classes are generally underrepresented because
they are deficient in the skills and experience for leadership and political manipulation, and the upper classes because they tend to be the
satisfied elements that resist basic changes that a mass uprising would
support. The upper classes are often content to remain aloof from the

[47] *Ibid.*, pp. 115-117.
[48] North and Pool, *op. cit.*, p. 383.
[49] Brinton, *op. cit.*, p. 102.
[50] George K. Schueller, "The Politburo," in Lasswell and Lerner, *op. cit.*, pp.
111-113.
[51] Frank Jellinek, *The Paris Commune of 1871* (London: Victor Gollancz, Ltd.,
1937), p. 173.
[52] North and Pool, *op. cit.*, p. 383.

executions of *coups d'état* since they realize that coups normally involve little more than a change in government personnel. The leaders of the French Revolution were not very different from the men who really ran the *ancien régime*—"the literate bourgeoisie from which were ultimately recruited the bureaucracy." [53] On the other hand, upper-class leadership is conspicuous in counterrevolutions and also in those national independence movements where intraelital conflict occurs.[54]

Elton holds that revolutionary leaders come from a class that is already acquiring power, not from the downtrodden.[55] Normally this group is some sector of the middle classes that is upwardly striving and finds its way blocked. Since the mid-nineteenth century, with the spread of radical and socialist ideas, the extension of education, and the growth of working-class movements, a few leaders have emerged from both the urban and rural lower classes. The middle-class leader has been and remains predominant, however. If "men of words" comprise the first generation of revolutionary leaders, we can expect them to be writers, teachers, students, priests and ministers, intellectuals, or in some societies, simply the literate.[56] Eric Hoffer maintains, moreover, that these "men of words" tend to be the noncreative within their profession or calling. The creative man of words may complain, but he is attached to the present; he desires to reform, not destroy. The intellectual who wants to create but lacks ability cannot abide a stable social order.[57]

Students are particularly susceptible to revolutionary ideology in unstable societies. Anxious about their own future with its limited opportunities, moved by a sense of responsibility as an educated elite in backward societies, motivated by nationalism in economically dependent countries, students are frequently the center of revolutionary ferment. In Latin America students have many times called for the overthrow of their governments. However, their age and lack of social standing have militated against their organizing and leading mass movements, and once they successfully complete their education, most are quickly absorbed into the power structure.[58] Where revolutionary

[53] Brinton, *op. cit.*, p. 107.

[54] See Charles Tilly, *The Vendée* (Cambridge: Harvard University Press, 1964), p. 330, and Sergio Villalobos R., "The Creole Desire for Office," in R. A. Humphreys and John Lynch (eds.), *The Origins of the Latin American Revolutions 1808-1826* (New York: Alfred A. Knopf, Inc., 1965), pp. 250-255.

[55] Elton, *op. cit.*, p. 11.

[56] Hoffer, *op. cit.*, p. 121.

[57] *Ibid.*, pp. 131-132.

[58] See K. H. Silvert, "The University Student," in John J. Johnson (ed.), *Continuity and Change in Latin America* (Stanford: Stanford University Press, 1964), p. 226.

conditions are ripe, that is, where popular unrest is already deep and wide as in Guatemala in 1944, France in 1848, and Hungary in 1956, students can supply the spark that ignites the revolution.

In his study of the membership of the Jacobin Clubs in France, Brinton discovered that in both the moderate and radical phases of the Revolution, middle-class elements predominated, although there was a tendency to recruit from somewhat lower social strata in the violent period (1793-1795). The "Jacobin was neither noble nor beggar . . . but almost anything in between." [59] In fact, Brinton maintains, they represented "the abler, more ambitious, and successful of the inhabitants of a given town." [60] The same conditions hold basically for the other three revolutions that Brinton studied. The English Puritan Revolution was led and supported by men of respectability and economic prosperity, by squires and merchants, and by some great lords. Even in its later more radical phase, the leaders were predominantly gentlemen, with the proletarian elements standing aloof from the conflict. The poorer peasants sided with the king. Of the 56 signers of the American Declaration of Independence, 33 held college degrees and only four had little or no formal education. Nearly all were economically well off. Samuel Adams, one of the most radical leaders of the revolution, came from a prosperous merchant family. Many of the southern leaders were plantation owners, local aristocrats, or comfortable piedmont farmers like Patrick Henry. Even the Russian revolutionists fit the pattern. There were a few nobles and wealthy commoners like Prince Lvov and Tereschenko, but the bulk of the leaders, whether moderate or radical, were middle-level intellectuals, officials, and lawyers. Kerensky was a lawyer from a provincial bureaucratic family. Lenin came from the same social class, upper bourgeoisie. Most were educated, even some of those of peasant origin such as Stalin. Trotsky and Kamenev were well educated intellectuals; Chicherin and Dzerzhinsky were aristocrats.[61]

Although the Chinese Revolution divided into two competing and hostile factions, the Communists and the Kuomintang, both wings recruited their leaders originally from the same social stratum, the culturally alienated intellectuals of well-to-do family backgrounds. The revolution originated in the social and economic disintegration that came with the introduction of Western culture; and landlords, scholars, bureaucrats, merchants, moneylenders, and the new capitalists in the coastal towns all demanded change. The Kuomintang, a middle-class,

[59] Crane Brinton, *The Jacobins: An Essay in the New History* (New York: The Macmillan Company, 1930), p. 70.

[60] Brinton, *The Anatomy of Revolution*, p. 102.

[61] *Ibid.*, pp. 106-110.

national revolutionary movement, but Western-oriented, was headed overwhelmingly by urban types, idealistic intellectuals, and treaty-port merchants, all under the leadership of Dr. Sun Yat-sen. During the 1920's the movement came temporarily under Russian influence and grew more radical, but the landholders and merchants seized control and returned it to a more moderate stance. Nevertheless, while the Central Executive Committee in 1924 had recruited only 10 percent of its members from the lower middle and lower classes, in 1929 it had more than 31 percent from those classes. The Communist movement was and remained radical, drawing more heavily for its leaders from rural areas as time passed. Its Politburo was one-third peasant origin before 1929, and two-thirds by 1945, the increase effected largely by the growing predominance of the military elements in the party.[62]

In Latin America, the top leadership of all three social revolutions (Mexico, Bolivia, and Cuba) came predominantly from the educated middle classes of lawyers, schoolteachers, bureaucrats, politicians, and small landowners. A few like Pancho Villa came from the lower class and a few like Madero came from the upper class. Virtually none came from the military establishments, although some officers joined the Mexican and Bolivian revolutionary forces. On the contrary, in the many coups that have occurred, the military have figured prominently. Whether motivated by ambition, patriotism, or fear, the military forces cannot remain indifferent to social and political unrest in Latin America today. On the other hand, few if any coups in Latin America since the Second World War have been solely military affairs, whatever the outward appearances. Behind most military takeovers of government, disgruntled civilian leaders have played important roles. Ambitious politicians want a share of power, merchants and business interests desire tax and trade benefits, organized groups of all types expect some rewards for participating in an overthrow of government. The civilian leadership in such coups represents a broad spectrum of the urban, upwardly striving middle classes.[63] A few military officers also spearheaded the partial social revolutions in Guatemala (1944-1954) and in Argentina (1945-1955), but these upheavals never had the wholehearted support of the officer corps and were eventually overturned by the military.[64]

---

[62] North and Pool, op. cit., pp. 320, 325-327, 376-377, 388-389.

[63] Edwin Lieuwin, Generals vs. Presidents: Neomilitarism in Latin America (New York: Frederick A. Praeger, Inc., 1964), p. 102.

[64] John D. Martz, Central America: The Crisis and the Challenge (Chapel Hill: University of North Carolina Press, 1959), pp. 59-61; Arthur P. Whitaker, Argentina (Englewood Cliffs, N.J.: Prentice-Hall, Inc., 1964), pp. 143-149.

The Rank and File of Revolution

Except at the very top and the very bottom, all revolutionists are both leaders and followers. In most social revolutions the social distinctions between leaders and followers are not great; in coups, jacqueries, and millenarianist outbreaks they are often indistinguishable. In riots and crowd actions, a loose kind of leadership sometimes emerges from the mass itself and therefore is identifiable with the general movement; at other times the leadership is distinctly above the general rank and file in social and economic status. For the most part revolutionists are not "riff-raff, scoundrels, scum of the earth." [65] There are of course criminal types associated with every mass revolution as there is with every mass movement. The worst evidence of brutality and bloodlust is "more often found among the jailers, thugs, and hangers-on of revolution. . . ." [66]

Peasants are ideologically innocent; they seldom hatch revolutions. In eighteenth-century France, where the peasantry had been acquiring land, many rural families joined the urban bourgeois-led revolution, burning chateaux and particularly their dues and tax rolls. Once the peasantry had acquired the land in their particular area, they lost interest in the revolution and in time became the backbone of French conservatism. On occasion the more oppressed and abused peasants may well throw in their lot with counterrevolutionary forces, particularly if the local elites are revolutionists. Such appears to explain the support of royalist forces by some Indian communities in what is today Peru and Colombia during the wars for independence.[67] The poorer peasants in the North and West in England joined the king's forces in the Puritan Revolution, while the prosperous peasants of Russia joined the moderate Social Revolutionaries.[68] It has been recently proposed that many peasants supported the royalist-led counterrevolution in the Vendée (1793-1795) because in that area the bourgeoisie had acquired large tracts of land formerly belonging to the church and the nobility.[69]

European peasants have been interested in freedom from serfdom and ownership of land. Revolutionary social slogans other than these have failed to arouse interest. In the Balkans, national liberation from Turkish overlordship had little appeal as a goal to the Christian

[65] Brinton, *The Anatomy of Revolution*, p. 127.
[66] *Ibid.*, p. 118.
[67] John Francis Bannon and Peter Masten Dunne, *Latin America: An Historical Survey* (Milwaukee: Bruce Publishing Co., 1950), pp. 308-309.
[68] Brinton, *The Anatomy of Revolution*, pp. 103-105.
[69] Tilly, *op. cit.*, pp. 120-121.

peasant. He made little distinction between his Christian overlord and the Turkish government official.[70] After 1848, disillusioned by the local nobility, the Rumanian peasant became a truly counterrevolutionary force, "reverting to the jacquerie as the revolutionary instrument for attaining the actual emancipation theoretically advocated but rejected in practice" by the local landowners.[71] In the early twentieth century the Macedonian peasant responded in the same pragmatic way. He rose against the Turks where government oppression was particularly severe, and where the agitators offered acceptable terms. Where the leaders showed little interest in peasant problems, and where the possibility of success was remote, the peasant rejected the call to arms.[72]

The urban working class developed revolutionary sectors only in the late nineteenth century. The English proletariat stood apart from the seventeenth-century Puritan Revolution although artisan groups tended to join the Roundheads. In the French Revolution the nonindustrial wage earners played no significant role. They hungered and they rioted but they followed bourgeois leadership. The only alternative in the late eighteenth century to middle-class revolution in France was the "sansculottes," a primarily "urban movement of the labouring poor, small craftsmen, shopkeepers, artisans, tiny entrepreneurs and the like." [73] Organized in Paris, they "provided the main striking-force of the revolution—the actual demonstrators, rioters, constructors of barricades." [74] The sansculottes stood between the bourgeoisie and the proletariat, and although they helped to formulate policy, they represented a dying movement since the day of the small craftsman and artisan was rapidly passing.[75] By the mid-nineteenth century radical political ideas and organization had begun to spread among urban working groups. The working class in Paris flexed its muscles for the first time in the revolution of 1848, and in 1871 stood off all of France in bloody battle for several weeks. In both cases they were overcome by the more conservative provincials. In Russia, however, the revolution was won by organized sectors of the urban working class under radical middle-class leadership, while the Argentine revolution of 1945 was a victory of the same class under more moderate military leadership.

[70] Stephen Fischer-Galati, "The Peasantry as a Revolutionary Force in the Balkans," *Journal of Central European Affairs*, Vol. 23 (1963), p. 21.

[71] *Ibid.*, p. 18.

[72] *Ibid.*, p. 20.

[73] Eric J. Hobsbawm, *The Age of Revolution, 1789-1848* (Cleveland: The World Publishing Co., 1962), p. 63.

[74] *Ibid.*

[75] *Ibid.*

Middle classes have frequently provided not only the leadership but the backbone of revolution. This class completely dominated the French Revolution, as we have seen by the composition of the Jacobin Clubs. It has been argued that until Napoleon, the French Revolution had no leaders. As Eric Hobsbawm says, "a striking consensus of general ideas among a fairly coherent social group gave the revolutionary movement effective unity. This group was the 'bourgeoisie.' . . ." [76] The revolution of 1848 was eventually dominated by this same class and the French Third Republic, established with the overthrow, first of Napoleon III, and then of the Commune, was solidly middle-class-oriented. Yeoman farmers and artisan groups supported the American Revolution, and while these same types supported the Russian Revolution in its early stages, they were wiped out as a class once the more radical Bolsheviks seized power. Students, a significant force in some revolutions—for example, in Hungary in 1956—are almost by definition middle class whatever their origins may have been. A variety of middle-class elements, civil and military, have virtually monopolized the coups of Latin America; the same could be said of much of the Middle East and Asia.

Feliks Gross uses the term "Catalinarian" to designate a large sector of revolutionary-minded middle-class Europeans who appeared after the First World War. He describes them as "young, power hungry, intellectuals and their fellow travelers, who are dissatisfied and unable to find employment." [77] Many could not be absorbed into the weak economies of postwar Europe, and begin to fill the ranks of the Spanish Falange, the German SA, and the Rumanian Iron Guard. Unsuccessful poets and writers, theorists, and ideologists made up the top level of the Catalinarians. Their followers were fanatics of various sorts, students, demobilized officers, and bureaucrats slow to advance. A revolutionary regime, they hoped, would open opportunities for power and status; ideological dissatisfaction and the urge for power proved irresistible. With the success of Hitler and Mussolini these Catalinarians filled the party "cadres," and after the Second World War many gravitated to the Communist parties not only because of the renewed promise of power and status, but also because of the emotional and ideological appeal generated by these parties.[78]

According to Eric Hoffer, the primary characteristic of revolutionaries, whether leaders or followers, is frustration. Obviously, however, different situations and different conditions produce different kinds

[76] *Ibid.*, p. 58.
[77] Feliks Gross, *The Seizure of Political Power in a Century of Revolutions* (New York: The Philosophical Library, 1958), p. 388.
[78] *Ibid.*, pp. 389-390.

of frustrations. Peasants desire land and freedom from personal interference; urban workers want jobs, better pay, more food, better clothing and shelter; the middle classes want respectability, political influence, government positions.

> For men to plunge headlong into an undertaking of vast change, they must be intensely discontented yet not destitute, and they must have the feeling that by the possession of some potent doctrine, infallible leaders or some new technique they have access to a source of irresistible power. They must also have an extravagant conception of the prospects and potentialities of the future. Finally, they must be wholly ignorant of the difficulties involved in their vast undertaking.[79]

Hoffer adds that the destruction and disorder that accompany mass movements have led us to think of the rank and file as lawless. Nothing is further from the truth, he says, since personal truculence would indicate a high level of individualism. "The true believer, no matter how rowdy and violent his acts, is basically an obedient and submissive person." [80] Insecure people are more willing to obey than the self-confident, and to them freedom from responsibility is more attractive than freedom from restraint. "Moreover, submission by all to a supreme leader is an approach to their ideal of equality." [81] And once the frustrated follower is completely immersed in the group, he is no longer frustrated. Hobsbawm basically agrees when he says that "utopianism is probably a necessary social device for generating the superhuman effort without which no major revolution is achieved." [82] Probably, he adds, the French and Russian revolutionaries would not have fought had they known what sacrifices would be required of them.

A study of a riot at a Japanese relocation camp at Manzanar, California, in 1942 throws further light on the personality and characteristics of revolutionists. Rioters comprising about one-fourth the camp population were activists, the elite in a discontented society. The non-rioters were interested spectators. The rioters more frequently were those who had failed to establish strong ties either to Japanese or American cultural groups and were intensely searching for such ties in group activities. They were relatively lacking in economic stakes, relatively younger, relatively freer from family responsibilities. They

---

[79] Hoffer, *op. cit.*, p. 20.
[80] *Ibid.*, pp. 108-109.
[81] *Ibid.*, p. 109.
[82] Eric J. Hobsbawm, *Primitive Rebels* (New York: Frederick A. Praeger, Inc., 1963), pp. 60-61.

tended to be more restless and dissatisfied, reacting more strongly to unjust conditions. As the authors summed up their findings: "It is not the conditions but the reaction to conditions which made the difference between . . . becoming a rioter or staying home." [83]

What is the fate of revolutionary followers? Do they survive the revolutionary onslaught in meaningful ways? Are the characteristics they display in revolution those needed in the period of consolidation? It is interesting to note the fate of Lenin's early followers, whom Adam Ulam characterizes as "the young, the activist, and the unreflective." [84] He goes on to say that few among Lenin's companions of his early years had "any independent moral or intellectual stature, as he himself was to recognize after 1917 when most of the survivors of the small band were relegated to very minor Soviet positions." [85] Castro too found his student followers of Havana and even many of his 26th of July people expendable once victory was achieved. Nevertheless, the evidence does not warrant easy generalizations; in some cases revolutionary followers are quickly jettisoned once success has been won, but in other cases they hold on to become substantial participants in the consolidation of the revolution.

Summary and Conclusions

From this review of the basic literature on revolutionaries several patterns clearly emerge. First of all revolts seldom occur as a result of conspiratorial activity alone. Normally political societies must be in some state of disequilibrium or "dysfunction" before would-be leaders of rebellion are able to overthrow the established order. On the other hand, a "time of troubles" does not automatically produce revolution. Certain types of persons must appear on the scene to articulate the problem, to focus the discontent, to suggest alternatives, and to rationalize the need for change. Other types, more daring, must plan for violence, lead the actual attack on the regime, and carry the rebellion through to victory. And finally, still other types must emerge to consolidate the new order and carry out at least some of the promises made in the earler stages. These categories of leaders do not correspond directly to any particular individuals, but rather are conceptual constructs characterizing the kinds of qualities necessary to produce suc-

[83] George Wada and James C. Davies, "Riots and Rioters," *The Western Political Quarterly*, Vol. 10 (1957), p. 873.
[84] Adam B. Ulam, *The Bolsheviks* (New York: The Macmillan Co., 1965), p. 200.
[85] *Ibid.*

cessful revolutions. Generally, the personnel turns over as the revolt progresses, but on occasion the rare individual appears who combines in his own person the various qualifications of our idealized types.

Because of the nature of these activities certain personality types tend to predominate among revolutionaries. The agitators have to be men of some education, if not intellectuals, to create ideology or at least to transform specific complaints into generalized criticism of the regime. The leaders of revolts, if not fanatics, must be men of firm determination, considerable self-esteem, and confidence in the rightness of their cause. They are normally frustrated men. The consolidators have to be men of stability, political acumen, and flexibility.

Revolutionary leaders are usually men of early middle age, that is, men of considerable maturity, but not yet old enough to have been co-opted into the ruling elite. Most often they are middle class in origin, because the upper classes are on the whole satisfied with society and the lower classes too lacking in skills to create a revolutionary movement.

The rank and file of revolution are hard to categorize except to say that like their leaders they are frustrated people. It is easier to say what they are not than what they are. They are not the dregs of society, and they are usually not peasants. Under some circumstances the peasantry of a country can be revolutionized, but once their simple basic demands are met, they quickly revert to conservatism. Until the late nineteenth century the urban masses were difficult to revolutionize, but today they can be mobilized and used without too much difficulty. Nonetheless, the middle classes still form the backbone of most revolutions and rebellions. Within the middle class, students are often prominent among revolutionary elements, especially in underdeveloped areas. In coups the military are naturally conspicuous, although middle-class civilian elements frequently play important behind-the-scenes roles. As a final summation we can say that revolutionaries are basically the ambitious and somewhat talented but frustrated and embittered elements in a society who are given opportunities to advocate and to engage in violence against the established order by weaknesses or "dysfunctions" in that very order itself. Revolutionaries make revolutions, but only when conditions are "ripe," and ripeness has no single definition.

6

The Ideology of Revolution

"There can be no revolutionary action," Lenin argued, "without a revolutionary theory." [1] More accurately, there can be no revolution without accompanying *guidance* and *justification*. The blend of these esssential ingredients will, of course, vary widely. The Bolshevik revolution in Russia in 1917 was mounted on an enormous body of doctrine, philosophy, and theory, but in spite of this Lenin and his followers had to improvise a great deal in consummating their revolution. It need not be added that the revolution itself spawned an enormous body of justification, *ad nauseam*. On the other hand, there was little to guide the small body of Egyptian army officers who overthrew Farouk in 1952 although it did not take Lt. Colonel Gamal Abdul Nasser long to compose his *Philosophy of the Revolution,* a justification of what he and his fellow conspirators had done. Similarly, the American revolutionaries in the 1770's drew upon a modest repertoire of political guidance in their insurrection against George III; they hastened to bulwark their justification of revolution by a variety of pamphlets, documents, and proclamations, of which the Declaration of Independence is the most famous. Every revolution proceeds upon whatever guidance—plans, philosophies, martyrology, doctrines—is available and compatible to its functionaries; but every revolution also produces a plethora of justification. Whatever has been done must be made compatible with the national destiny, the forces of progress, the rights of mankind, and *pari passu,* the voice of the people.

This guidance and justification takes the form of *ideology.* Ideology is, as Daniel Bell has told us, "the conversion of ideas into social

[1] Quoted in E. H. Carr, *Studies in Revolution* (New York: Grosset & Dunlap, Inc., 1964), p. 149.

levers." [2] It is, moreover, that congeries of ideas, vague, ambiguous, and often irrational, that large numbers of individuals can espouse and endorse, either in defense of or attack on the political and social milieu of which they are a part. An ideology must "simplify ideas, establish a claim to truth, and, in the union of the two, demand a commitment to action." [3] Ideology seems to be a necessary adjunct of men acting in concert with one another, at least in any great numbers. Even American political parties find it necessary to use ideology in their platforms.

Revolution is the violent upheaval of an established order, involving the shattering of myths and inevitably the production of new ones. There is a pressing need to justify the violence and the destruction that accompanies revolution. Even a relatively peaceful "palace" revolution or bloodless coup of "colonels" requires some explanation couched in terms easily assimilable by (and acceptable to) a populace that may well be suspicious and hostile to those who have upset order and stability. The explanation is ideological. "What gives ideology its force is its passion." [4] As Bell has said, ideology taps emotion, and "fuses . . . [its] energies and channels them into politics." [5] Its connection with revolution, then, seems natural.

Few Americans question the American Revolution today; we have had, after all, nearly two centuries to construct the justificatory myth. [6] Any revolution in consolidation will produce such a myth, ultimately encrusted with a patina of objective and apodictic qualities. But two centuries of acceptance can hardly be produced at once. Those who have made a revolution must jerry-build and improvise, hurrying into being what seems necessary to maximize acceptance of their changes.

The first, most urgent task of successful revolutionaries is to offer reassurances to their own people and often, in other ways, to foreign governments. Such reassurances must assert that the violence has ended (whether or not in fact it has), that all things are under control, and that all the country (including, most importantly, the armed forces) supports the new regime. There must also be reassurances that the old, discarded reactionaries (as the vanquished are usually termed) will be punished, that the forces of progress will now be unleashed and

[2] Daniel Bell, *The End of Ideology* (New York: The Free Press, 1960), p. 370. *See also* David E. Apter (ed.), *Ideology and Discontent* (New York: The Free Press, 1964). Ideology "links particular actions and mundane practices with a wider set of meanings and, by doing so, lends a more honorable and dignified complexion to social conduct" (Apter, p. 16).

[3] Bell, *op. cit.*, p. 372.

[4] *Ibid.*, p. 371.

[5] *Ibid.*

[6] *See* Bernard Bailyn, *The Ideological Origins of the American Revolution* (Cambridge: Harvard University Press, 1967).

that the ordinary processes of government will soon return to "normal." It is thus vitally important for the revolutionaries of today to have control of radio, television, and the press. The first communications are perforce hurriedly and consequently often sloppily put together. These early messages ultimately make way for more carefully prepared materials. As the revolutionary leadership becomes more crystallized, it can select its audiences more carefully and can, with less insecurity, prepare its intellectual and emotional positions of defense. Newspaper statements are thus superseded by elaborate pronouncements by the leader or his underlings. A *philosophy* of the revolution is prepared—or emanates from heterogeneous sources—in which all needs and developments find their proper place.[7]

There is also, of course, antirevolutionary ideology. Most governments indulge in self-laudatory propaganda; all attempt to denigrate revolution by labeling it treason. "Good citizens" are reminded of their responsibilities to "obey the law." There is nothing more subversive or reprehensible, it is argued, than the advocacy of overthrowing a government by force. Even governments born in revolutionary travail quickly learn to insist that the season for revoltuion has passed and that the recently established status quo must be maintained. In both historical Islam and Christianity the weight of God's authority was attached to the maintenance of legitimacy. It was better to endure a bad ruler than to install a good one by force. Those philosophers, like John of Salisbury, who advocated tyrannicide, were quite rare indeed.

To be effective and persuasive, an ideology need not be rational or consistent. But like religion (which often serves as a basis for ideology) it must facilitate the reconciliation of the individual with his *acts* (or those he desires or supports). For revolutionaries it is the vehicle for justifying the violent overthrow of legitimacy. It supplies the *why* and the *ought* for revolutionary action. It is not exclusively or necessarily a theory of how revolution is to be mounted—although it often contains such theory—but rather it is that mass of doctrine that enables a variety of men to espouse a simple cause and to reduce their apprehensions for jeopardizing the stability of an old regime.

The Need for Revolutionary Justification

All revolutionaries find it necessary to defend what they have done and to consolidate their achievements. In this sense they cease to be revolutionaries, for their task now is to defend an established order,

[7] There is an enormous literature on communication. *See*, for example, Karl W. Deutsch, *The Nerves of Government* (New York: The Free Press, 1963).

their own. Their ideology may contain the clarion call to revolution but only for other climes and times.

The justification that is produced is rarely candid. That is, those who have seized power rarely describe their motives in any but the most selfless terms. Revolutionary strongmen never say that they have mounted a revolution because they are power-hungry, or that they are ambitious or that they have wanted to impose their views on a reluctant citizenry. Rather they emphasize the modesty of their role and their reluctance to act at all. They usually argue that they have acted out of deference to the will of others. Nevertheless, from such humble beginnings they have somehow found the answers to their nation's problems and the true way to its ultimate destiny.

Among modern revolutions the French and Russian have been the major producers of ideology. The actual events of each were merely the storm centers of several centuries of ideology, in both cases preceding as well as succeeding the actual, physical transfer of power; the revolutionary doctrines of the French Revolution were also the antecedents of the events in Russia.

In France the revolution was never so complete, or so fully agreed upon, that there was not the almost constant need to explain and justify events to a populace both fragmented and frightened. The Convention (National Assembly) was itself a constant source of such justification, which emanated from the endless rounds of debate and speechmaking; but there were also the famous clubs—for example, the Jacobin Clubs—where political rivals would spar in the never-ending struggle for dominance among the factions that made up revolutionary France. What was said in the Convention, in the clubs, or merely at some street-corner rally would likely appear, with commentary and embellishments, in one or another newspaper or in the constant stream of pamphlets and handbills. Perhaps the most influential journalist of the times was Camille Desmoulins, who edited the famous *Le vieux Cordelier,* and who died with Danton on the guillotine in April, 1794.

> The Revolution created literary styles—political eloquence and journalism—and suggested or supplied themes to authors: the Tennis Court Oath to André Chénier, Charles IX to his brother (Marie-Joseph), and Philinte to Fabre d'Églantine. Propagandists made use of gazettes, pamphlets, processions, and festivals, along with the theatre. [There were also t]imely plays, violently hostile to the nobility, then to kings, at times anticlerical, and after 9 Thermidor, anti-Jacobin. . . .[8]

[8] Georges Lefebvre, *The French Revolution from 1793 to 1799* (New York: Columbia University Press, 1964), pp. 300-301.

Some of these revolutionary communications were melodramatic. Thus, Marat:

> I know there is a price on my head, set by the rascals who are at the head of affairs of State; five hundred spies seek for me night and day; well, if they find me and hold me they will cut my throat, and I shall die a martyr for liberty; it shall not be said that the country is dying and the Friend of the People has kept a cowardly silence.[9]

Or they were frantic:

> Friends, we are betrayed! To arms! To arms! Now is the terrible hour when the country's defenders must conquer or find their graves in the bleeding ruins of the republic. Frenchmen, never was your liberty in greater peril! Our enemies have at last set the seal on their black perfidy. . . .[10]

There was Desmoulins' last article, written days before his death:

> . . . I have not changed my principles at all, I still believe what I wrote in one of my earliest numbers; the great remedy for the license of the press is the liberty of the press. . . . Political liberty has no better arsenal than the press . . . in the war of the pen: only the artillery of the good cause destroys all its opponents.[11]

Or there was the *Manifeste des Égaux* of Babeuf:

> EQUALITY! First need of nature, first demand of man, and chief bond of all legitimate society! . . . We are all equal, are we not? . . . Well, henceforward we are going to live and die equal as we were born; we desire real equality or death: that is what we want. . . . And we shall have this real equality at all costs. Woe to those who stand between it and us! Woe to those who resist so strong a desire! . . . The French Revolution is but the precursor of another revolution, far greater, far more solemn, which will be the last. . . . The people marched over the corpses of the kings and priests who banded against them. They will do the same to the new tyrants and new political Tartuffes who sit in the seats of the others.[12]

The great ideological document of the French Revolution was the Declaration of the Rights of Man. The Bastille had fallen on July 14

[9] R. W. Postgate, *Revolution from 1789 to 1906* (London: Grant Richards, Ltd., 1920), p. 32.

[10] *Ibid.*, p. 42.

[11] *Ibid.*, p. 52.

[12] *Ibid.*, p. 54.

and within days the National Assembly began debating that which was to become the Declaration, which was, in the words of R. W. Postgate, "[T]he Assembly's last unanimous act—[and] certainly its most important one." [13] It contained "scarcely a phrase which was not a revolutionary challenge, yet the document was adopted with practical unanimity." [14] The King, Louis XVI, was persuaded—perhaps "forced" is a better word—to sign it only in October; but with little delay it became a dangerous revolutionary instrument throughout much of the world. Short, pithy, blunt, and intoxicating, it was translated into literally all languages and distributed in huge numbers. Its presence and its message were felt for years; even in the middle of the twentieth century it has much more than an antiquarian interest. Although revolutionary, there was little in it that was new; it was certainly related to American themes of human and natural rights; similarly it smacked of the words of Thomas Paine, whose *The Rights of Man* (which contains the Declaration) is often confused with it.[15] It is hardly necessary to detail the Declaration here; suffice it to say that it is one of the most significant ideological instruments to appear in the last several centuries; and it appeared, it may be added, because the members of the French Assembly needed to justify to themselves and to the world the revolution they were making.

In Russia there is no lack of pre- and postrevolutionary guidance and justification: propaganda, revolutionary literature, and ideology. The Italian scholar, Franco Venturi, has devoted a massive tome to the theme that there was a revolutionary (which he terms populist and socialist) continuity from at least the time of the Decembrists down to the revolution in 1917.[16] One needs to mention only such names as Herzen, Bakunin, Chernyshevsky, Schapov, Nechaev, and Tkachev in the early and middle period and Plekhanov, Axelrod, and Zasulich followed by Lenin, Martov, and Trotsky in the later years to indicate the great continuity in revolutionary fervor that ultimately culminated in the Russian Revolution. Indeed, by 1917, there had been enough theory created, enough ideology generated to justify any kind of revolution in Russia. But the men who eventually won control of the revolution were men of words as well as of action, and they have left us enormous quantities of ideological materials that still, in many ways, "shake" the world. The Russian Revolution as a Marxian revolution drew upon not

[13] *Ibid.*, p. 13.
[14] *Ibid.*
[15] A convenient edition is Thomas Paine, *The Rights of Man* (New York: E. P. Dutton & Co., Inc., 1951). This is the Everyman edition.
[16] Franco Venturi, *Roots of Revolution* (New York: Grosset & Dunlap, Inc., 1966).

only the indigenous populist sources in Russia but also upon the body of doctrine that Marx and Engels had bequeathed the world.

But these have been the classic revolutions; the world has produced many others. And all in their way have generated their quotas of ideology. To look at only twentieth-century phenomena, there is no dearth of examples. The Irish expelled the British to the accompaniment of fervent propaganda and literature. The Nazi period in Germany resulted in a large amount of pseudoscience and pseudophilosophy that best is described as ideology—Alfred Rosenberg's *Der Mythus des 20. Jahrhunderts* is as good an example as any. The Peronistas in Argentina busied themselves with rationalizing the changes they had made; they were successful enough that Peronism is still a powerful force in Argentina in the 1960's. The Aprista movement in Peru (of Haya de la Torre) was another generator of ideology in Latin America. The Chinese have been unusually productive of ideology in their multiple revolutions of the twentieth century; the names Sun Yat-sen, Chiang Kai-shek, and Mao Tse-tung will suggest a certain heterogeneity in their approach. Maoism, or its *avant garde* variants, is now in the ascendant; it offers a claim to the mantle of all communism and specifically produces formulas for the successful application of revolution to agrarian countries. There have been many in Asia who have been impressed with what the Chinese have done and who have absorbed their ideology. Indonesia is another nation with much contemporary revolutionary travail; the rise and fall of Sukarno alone can be written in ideological terms.

Every political system produces ideology; those in revolutionary turmoil are even more likely to add to the normal ideological output. Every political change requires justifications—even stagnation seems to require reassurance—and those changes associated with revolution are precisely the ones requiring enormous justification. It is seldom easy to sort out this revolutionary ideology, especially in the early days of a revolution. What will be discarded and what will be kept to become a permanent part of the reconstruction myth? What is significant; more importantly, what is successful in mollifying not only those aroused by the revolution but the other population sectors whose long-run approbation is essential to the stability of the new regime?

Perhaps it is here appropriate to remark that there has been a shift in the direction of revolutionary ideology over the last several centuries. Ideology is largely directed toward those for whom a revolution is made or for whom it benefits. Yet prior to the eighteenth century revolutions were rarely made for or by any other than fragments of the elite. Now and then peasants might get out of hand; but they were almost always "put in their place." And as we all know the barons who gathered at

Runnymede in 1215 to force Magna Carta on King John were hardly concerned with ordinary Englishmen; it is fortuitous that their efforts and their ideology, three-quarters of a millennium later, has been put to a more proletarian use. Hanna Arendt has argued simply that there were no revolutions before the eighteenth century and that the only purpose of revolution is the attainment of freedom. The *sine qua non* of her "revolution" is the presence of great masses of people—as beneficiaries or participants—who hitherto have not shared either in the exercise of government or its benefits. Terminology is unimportant; what should be noted is that, from the point of view of those who have stakes in the enterprise, the nature of revolution has changed. The American Revolution despite its limited social aspects introduced the wedge of mass involvement in political action. The French Revolution carried the process still further, and the continuing revolutionary turmoil of the nineteenth and twentieth centuries culminating in the Russian Revolution and the drive for independence of colonial areas have at last thrown up the final amorphous masses of people as a proper subject for revolution.

This is not to suggest that current coups and revolutions are largely mass inspired. What it does mean, though, is that more revolutions are undertaken in the name of the "people" and more of their objectives and ends are couched in terms appropriate to peasants and urban workers. This may be done in order to enlist ultimate mass political support; Perón's use of Argentine labor was for this purpose. Or it may be done simply to forestall unrest; Manfred Halpern terms land reform in the Middle East as a "prophylactic against agitation." [17] Or it may occur because it is fashionable in the mid-twentieth century to offer an ideological genuflection to the masses. It hardly matters that peasants rarely make revolutions themselves; they seldom have access to or the skills to use modern military equipment. But even the most inert and passive mass of people may become restive and by their existence alone make the task of government an impossible one and thus make revolution more likely. The following examples point this up. About fifteen million men answered the call to arms in Russia during World War I. The bulk of these were peasants and urban workers. It was their desertions, mutinies, and attitudes that facilitated the actual revolution in 1917. In Vietnam a restless, uprooted peasantry is already the product of the protracted war there; regardless of the ultimate political resolution, the presence of this agitated peasantry will enormously complicate the task of whatever future government Vietnam may possess.

[17] Manfred Halpern, *The Politics of Social Change in the Middle East and North Africa* (Princeton: Princeton University Press, 1963), p. 97.

Marxian Revolutionary Ideology

. . . the Communists everywhere support every revolutionary movement against the existing social and political order of things. . . . The
Communists disdain to conceal their views and aims. They openly declare that their ends can be attained only by the forcible overthrow of
all existing social conditions. Let the ruling classes tremble at a communist revolution. The proletarians have nothing to lose but their chains.
They have a world to win. . . . Workingmen of all countries, unite! [18]

These words of Karl Marx and Friedrich Engels are from *The Communist Manifesto*, published in 1848. More than a century later they
still apparently have the power of arousing men; certainly they retain
the power to frighten others.
But as Robert C. Tucker has said,

The idea of revolution is present in nearly everything that Marx wrote.
It is the theoretical axis of his early philosophical writings. It is the
leitmotif of his great political pamphlets on the 1848 events, the *coup
d'état* of Louis Bonaparte, and the Paris Commune. It informs almost
all that he has to say on the strategy and tactics of the Communist
movement. It is a favorite subject in the voluminous correspondence
that he carried on with Engels and others. And his major work, *Capital*,
together with his other economic writings, is essentially a political
economy of revolution, an inquiry into the conditions of capitalism's
revolutionary self destruction. In a basic sense, therefore, revolution
was the master theme of Marx's thought, and an exposition of the
Marxian revolutionary idea in complete form would be nothing other
than an exposition of Marxism itself as a theoretical system.[19]

Marx was of course concerned with the social transformation of man;
the revolutions that interested him were consequently social revolutions
and not *coups d'état* and other political alterations in the ruling elite.
Essentially he concocted a theory of history based on the notion of the
"class struggle" and formulated in Hegelian dialectics, that made these
social transformations ultimately inevitable. Mankind would, he argued,
evolve through certain economic stages, of which capitalism is the
penultimate. But capitalism would contain "the seeds of its own de-

[18] V. Adoratsky (ed.), *Manifesto of the Communist Party* in *Karl Marx: Selected
Works*, Vol. 1 (New York: International Publishers, n. d.), p. 241.
[19] Robert C. Tucker, "The Marxian Revolutionary Idea," in Carl J. Friedrich
(ed.), *Revolution* (Nomos VIII) (New York: Atherton Press, 1966), pp. 218-
219.

struction" and would ultimately have to make way for "the dictatorship of the proletariat," the "classless society," and "the withering away
of the state"; in short, it would be replaced by eternal communism.

Such an intellectual analysis of history is hardly a clarion call to
revolution, and its sober recital resembles very little the stirring words
of *The Communist Manifesto.* But as an ideological assertion that revolution is inevitable, it can have (and has had) an incredible impact
upon people searching for some justification of their revolutionary
moods.

The unimaginative interpretation of orthodox Marxist revolutionary
theory suggests that there is little that can be done to affect the dialectics of history; specifically it meant to some Russian Marxists, *circa*
1900, that since capitalism was not very highly developed in Russia,
the way to gain revolution was to speed the development of capitalism.
Indeed, Marx had never understood peasants as he had the urban
worker; he had no formula for agrarian revolution. But as Frances
Becker pointed out some thirty years ago, Marx himself was less Marxist than his followers: he believed that "[m]an makes his own history"[20] and that "[c]ircumstances may be altered by men."[21] There is
no question that Lenin, the successful revolutionary in Russia, found it
necessary to embark upon the seas of Marxian innovation in order to
have a revolution at all. Lenin improved upon Marx's formula in a
number of ways but essentially he suggested the necessity of utilizing
a small conspiratorial elite to mount the revolution in the name of and
for the proletariat.[22]

The conditions in Western Europe that Marx had studied so avidly
hardly obtained in Russia; but as it turned out, the Leninist recom-
mendations were of only limited value in China. A wholly new concept
of communist revolution was apparently needed and this Mao Tse-tung
supplied, at least for Asia. The result was what Chalmers Johnson calls
the *militarized mass insurrection;* it finds its current example in Vietnam. Instead of seizing the reins of government, those who are seeking
revolution start with the simplest guerrilla tactics and eventually enlist
enough popular support to challenge militarily the armed forces of the
regime. The result is civil war, or a war of colonial liberation. If the
insurgents win in this struggle, they have consummated a revolution;

[20] From *The Eighteenth Brumaire,* quoted in Frances Bennet Becker, "Lenin's
Application of Marx's Theory of Revolutionary Tactics," *American Sociological
Review,* Vol. 2 (1937), p. 353.
[21] From "On Feuerbach," in Friedrich Engels, *Feuerbach: The Roots of the
Socialist Philosophy,* quoted in *ibid.,* p. 353.
[22] *See,* for example, Bertram D. Wolfe, "'War is the Womb of Revolution':
Lenin 'Consults' Hegel," *The Antioch Review,* Vol. 16 (1956), pp. 190-197.

if not, as in Greece after the Second World War, they sink onto "the dustheap of history." [23]

Marxian (and neo-Marxian) revolutionary ideology is a rich vein of doctrine with many manifestations of guidance and justification. It contains a "scientific" theory of revolution for advanced as well as for undeveloped urban and primitive peasant societies. It offers a *Weltbild* transcending the political system, with implications for literature, science, and technology. It is chiliastic yet it contains an abundance of "here and now" programs for social and economic betterment. Its myth is an appealing one to many peoples in the twentieth century, and it remains the most potent revolutionary force in modern history. And it exists in sufficient a number of forms—Trotskyism, Stalinism, Maoism —to be pervasive.[24]

Nationalist Ideology

Nationalism is not something that automatically blossoms where a community of language and culture exists; nor is it "a doctrine invented in Europe at the beginning of the nineteenth century." [25] Perhaps much of nationalism in underdeveloped areas is nothing more, psychologically, than shared, semiarticulated discontent, based on real or fancied grievances and conveniently directed against the "outsiders" who have exploited "natives." Nationalism often must have a target for its spleen; where there is a colonial power, a dominant foreign economic interest, an old regime that can be considered a thing apart, nationalist energies can easily be focused against these "external," exploiting forces. Where community of language or culture exists, it is manifestly easier to share discontent, to communicate dissatisfaction, and to locate the target for the community's ire. Yet nationalism can arise with little community to aid it; subsaharan Africa offers a number of contemporary examples of this.

It is hardly surprising that many revolutions are termed "nationalistic" or that the ideology they produce is called "nationalist." A common attempt on the part of every successful revolutionary government seeks mass commitment and support. It is tempting on the part of such

---

[23] *See* the article by Ralph Sanders, "Mass Support and Communist Insurrection," *Orbis,* Vol. 9 (1965), pp. 214-231.

[24] An interesting article on contemporary Soviet ideology is Alfred G. Meyer, "The Function of Ideology in the Soviet Political System," *Soviet Studies,* Vol. 17 (1966), pp. 273-285.

[25] Elie Kedourie, *Nationalism* (*rev. ed.*; New York: Frederick A. Praeger, Inc., 1961), p. 9.

a government to view the revolution or its goals as being the object of danger from foreign or outside forces. The inevitable result is nationalist literature and ideology. Some nationalism then seems to be the inevitable product of revolution, regardless of the genesis of the revolution itself.

Speaking of African nationalist literature, Thomas Hodgkin suggests that "there is, to a large extent, a common political language; common themes continually recur." [26] Hodgkin has summarized these themes in a most interesting fashion. Although they are too long to quote fully here, fragments can be paraphrased as follows: African peoples are "nations" that have been controlled by "imperialist" powers through "domination," "exploitation," and "racial discrimination." But a "nation" has an "inalienable right" to govern itself; in order to secure "independence" a "national liberation movement" must be generated. This movement for "political emancipation" is backed by the "popular will"; it is "democratic" and "socialist." Once "colonialism" has been eliminated and "Balkanization" avoided, the great "African Commonwealth" will be achieved.[27]

It seems helpful to quote a contemporary (1964) revolutionary, nationalist document. It is a call to revolution for the people of Mozambique against the Portuguese, who incidentally consider Mozambique to be an integral part of Portugal. The language should be noted; reference to the Portuguese as "strangers" who should "get out" is particularly significant.

> Our armed *struggle* has begun.
>
> It began as FRELIMO [Congress of the Mozambican Liberation Front] had planned—organized and determined.
>
> At the exact moment, after FRELIMO had prepared the minimum military and political conditions within Mozambique, *the people,* under FRELIMO's leadership *took up arms* and attacked.
>
> Up till then, *our struggle* was on the plane of negotiation, that is, attempted negotiation. It was only after exhausting all possibilities of a peaceful solution that we decided to take up arms. We are now sure that this is the only means by which *to convince the Portuguese people in Mozambique to get out, to give back what belongs to us, to restore to us our land.*

[26] Thomas Hodgkin, "The Language of African Nationalism," in Kenneth Kirkwood (ed.), *African Affairs* (London: Chatto & Windus, Ltd., 1961), pp. 22-40; reprinted in William John Hanna (ed.), *Independent Black Africa: The Politics of Freedom* (Chicago: Rand McNally & Co., 1964), p. 236.

[27] Quoted and paraphrased from Hanna, *op. cit.,* pp. 236-237. A most valuable book on African "socialist" themes is William H. Friedland and Carl G. Rosberg, Jr. (eds.), *African Socialism* (Stanford: Stanford University Press, 1964).

We are aware of the difficulties we shall have to face: 35,000 Portuguese soldiers equipped with the most modern arms, cannons and tanks, jet planes, napalm bombs; police instructed in the *Nazi techniques of repression and control;* colonials specially trained in the "caça ao negro" ("hunt for the black man"). This entire apparatus has already begun to work against us with its great strength.

Only, when we decided to confront *Portuguese colonialism*—when we resolved by a conscious and pondered decision to destroy the world of *oppression and misery* that *strangers* established in *our country,* to build a world of *Justice* and *Equality,* we had already weighed the forces of repression. We knew that for many of us *death would be the price of that ideal.* We are ready to pay any price for it.

For us, we have the strength that comes to us from *our ideals of Liberty.* We have aid that other *peace-loving peoples* of the world give to us. We have the history and the example of other peoples: our Algerian brothers one day decided also to be *free,* and they succeeded, fighting against one of the most powerful colonialist armies of the world.

We have nothing to lose. Existence itself has no meaning in a *regime of servitude.* We have nothing to lose but the chains that destroy *our dignity.*

We shall never turn back. Nothing can stop *our revolution.* The Mozambican revolution is *an immense movement—irreversible* as a *force of nature*—with *roots* in the *will* and in the *aspirations* of each Mozambican.

Our armed struggle has begun. It will not cease before Mozambique is *independent.*

With *quiet confidence,* with no fanfare, but with a certainty and a determination which transcend the words and the gestures, we proclaim: *The Mozambican people will win. Mozambique will be free.*[28]

In many ways, nationalist literature is *sui generis* but also eclectic. Arab nationalism offers us a good example. The kinds of ideas and events and happenings that are used to create a sense of community among the Arabs can be shared with no other peoples of the world. However, many of their themes and terminology have been borrowed from other peoples and their nationalist movements.

Make-shift Ideology

When acceptable justificatory ideology is not available, something else must be concocted or devised. Moreover in the acceptance of any

---

[28] Quoted from "Voices of Revolution" (no author), *The Harvard Review,* Vol. 4 (1966), p. 123. Italics are those of the authors.

ideology some parts of it inevitably are altered by the acceptance. An acceptable ideology is usually one ambiguous enough to satisfy a wide variety of people, but what this really means is that those adopting an ideology for their own must be able to read into it what they would like to see. The proliferation of heresy within the Marxian system is well known.

Makeshift justification (ideology) is simply a budget of arguments that, at the moment, seem to make sense, that seem to be accepted and seem to reduce the political anxiety of the populace. Such arguments are rarely produced in any finished form. It is not unusual for revolutionary leaders to move from one doctrinal position to another with great rapidity as they become more cognizant of their own strength and of the reactions to the acts that they have done. Thus the early revolutionaries in France were monarchists and only discarded the King when it became apparent that he was no longer of any great value to them. And in modern Spain Franco has been the great pragmatist toying over the years with all sorts of ideas and positions, as the current situation seemed to require.

Makeshift ideology is the practical product of the chaotic nature of revolution itself; no formula will suffice for all peoples at all times. But makeshift doctrines also come into being when revolutionary leaders are ignorant of ideology or those to whom they direct their efforts are ignorant of the terms in which they couch their appeals. The Marxists have often argued that it is necessary to agitate among the peasants and workers and to indoctrinate them with correct ideas. But this suggestion rarely helps the army colonel (*né*, a corporal in a colonial black regiment) who has just led his 500-man army in a coup against his government. He is eager to justify his action but he may know little about standard ideological formulas, and the masses under him know even less. It is precisely their inertness and indifference that may give him time to concoct some appeal to their senses and their prejudices. If the appeal is successful the strongman has become an ideologue; but his ideology is makeshift. Contemporary Africa offers a number of examples of this type of hurriedly constructed ideology.[29]

Often these ideological efforts are attached to words or phrases that have universal appeal even if they are but dimly understood. Such a word is *democracy*—or *people, socialism,* and *anticolonialism,* among many others. In a narrower sense *Arabism, land reform, republicanism,* or *Christianity* may serve as labels for a more heterogeneous ideological

[29] When the *Force Publique* mutinied in the Congo in July 1960, it was perhaps to discover a pragmatic meaning for the "independence" that the Congolese had recently won; for many independence was best symbolized by meting out indignities to white Belgian women.

mixture. Often the labels acquire adjectives; thus *African Socialism* or *Arab Socialism*. There are also ideas that demand lip service in any new ideology. It would be difficult for any Arab leader today not to endorse *Arab Unity* or denounce *Zionism*. And in the broad world of Africa and Asia, the concept of *neutralism,* whatever it may mean in practice, must receive its accolades. But these are not serious restrictions. Ideology is entwined with myth anyway; what is important is the popular acceptance of some explanation for revolutionary violence. Few revolutionary leaders fail to come up with some reasonably successful formula.

And, as Daniel Bell has argued,

> The extraordinary fact is that while the old nineteenth-century ideologies and intellectual debates have become exhausted, the rising states of Asia and Africa are fashioning new ideologies with a different appeal for their own people. These are the ideologies of industrialization, modernization, Pan-Arabism, color, and nationalism. In the distinctive difference between the two kinds of ideologies lies the great political and social problems of the second half of the twentieth century. The ideologies of the nineteenth century were universalistic, humanistic, and fashioned by intellectuals. The mass ideologies of Asia and Africa are parochial, instrumental, and created by political leaders. The driving forces of the old ideologies were social equality and, in the largest sense, freedom. The impulsions of the new ideologies are economic development and national power.[30]

Perhaps an example of makeshift ideology would be pertinent here. In 1960 the ruler of Nepal, King Mahendra, abolished the then "parliamentary" system on the grounds that it was "unsuited to Nepal's political climate." Reminiscent of President Ayub's Basic Democracies in Pakistan, the king's new system was called Panchayat Democracy. Accompanying the new system was a plethora of promises, including land reform and an attempt to impose limits on land rents. The king's act in 1960, in which he threw out a prime minister backed by a majority party and banned all political parties, was a coup, in that he unconstitutionally seized the bulk of the power mechanisms of the government for himself. He then "needed to put some ideological flesh on the bare bones of power" [31] and set about to justify his coup by arguing that the old system was bad for Nepal and that his new system (sometimes referred to as "Nepalism") was more democratic, more

---

[30] Bell, *op. cit.,* p. 373. *See also* David J. Thomas, "Ideology—Death or Transfiguration?" *The Harvard Review,* Vol. 4 (1966), pp. 88-95.

[31] J. Anthony Lukas writing in *The New York Times,* October 24, 1966. All quotes are from this article.

effective, and more likely to be successful. The resultant ideology was makeshift.

Summary

Those who seek to overthrow a government need guidance and support. Ideology helps by justifying revolution and by providing guidelines for its consummation. Never to be understated is the necessity for postrevolutionary explanation, in a form that will gather popular support. Ideology is thus inevitably generated by revolution.

The most widespread and effective revolutionary ideology today is that congeries of beliefs labeled Marxian. But Marx's original beliefs and exhortations have been "revised" by some (Bernstein, for example), interpreted by others (Lenin), and virtually superseded by still others (Mao Tse-tung). But all are labeled as Marxian and are in their various forms the outstanding revolutionary doctrine extant. Moreover, contemporary revolutionary ideology is necessarily nationalist. Although often unique, such nationalist ideology is commonly eclectic, borrowing terms and themes from the surrounding world.

But revolution spawns ideology as well as utilizing it. Much of this is makeshift in the sense that it is put together hurriedly and pragmatically. Its only criterion of value is whether it succeeds or not; whether in fact it will facilitate the building of popular support. A great portion of the new ideologies today, especially in Africa and Asia, are of this variety.

II

CASE STUDIES IN REVOLUTION

This section presents four case studies of modern revolution: the Mexican, the Turkish, the Egyptian, and the Cuban. They represent the most significant examples of revolution within the areas of the authors' special interests. The Turkish and Egyptian revolutions have had greater impacts on their societies than any other upheavals in the Middle East. And with the possible exception of the Bolivian, the Mexican and Cuban revolutions stand alone as exemplars of social revolution in Latin America. Presented here in chronological order, they point up many of the similarities of all revolutions, yet also many of the unique qualities that stem from their different cultural areas, the personalities of their leaders, the machinations of foreign powers, and the depth of their individual dysfunctions. Each chapter will offer a modest historical context to revolution and an analysis of the factors of revolution: the use of violence, the stages of its development, the nature of leadership and its followers, the impact of ideology.

7

The Mexican Revolution

The year 1910 marked the centenary of Mexico's independence and the twenty-sixth consecutive year of the reign of dictator Porfirio Díaz. The country appeared stable and prosperous. Newly constructed communications systems crisscrossed the land. Industrialization was well under way, trade was flourishing, and the peso ranked among the world's sounder currencies. Despite this progress, the standard of revolt was raised that year by a little-known political aspirant and within a few months the regime fell. Civil war then wracked the country for almost ten years. The struggle for power was fought not only between the revolutionaries and the supporters of the old regime, but among the revolutionaries themselves. By defeat or by assassination would-be rulers were eliminated until in 1920 one stood supreme, General Alvaro Obregón. For the next decade and a half Obregón and his associate and heir, General Plutarco Elías Calles, dominated the country.

The Mexican Revolution seemed over. Obregón, and especially Calles, made peace of sorts with most of their former adversaries. Land reform, one of the great promises of the Revolution, slowed almost to a halt; labor unions, which had gained recognition in the period of strife, were tightly controlled. All that the Revolution appeared to have accomplished was the loss of a million lives, the enormous destruction of property, and a slight broadening of the political base.

Then in 1935, the revolutionary movement made a dramatic recovery. President Lázaro Cárdenas, a protégé of Calles, threw off the controls of his chief. The next five years witnessed the climax of the Revolution. The regime distributed millions of acres of land, and broke forever the power of the landed aristocracy. Lombardo Toledano, a Marxist intellectual, reorganized labor, while Cárdenas gave the official party a social base resting on the peasantry, organized labor, the army, and professional associations. The government also nationalized several major sectors of the economy, launched a massive program against il- literacy, and tried to raise general health and income levels. In this period of revolutionary change, reforms were carried out with a mini- mum of disorder and turmoil.

When Cárdenas stepped down in 1940, the Revolution entered still another phase, or as most Mexican intellectuals insist, it died. Since 1940 government leaders have concentrated on the twin programs of political stability and economic development. Political leaders have kept their ears to the ground for rumblings of dissatisfaction and have attempted to fulfill at least minimal demands. Resources are scarce, but productivity increases for the past quarter of a century have kept well ahead of rapid population increase. Despite a growing gap between rich and poor, enough distribution to the lower classes has continued to keep the country politically stable.

What happened to Mexico in 1910? After 35 years of peace, astonish- ing economic gains, and the beginnings of national integration, why did the country virtually fall apart, wreak havoc on its productive plant, butcher its people, and antagonize its mighty neighbor? What internal stresses and strains within the Díaz period were covered over by the façade of well-being that appeared so remarkable to foreign observers?

Force, Violence, and Terror in Mexican Politics

Mexico today is enjoying the longest era of political tranquility in its history. The country experienced its last successful *coup d'état* against an incumbent administration in 1920, its last serious revolt in 1929. Mexico, however, has not always been so peaceful. In fact, until 1920 it ranked among the most turbulent countries of Latin America.

Throughout the nineteenth century, force and violence constituted the normal means of retaining and holding power. Independence from Spain had hardly been achieved when the commanding general of the victorious national forces assumed the title of emperor. His dowdy court and somewhat shabby nobility failed to gain his regime popular support, and he soon fell. Mexican politicians next experimented with representative government under the Constitution of 1824. Only one president elected under this document served out his full term.

The years between 1828 and 1855 saw a succession of basic charters, presidents, coups, and proclamations. No regime and no constitution in this period could command the sustained loyalty and respect of the majority of the politically active population. One man, Antonio López de Santa Anna, through certain charismatic qualities, could engender mass enthusiasm. But he could never hold this support for long. Furthermore, his political, military, and administrative gifts were few. His enemies under the banner of Liberalism overthrew him finally in 1855.

The overthrow of the tyrant did not, however, usher in a period of peace and democracy. Given the lack of political and social consensus, it could not have been otherwise. Authority continued to rest on naked force, not on expressions of popular will. A full-scale civil war broke out in 1858, and for three years laid waste the country. The Liberal Party, with its national leader Benito Juárez, emerged victorious over the Conservatives, but scarcely had the country begun to recover from civil war than foreign creditors, especially the French, began to insist on resumption of debt payments. When Juárez demurred, French troops began systematically to occupy the country, and set up a puppet regime. The French soon controlled the cities and major roads, but the countryside remained in the hands of the Juárez forces. When the French were finally forced to withdraw, their puppet government of the Emperor Maximilian quickly collapsed in 1867.

Juárez was now unchallenged as Mexico's national leader. Calling for national unity, he confirmed Conservative families in the possession of their properties, permitted opposition groups a degree of political freedom, and scheduled elections. For the remaining five years of his life Juárez held the country together, but with his passing the latent factionalism among the Liberals erupted. Several minor uprisings were followed by a successful revolt led by General Porfirio Díaz in 1876. Díaz then had himself elected president for one term, and "imposed" a comrade in arms for the next. In 1884 Díaz stood again for the presidency and remained in power, holding elections at appropriate times, until his overthrow in 1911.[1]

Mexican political history reveals several notable characteristics in the use of force and violence. First, political authority in the nineteenth and early twentieth centuries rested almost exclusively on brute force. There were some exceptions, of course. Certainly Juárez commanded a high degree of moral authority, particularly after 1867. Díaz, too, ruled for some years with broad support. Only after 1900 did widespread discontent manifest itself. Few other Mexican leaders possessed similar authority. Few were ever free from the danger of deposition. None rested upon free and open elections.

Secondly, most governmental changes were effected by *coups d'état* in which only the personnel changed. Three revolts, however, consti-

[1] The most exhaustive study of the Díaz period is the multivolumed *Historia Moderna de México* edited by Daniel Cosío Villegas (Mexico: Editorial Hermes, 1955-1965).

tuted more serious types of revolution. The independence movement (1810-1821) substituted home rule for colonial rule and eventually republicanism for monarchy. It did not, however, seriously disturb the socioeconomic structure, although it introduced new slogans and used new idioms. The revolt of 1855 and its aftermath broke the power monopoly of the landed aristocracy in favor of urban professionals "inspired" by European liberalism. The latter did not destroy the old families but acquired confiscated church properties and Indian lands to become themselves landed proprietors. By 1910 the two factions were hard to distinguish. Finally, the Revolution of 1910, a thoroughgoing social revolution, broke the power of the then ruling elites. New political groups emerged, and new myths accompanied the political and social reforms.

Thirdly, despite the force and violence, despite the brutality and destructiveness, despite the social upheavals that these conflicts have created, there has been little terror in Mexico's political history. Perhaps two million people were killed in these struggles, but neither incumbents nor their opponents resorted to systematic terrorization of the civilian population. Only after 1910 did any assassinations of chief executives occur: two in the period 1913-1920, and a president-elect in 1928. Individual acts of brutality and slaughter were common, but terror was seldom a feature of these revolts.

Causes of the Mexican Revolution

Multiple "dysfunctions" were troubling Mexico in the first decade of the twentieth century. Foreign investments had created a new type of colonialism that aroused much resentment. In addition, economic crises struck the country after 1900, causing uncertainty among elite sectors and violence among newly organized urban workers and miners. The peasantry suffered silently. The dictator was aging—and a new generation was seeking its place in the sun. By 1910 various sectors of the population were ready to overthrow the regime or at least acquiesce in its demise.

Throughout the nineteenth century Mexican leaders watched with dismay as the United States expanded in territory, population, and wealth. Some were farsighted enough to insist that Mexico had to attract industry, develop its mining and agricultural areas, and expand its commerce to hold off the threat from the north. Few plans ever materialized, and continued civil strife contributed to Mexico's decline relative to the United States. With the advent of the Porfirian age, Mexico was exhausted materially and spiritually. Díaz sensed a strong

desire for peace and recognized that an appeal for national development would not only contribute to national prestige and defense, but
would also provide a common rallying point for most Mexicans. Cooperation with Díaz meant opportunities for all to share in the building
of the nation and in the profits to be made. Resistance brought swift
and severe repression. To finance his program Díaz enticed foreign
capital and technologists to Mexico with bountiful rewards. To avoid
the danger of domination by one country, Díaz tried to attract assistance from many, but by the end of the regime the United States was
clearly predominant.[2] Railroads, oil, public utilities, and mining were
all controlled by foreign interests with a few Mexicans holding positions
but with no real influence in the companies. In addition, millions of
acres of government lands also passed to foreigners for development
purposes. A common saying arose that Mexico was the mother of
foreigners and stepmother to her own children. The grants and concessions awarded to foreign firms became widely resented. Especially
did hostility grow as the group that influenced the dictator grew
smaller, as a sense of nationalism increased, and as the enormity of
foreign influence revealed itself. Among the intellectuals and political
leaders, many utilized the outbreak of rebellion to launch attacks on the
economic imperialists. They wrote their economic nationalism into
those sections of the Constitution of 1917 that vests ultimate ownership
of land and minerals in the nation and insists on the social responsibility of property.

Obviously the prosperity of the prerevolutionary years was narrowly
based. Not only did foreigners largely control the process of economic
growth and development, they distorted it. Foreign capital was attracted to those enterprises in which profits could be extracted quickly:
minerals, utilities, commerce, and large-scale agriculture, especially
ranching. Industry with its large risks was not very attractive. While
profits accrued to the foreigners and their Mexican associates and
collaborators, the bulk of the population in no way shared in the economic modernization programs. Illiteracy still ranged around 90 percent in 1910, and the real income of the peasantry had declined drastically from a century before. Furthermore, most peasant villages had
lost their communal lands during the Porfirian era under the same laws
that had stripped the Church. The small but growing middle class also
experienced a sense of frustration and "cramp." Aspiring to upper-class
status, they could ill afford the symbols and signs of that status with the
rewards offered for their skills in the bureaucracy, in the professions, or
in managerial posts. Finally, sectors of the elite itself were becoming

[2] David M. Pletcher, *Rails, Mines, and Progress: Seven American Promoters in
Mexico, 1867-1911* (Ithaca: Cornell University Press, 1958), p. 3.

restive in the last decade of the *Porfiriato*. The rate of industrial growth
slowed after 1900, the customary credit to the *hacendado* was cur-
tailed, and internal consumption dropped appreciably.[3] None of these
alone constituted the cause of the Revolution, but they contributed to a
loss of enthusiasm for the regime even among the elite.

The theoretical justification for the Díaz dictatorship was furnished
in the early 1880's by a group of young educators, philosophers, and
politicians imbued with Positivism. They opposed revolution and disorder as antiscientific, and argued that the Mexican people were not
ready for political democracy. They also advocated economic development. In time, some of these men came to form Díaz' most trusted circle
of advisers. By 1910, however, order and progress in the Díaz style had
begun to lose some of its attractiveness. Increasingly political leaders
were questioning the doctrine of indefinite dictatorship. Others, more
practical-minded, frankly sought political power, or worried about
renewed violence with the passing of Díaz. Liberal idealists wished to
establish a democratic regime; more radical agitators advocated a
complete political and social restructuring of the nation.

For reasons still obscure Díaz promised in 1908 that free and open
elections would be held at the end of his term in 1910. This pronounce-
ment opened the floodgates for political speculation and maneuverings.
Supporters as well as opponents of the dictator began to prepare for
political campaigning, but Díaz soon reversed himself and announced
that he would run again. Political opposition coalesced around Francisco Madero, a wealthy landowner, whose primary concern was the
establishment of political democracy. The elections were held but
rigged, with Díaz the winner. Just prior to the balloting Madero had
been jailed, but in October he escaped, fled to the United States, and
issued a proclamation of rebellion. Small revolutionary bands rose up
everywhere. The vaunted army of the regime proved incapable of
meeting the challenge. It lacked modern equipment and training, and
was undermined by corruption. Against widely scattered outbreaks led
by determined men, federal troops could not control the situation.
Finally the wavering of civilian support forced the government to
capitulate.[4]

What had happened to the government's civilian support? The forces
that supported Díaz were never unified, and the dictator played them
off against each other. Positivists, Jacobins, and Catholics continued

[3] James D. Cockcroft, "Intellectuals in the Mexican Revolution: The San Luis
Potosí Group and the Partido Liberal Mexicano, 1900-1913" (Stanford University:
Unpublished Ph.D. Dissertation, 1966), pp. 52-53.
[4] The best biography of Madero is unquestionably Stanley R. Ross, *Francisco I.
Madero: Apostle of Democracy* (New York: Columbia University Press, 1955).

their quarrels beneath the surface. The Jacobins, particularly, chafed under a regime that frequently winked at Catholic violations of the anticlerical laws. In the 1880's and early 1890's, however, economic progress was truly astounding and sufficiently attractive to persuade most Mexicans to keep the peace. Those who complained about the despoliation of the peasantry, the exploitation of workers, or the sell-out to foreigners were silenced by the clank of arms and the chink of money. But by 1900, order had solidified into rigidity and the rate of progress had begun to decline. Elements of the elite, even some who had benefited from the regime, began to suffer from its defects. Many felt their positions threatened and were uncertain how best to protect their interests. The triggering element of Madero's uprising galvanized a number of the discontented into action to bring down the regime; few could be found to support it with enthusiasm.

Stages of the Revolution

The Mexican Revolution is virtually unique in the manner in which it has passed through its various stages. In a way, the thesis of Crane Brinton—that growing radicalization in revolutionary movements is followed by conservative reaction—explains the Mexican Revolution, but hardly so neatly. Certainly the victory of Madero over Díaz was soon followed by demands for deeper changes other than political, but the civil war that raged to 1920 cannot be interpreted as moderate vs. radicals vs. conservatives. In part it was a struggle for power among military chieftains with little ideology or program; but it was also a struggle among political leaders and intellectuals who were often attached to military chiefs. By 1920, relatively conservative forces within the revolutionary movement had gained the ascendency, and within a decade it seemed that a new elite had emerged. However, reforming president Cárdenas, taking office in 1934, thoroughly "revolutionized" the country for the first time in social and economic terms. When he stepped down in 1940, a new thermidor took place that has lasted to the present. In other words, the Mexican Revolution was played out in two distinct movements, each comprising a period of change followed by a conservative backswing.

The Mexican Revolution began on November 18, 1910, when an armed force in support of Francisco Madero's call for rebellion resisted local authorities in Puebla. Within a week a dozen or more scattered uprisings proclaimed Madero's Plan de San Luis Potosí. In its early stages, however, the uprising took on some of the aspects of a comic opera. Lack of coordination with many of his supporters within Mexico and the failure of his first call for popular support almost forced Madero to abandon his cause. In fact he did not enter Mexico from the United States on November 20 as planned because of the discouraging news that the authorities had rounded up many of his followers. Despite its first successes, the Díaz government could not cope with all points of resistance, particularly in the north. The longer that rebel forces could remain in the field threatening communication and supply lines, pinning down federal troops, and inspiring sympathizers to enter the conflict, the greater their chances of success. By the time Madero's forces captured Ciudad Juárez, "the coup de grâce for the Díaz regime," rebel bands were active in 26 of the 31 federal states and territories, and in most of these they controlled more than half the area.[5]

In the spring of 1911 the Mexican political situation had become extremely fluid. The dictatorship had collapsed but no permanent regime immediately replaced it. Madero, true to his democratic ideals, set up a provisional government to convoke elections. The revolution that he had begun, however, had unleashed forces and movements far more radical than he had anticipated. In addition, victory had come so quickly and by such widely dispersed revolutionary forces that discipline and organization had not properly developed. There existed no recognized overall military command, and "Madero remained, at best, a symbol rather than a chief of the revolution which he had initiated."[6]

According to schedule the provisional government held the presidential election in October, described as "among the cleanest, most enthusiastic, and most democratic elections in Mexican history."[7] Madero, elected with virtually no opposition was sworn into office on November 6. During the five months of the provisional government, however, his supporters had begun to quarrel among themselves, conservatives began to regroup, and Madero himself had lost some of his original popularity. Law and order remained to be restored, but Madero never succeeded completely in establishing his authority. He met the demands of neither extreme, and his inability and unwillingness to suppress the radicals gave the pretext to the conservatives, led by the army, to overthrow his government in February, 1913. Shortly thereafter he and his vice-president were assassinated.

The military dictatorship, headed by General Victoriano Huerta, that succeeded Madero openly endorsed the authoritarian policies of the Díaz regime. Madero's overthrow and murder had the effect, however, of temporarily uniting the several quarreling factions of the revolution. Moreover, in March, 1913, the moralistic Woodrow Wilson

[5] *Ibid.*, p. 166.
[6] *Ibid.*, p. 167.
[7] *Ibid.*, pp. 215-216.

succeeded the more pragmatic William Howard Taft as president of the United States. Wilson, incensed at the events of February, 1913, refused to recognize the Huerta regime and on two occasions sent troops into Mexico. At the same time Wilson supported the rather conservative Venustiano Carranza, one of the claimant successors of Madero. Carranza emerged the victor, but fell in 1920 by the hand of his most successful general, Alvaro Obregón.

Agitation and unrest among the lower classes had occurred with some regularity in many parts of the country since the beginning of the century. Two states constituted the main centers of discontent: Morelos in the south and Chihuahua in the north. In Morelos the troubles centered about land ownership and working conditions on the large sugar estates. Madero's uprising presented the embattled peasantry with their first opportunity for a redress of grievances after years of frustrating protests. Out of the turmoil emerged Emiliano Zapata "an uncultured peasant" but a natural leader. Skirmishes with Madero turned into civil war with Huerta and Carranza. Zapata himself was assassinated in 1919 but his Plan de Ayala calling for the return of the land to the villages was formally adopted as a national policy at the Aguascalientes Convention in October 1914, and its principles were included in the Constitution of 1917.[8] During this same period urban labor too began to organize. Labor agitation in the Díaz years centered around the mining towns in northern Mexico, but affected other enterprises such as railroads and textile mills. Strikes or other forms of protest were brutally suppressed. Labor organizations increased rapidly after the fall of Díaz, and in 1915 labor organizers signed a pact with Carranza to supply him with worker fighting battalions in return for support for labor demands. Labor guarantees, too, were written into the Constitution of 1917.[9]

The victory of Carranza, however, marked the first thermidor of the Mexican Revolution. Despite the 1917 Constitution, with its broad social programs and guarantees for peasants and workers, the regimes of Carranza, Obregón, and Calles were relatively conservative. Some peasants received land, some benefits accrued to labor, but both groups were tightly controlled and the basic socioeconomic structure remained untouched. The promotion of education, the rediscovery of the Indian as an integral part of the national heritage, and attacks on the Church marked the primary "revolutionary" activity of the 1920's. The new generation of political and military leaders seemed to be settling down

[8] John H. McNeely, "Origins of the Zapata Revolt in Morelos," *The Hispanic American Historical Review*, Vol. 46 (1966), pp. 153-169.

[9] M. R. Clark, *Organized Labor in Mexico* (Chapel Hill: University of North Carolina Press, 1934).

comfortably side by side with older elite families. When President-elect Obregón was assassinated in 1928, President Calles and his military subordinates quickly organized a new political party and provided for the appointment of an interim president. With perspective, it is now clear that the founding of the official party in 1929 laid the foundation for the institutionalization of the revolution. Calles ruled Mexico as the power behind the throne, and in 1934 had a protégé elected president. The new president, Lázaro Cárdenas, however, in 1935 effected a quiet sort of coup that resulted in Calles' retirement from the political scene.

Once he had settled the question of power, Cárdenas set to work on reform. One of his first acts, rather surprisingly, was to make peace with the Church. Cárdenas had no intention of repealing the anti-clerical laws, but he did call a halt to their more radical interpretations. Cárdenas then sponsored a thorough regrouping of the labor movement, formed a national peasant confederation, and reorganized the official party. He also parceled land to peasant communes by the millions of acres, and in the process almost completely destroyed the hacienda system. Labor was given a prominent position in public affairs, wages were raised, and benefits extended. Education was pushed and illiteracy attacked; health measures were inaugurated; and protection was extended to women and children in the labor market. As the capstone to his administration, Cárdenas in 1938 nationalized the oil industry after a bitter quarrel with its foreign owners. The nationalized oil industry has since become one of the primary symbols of both the Mexican Revolution and Mexican nationalism.[10]

Had he so desired, Cárdenas could have succeeded himself. He chose rather to name as his successor General Manuel Avila Camacho. Camacho was widely known to harbor rather conservative views, and it has remained something of a mystery why Cárdenas selected him. As it has turned out, all presidents since Cárdenas have followed moderately conservative policies. The end of the Cárdenas administration marked the second thermidor.

Since 1940 more emphasis has been placed on economic growth than on redistribution of existing wealth. The government and the official party have continued the reform programs instituted by Cárdenas in education, health, land reform, and labor benefits, but in the economic boom that the country has experienced since 1940, a greatly disproportionate share of new wealth has accrued to the business community and commercial farm operators. Although overall living standards have risen somewhat, the lot of the peasantry is still unbelievably

[10] Howard F. Cline, *The United States and Mexico* (rev. ed.) (New York: Atheneum Publishers, 1963), pp. 216-238.

wretched and the gap between rich and poor has been widened. With emphasis on stability and moderation, the regimes since 1940 have extended social and economic benefits to the lower classes in rough ratio to their potential for upsetting the system. As population continues to grow at the fantastic rate of 3.5 percent per year, the question arises as to whether the rulers of Mexico will be able to make and enforce the hard decisions in the coming years to satisfy some of the demands of the lower 50 percent. That response may well supply the answer as to whether Mexico will have to confront a third period of radicalization, and, if so, whether it will be peaceful as in the 1930's or bloody as in the 1910's.[11]

Leaders and Followers

Sporadic resistance plagued the Díaz dictatorship throughout the nineteenth century. After 1900, however, the opposition became more persistent, more widespread, and more deep-rooted. The social and economic disequilibrium of the nation was becoming more apparent, and "men of words" soon appeared to complain bitterly of the inequities. Foremost were the Flores Magón brothers, middle-class journalists and lawyers from Oaxaca, and Camilo Arriaga, a mining engineer of the upper class of San Luis Potosí. At first they addressed themselves primarily to those upper- and middle-class elements who were opposed to the inner circle of native and foreign political and business entrepreneurs surrounding Díaz. Frustrated in their reform efforts, they became more radical, some eventually espousing anarchism. As early as 1903 a few of these "precursors" were advocating revolution as the road to social reforms in behalf of the urban and rural poor.[12] They also formed political clubs, published newspapers, circulated pamphlets, sponsored strikes, and three times prior to 1910 led armed revolts against Díaz.[13]

In the meantime a more moderate opposition had organized in the northern state of Coahuila in 1904. Prominent among its leaders was Francisco Madero, then 31 years of age, and scion of a large landowning and mining family. Madero gradually became involved in the social problems of his region. Experience abroad had attracted him to Anglo-Saxon democracy, French equality, and spiritism with its emphasis on human welfare and progress.[14] His first forays into city and

[11] Howard F. Cline, *Mexico: Revolution to Evolution, 1940-1960* (London: Oxford University Press, 1962).
[12] Cockcroft, *op. cit.*, p. 13.
[13] Ross, *op. cit.*, p. 42.
[14] *Ibid.*, p. 10.

state politics ended in utter defeat as a consequence of electoral fraud on the part of the government. Undismayed, he supported opposition journalists and political leaders in various parts of the country. For a while he sent funds to the Flores Magón group, but abhorring revolution, broke with them in 1906 when they launched their first armed revolt. Madero continued his political opposition, nonetheless.

Cautious in opposing Díaz, Madero at first sought only the vice-presidency in the 1910 elections, but eventually he challenged the dictator for the presidency itself.[15] His book, *The Presidential Succession of 1910* had little literary merit or social significance, but "it catapulted its author, then little known, into national prominence . . . ,"[16] and made possible the rallying of diverse and scattered opposition groups around a central symbol. Madero's presidential campaign, his arrest and flight, and the publication of his call to arms, make of him not only a "man of words" and a precursor of the Revolution, but one of its principal organizers and leaders.

The revolutionary movement, however, had little unity. It comprised every shade of political thought from that of the business and land-holding groups who had joined only to topple Díaz, to that of the peasants and urban workers who advocated thoroughgoing social and economic changes. These several factions failed to resolve their differences and after victory only the prestige of Madero restrained them from full-scale hostilities. With the military *coup d'état* by Victoriano Huerta and the assassination of Madero in February 1913, civil war broke out. For a time the Madero followers rallied under the new leadership of Venustiano Carranza, governor of Coahuila, who proclaimed himself First Chief of the Constitutionalist Army. Although a property owner, a provincial, and a social conservative like Madero, Carranza differed significantly from him. Middle-class rather than of the elite, he was also taciturn, aloof, and "insufferably conscious of his own rectitude." Those who knew him either admired or hated him.[17]

The alliance of revolutionary forces under Carranza was shaky from the start. Zapata and his rebellious peasants remained in suspicious watchfulness of any forces that attempted to enter Morelos. Pancho Villa, "virile, earthy, passionate," proved a poor subordinate.[18] As Huerta's forces weakened in the spring and early summer of 1914, Villa and Carranza raced to occupy the capital. Carranza with his

[15] Cline, *The United States and Mexico*, pp. 119-120.
[16] Ross, *op. cit.*, p. 64.
[17] Robert E. Quirk, *The Mexican Revolution, 1914-1915: The Convention of Aguascalientes* (Bloomington: Indiana University Press, 1960), p. 10.
[18] *Ibid.*, p. 12.

military chief Alvaro Obregón, entered Mexico City in triumph in August, but in November was forced to withdraw to Veracruz under the combined attack of Villa and Zapata. These latter could agree on no political plan of action. Although great natural leaders, neither had any clear conception of what the new Mexico should be like. They were "politically naïve and socially insensitive." [19] Early in 1915 Carranza's forces began to recover. His able military chief, Alvaro Obregón, won the support of the newly organized labor forces that raised worker fighting battalions. Obregón, of provincial lower-middle-class background, had been a school teacher and industrial worker and had imbibed some socialist ideology. Partly through his influence the Carranza regime proclaimed several agrarian and labor decrees. In addition Obregón proved to be an able military administrator and tactician. By the end of 1915 he had confined Zapata in Morelos and driven Villa into Chihuahua.

With the triumph of his forces, Carranza set about regularizing his provisional regime. In 1916 he called together a constituent assembly to draw up a new constitution. In this stage the intellectuals finally came into their own. A number of young intellectuals, previously attracted to various revolutionary chieftains, now gathered around the victors, Carranza and Obregón. Nearly all shades of revolutionary opinion found representation at the constituent assembly, but the moderates predominated. "No one clique with a clearly defined and rigidly enforced orthodox ideology was able to consolidate its power as the elite group of trustees for the future." [20] Carranza was not to enjoy his triumph in peace. Several minor uprisings threatened his regime, and when he tried to name his successor to the presidency, Obregón turned against him. Carranza was assassinated in flight. Obregón and then Calles, both northerners like Carranza, continued the rule of the "northern dynasty" until 1934. Organizers of revolt and fighting men, they were also administrators and consolidators. The social programs of the Revolution slowed under their hegemony while economic recovery progressed rapidly. It appeared that the Revolution had entered its final phase.

Unexpectedly the revolutionary movement revived with the selection of General Lázaro Cárdenas as president in 1934. Born in a small village in Michoacán of a provincial middle-class family, Cárdenas had received a sixth-grade education. A teen-age supporter of Madero in 1910, he variously fought with Zapata, Villa, and Obregón. Nothing in

[19] Cline, *The United States and Mexico*, p. 137.
[20] *Ibid.*, p. 163.

his career prior to 1934 indicated that he would overthrow his sponsor, General Calles, or institute the radical restructuring of Mexican society that he carried out in five short years.

The Cárdenas era marked a decisive turning point, too, in terms of revolutionary leadership. From the outbreak of revolt in 1910 until 1934, northerners clearly dominated the country. Madero, Carranza, Villa, and Obregón were all from the north. Out of 34 representative leaders in the period 1910-1920, including military officers, civilian politicians, and intellectuals, one-half (17) originated in the north, 10 in the core, 5 in the south, and 2 in the west.[21] None were born in Mexico City. By contrast, a study of a selection of 14 prominent figures (including Cárdenas) in the 1934-1940 era, indicates a decided shift of control back to the core. Of these 14, 10 were born in the core, one each in the west and south, and only 2 in the north. Significantly, only one of these leaders was born in Mexico City. Only about 4 or 5 of the 34 in the early period were born in large towns or cities, but in the Cárdenas administration 6 of the 14 came from decidedly urban areas. Leadership changes are also clear in terms of class, background, education, and occupation. Of the 14 prominent leaders in the 1930's, 2 were military men, one a politician, one a labor leader up from the ranks, and the rest were university-educated with professional degrees. Of the latter, 9 were lawyers, and one an economist. Several had been university professors, one a rector of the National University, and another rector of a state university. All apparently received their opportunity for advancement in some way through the Revolution; none came from families prominent before 1910; all but one or two were of solid middle-class background. By contrast the men of 1910-1920 were a mixed lot. Madero and some of his close associates were from upper-middle- or upper-class families in the Díaz period. Lower-middle-class types were prominent in persons like Obregón, Aquiles Serdán, and Pablo Orozco. The young intellectuals that surrounded the military chiefs and wrote the Constitution of 1917 were generally of the comfortable middle class, while some of the military leaders like Zapata and Villa came from the lower classes. The latter two were virtually illiterate. Information on the early lives of the Revolutionaries of 1910 is hard to come by. Although well under half of the selected 34 had a professional degree, most had some education. School teachers were fairly prominent among their ranks, as were journalists, lawyers, and aspiring politicians. Few were tradesmen or manual laborers.

The age distribution of Mexican revolutionary leaders falls into the expected range. For the 1910-1920 years, a few were in their early

[21] These regional designations are adopted from Cline's model in *The United States and Mexico*, pp. 90 ff.

twenties, a few in their forties or early fifties, and the majority in their late twenties or in their thirties. The median age of our selected group was 34 years. For the Cárdenas period, the median age was 39.5 years.

In matters of temperament few of the revolutionary leaders were fanatics, or "true believers." Those that were rabid on some aspect or other of revolutionary goals either accommodated themselves to compromise or were swept aside in the course of the revolution. Ricardo Flores Magón and his anarchists made little headway after the fall of Díaz. Madero and Carranza were in many ways basically conservative but determined and even stubborn in their drive to overthrow tyranny and establish their own concepts of democratic government. Zapata dedicated himself to the destruction of the hacienda and the division of lands. He had some limited success in his own state but lacked the vision to enforce his ideas nationally. Calles had a streak of anticlerical fanaticism. Several bishops were uncompromising in their opposition to the Revolution, but Cárdenas eventually made peace with the more reasonable Archbishop Martínez and exiled Garrido Canabal, the extreme anticlerical boss of Tabasco state. Many revolutionary leaders, particularly the military chieftains, had no ideological programs. Of these Villa is the prime example. The Villas and the Zapatas, however, gave way to the Obregóns and the Calles. Even Cárdenas was succeeded by Avila Camacho and the conservative civilian presidents who have followed.

Ideology in the Mexican Revolution

The Mexican Revolution has produced not just a single "ideology," but a host of ideologies that are often contradictory. The country's military and civilian political leaders for almost 60 years, however, have in a very pragmatic way reconciled and compromised these ideological conflicts in their social and political programs. In doing so they pay lip service to all the major ideas and extol the merits of all the major ideologists spawned by the revolutionary movement.

From the beginning, the revolutionary movement was divided ideologically. Several groups were simply power-seekers, advocating free elections as the road to office. Many of Madero's followers fall into this category, but Madero himself sincerely believed in political democracy, summed up in the old slogan "Effective suffrage; no reelection." Beyond this, Madero's movement produced little ideology, although it gave some recognition to the problems of rural and urban poverty, illiteracy, and land distribution. Madero saw all these as subordinate to the political question, and confidently expected that they could be solved by democratic procedures once the people could freely elect a president and legislature.

Another opposition element to Díaz, the Flores Magón movement, produced a large body of ideology. Ricardo Flores Magón began his criticism of the Díaz government in the 1890's with attacks on specific abuses. Frustrated at every turn, Flores Magón began to widen his attacks to include the regime itself. From exile in the United States, Ricardo, his brother Enrique, and other followers organized the Mexican Liberal Party. In 1905 under the slogan of "Reform, Liberty, and Justice," they produced a party platform that included, in addition to traditional anticlerical propositions, proposals for social and economic reform including an agrarian program. From this point the Liberal Party moved on to labor agitation, including strikes and armed uprisings, and ended with "a visionary philosophical anarchism." [22] Although specific ideas of the Liberal Party gained currency once the revolution erupted, the party itself never became a significant political element. For most Mexicans, its total program was too radical.

A final element in the intellectual preparation of the Revolution arose from within the *Científicos* themselves. Foremost of these was Justo Sierra, the country's leading intellectual. These critics probably contributed more to the Revolution in terms of undermining the confidence of the intellectual supporters of the regime than in bringing recruits to the cause of rebellion.

Once Díaz was overthrown, a mad scramble ensued among the revolutionaries to construct the new Mexico along the lines of their own programs, plans, and ideologies. Unlike the French and Russian revolutions, the Mexican Revolution continued to be strongly influenced if not always dominated by its moderate elements. Madero and later Carranza remained cautious about introducing sudden and rapid changes into the social and economic fabric of the nation. Obregón and Calles, though making some concessions to the peasants and to urban labor, tied their interests basically to men of property while continuing to pay lip service to ideals of political equality, social justice, and a more equitable distribution of national resources. More conservative groups sought to nullify legal provisions for land distribution, benefits to labor, and government controls on private property. Catholics sought changes in the old anticlerical laws dating from the Juárez period, but their support of the Huerta coup resulted in their being totally discredited. Radicals sought the destruction of the hacienda system and the parceling of land to the Indian communities, control of industries by labor, national literacy and health programs,

[22] Ross, *op. cit.*, p. 41.

an overhauling and extension of the educational system, and the final destruction of the influence of the Catholic Church. Within organized labor circles anarchism grew strong, and among many intellectuals Marxism seemed to offer both practical and theoretical solutions to Mexico's grave problems.

Many of these ideologies, slogans, and programs found expression in the Constitution of 1917. Carranza, to win support, had obligated himself to some basic changes, including "municipal liberty, agrarian reform, labor legislation, nullification of foreign contracts and monopolies, tariff realignments, credits for Mexicans, and a series of promises of political readjustment." [23] Necessary though they had been to give him victory, Carranza had little enthusiasm for such reforms. Nevertheless, to regularize his own political position, he convoked a constituent assembly and promulgated the new constitution that it produced.

The Constitution of 1917 is a combination of new and old concepts. The political structure was copied with slight modification from the Constitution of 1857, which provided for a federal system with checks and balances. In the new charter, however, the powers of the president were substantially increased. The new constitution also repeated and enlarged the anticlerical provisions of the earlier charter, and again provided for a long list of individual and personal rights and privileges including the right of private property. Thus far the new constitution represented the traditional nineteenth-century liberal concerns for political democracy and individual rights. In the remaining one-third of the document, however, social and cultural guarantees represent a departure in constitution-making not only for Mexico but for all of Latin America. Articles 3, 27, and 123 were, and for long remained, the most highly controversial. The first of these placed on the national government the burden of providing free elementary education. It excluded the teaching of religion in the public schools and forbade religious institutions or members of religious organizations to conduct schools on any level except the university. Article 27 stressed the social nature of property, gave the state control of subsoil wealth, canceled grants and concessions made by Díaz, and provided for agrarian reform. Article 123 placed on the state the responsibility for encouraging a national labor movement and gave to the government the power to regulate it. The ideology behind this enactment came from Flores Magón, as well as from labor legislation in France, the United States, and New Zealand. "The basic principle of Article 123 was that labor was a status, a way of life, for which the minimum

[23] Cline, *The United States and Mexico*, p. 165.

essentials were now constitutionally guaranteed, rather than an economic commodity, subject to the market vagaries of supply and demand." [24]

Little new ideology has been generated since 1917. The basic charter
is so broad and all-inclusive that almost any program or plan of action
can be justified in terms of the Constitution or of the Revolution with
which it has become identified. The Revolution is at any moment what
the political leadership says it is. Cárdenas used a few new slogans
in his educational, land, labor, and oil reforms, but he found his basic
rationale in the Constitution. His successors have followed his policy,
but whereas Cárdenas attempted to tackle problems on a broad scale,
succeeding presidents have been content to identify themselves with
a "March to the Sea" or a "National Frontier Program." Whether social
security benefits are extended to a new village, a parcel of land divided,
a dam inaugurated, or a steel mill expanded, it is all attributed to the
Revolution. Since 1940 moderation, stability, economic development
have been the keynotes of the "Revolution." Many Mexican intellectuals insist that the Revolution is dead, but the political leaders continue to talk in terms of its myths, and these seemingly still have an
enormous hold on the minds of the masses.

International Repercussions of the Mexican Revolution

To the world at large the Mexican Revolution of 1910 appeared at
its inception to be simply another in a never-ending round of coups,
revolts, or barracks uprisings that have plagued Latin America since
independence. By the time that the full implications of the Revolution
were unfolding, the major European powers were thoroughly em-
broiled in their own problems. The United States, however, became
increasingly involved in the struggles of its southern neighbor. Although President Taft favored the Díaz regime when the Madero uprising began, the United States government quickly recognized Madero
once he was inaugurated, and a sympathetic border population had
assisted the revolutionaries from the beginning. [25] The Ambassador of
the United States to Mexico, however, strongly opposed Madero, and
used every occasion to undermine Washington's confidence in his administration. The exact role of the ambassador in the fall of the Madero
government is open to some dispute, but no one denies his support for
General Huerta who led the coup and succeeded to power. President

[24] *Ibid.*, p. 169.
[25] *Ibid.*, pp. 128-129.

Taft, however, held up diplomatic recognition until his term expired.

Woodrow Wilson brought to the presidency the magisterium of the classroom and the moralism of the pulpit. To him, "Huerta was the symbol for all that was wrong with Latin American governments." [26] Wilson withheld recognition, but offered to mediate between Huerta and Carranza. To Wilson "mediation" meant "getting Huerta to agree to hold an election in which he would not run." [27] When these efforts failed, Wilson's Mexican policy shifted largely to projects to eliminate Huerta. In February, 1914, he lifted the arms embargo on Mexico, and in April he used a minor incident involving United States naval forces in Tampico harbor to create a major crisis. When Huerta refused his demand for a 21-gun salute, Wilson ordered Veracruz occupied by Marines. With his main source of revenue removed, Huerta quickly weakened, and in July he fled the country. With Huerta gone Wilson drew his forces out of Veracruz.

Since the Constitutionalists were quarreling among themselves, Wilson remained undecided about whom to support. When Obregón defeated Villa, however, Wilson recognized Carranza as *de facto* president. Despite continuing disputes over property rights and claims, Mexican attacks on United States citizens, and a punitive military expedition in 1916 into Mexico, relations between Mexico and the United States remained reasonably stable, if not friendly, until Obregón carried off a successful coup against Carranza in 1920. Just as Taft had left Huerta to him, Wilson left Obregón to incoming President Warren G. Harding.

Disputes over claims and property rights growing out of the Revolution plagued these relations until the late 1930's. The revival of the church-state struggle in Mexico in the late 1920's led to demands among Catholics in the United States for their government to intervene one way or another. Other Americans propagated a "red scare," but the most serious issue undoubtedly involved the Mexican expropriation of the oil industry in 1938. By that time, however, President Franklin Roosevelt had firmly committed the country to a strong noninterventionist policy. Moreover, war clouds were gathering in Europe and Asia, and primary concerns of the United States were already beginning to shift away from the Western Hemisphere. After 1940 relations between the two countries further stabilized, and despite some differences of viewpoint and some continuing problems are among the most cordial in the hemisphere.

The Mexican Revolution has had only minor repercussions abroad,

---

[26] Robert E. Quirk, *An Affair of Honor: Woodrow Wilson and the Occupation of Veracruz* (New York: McGraw-Hill Book Company, 1964), p. 2.
[27] Cline, *The United States and Mexico*, p. 144.

except in the United States. During both phases of "revolutionary" change in Mexico, European and Asian powers were deeply involved in their own regional conflicts. The Mexicans themselves regarded their Revolution strictly for home consumption and gave little attention to proclaiming a universal doctrine or to exporting their reform measures. In a number of Latin American countries the social and economic provisions of the Mexican Constitution of 1917 served in broad outline as models for similar sections in their own constitutions. More important, the Bolivian revolutionaries of 1952 tried to copy some features of Mexican developments such as the agrarian reform, political party organization, and nationalization procedures. A few Bolivians studied Mexican methods, but the Mexican government gave little encouragement to such projects. Mexico made its Revolution for Mexicans and for no one else.

Conclusion

Not surprisingly the Mexican Revolution shares some common features with the upheavals and political convulsions that we have briefly scanned in the first part of this work.

There are also some striking specific differences. Mexico was perhaps the most violence-prone country of Latin America in the nineteenth century, and the peace and order at the end of the century was based largely on repression. Its revolution that destroyed that order was the most violent, prolonged, and destructive in Latin America. A striking feature of political violence in Mexico, however, has been the absence of terror so prominent in both the French and Russian revolutions. Bloodshed, brutality, slaughter, rape, destruction there certainly were, but no systematic attempt to terrorize noncombatants.

But the Revolution was more than a recurrence of political violence. Madero's revolt unleashed social forces that remade the image of the country. Almost no one foresaw the extent of the changes that would be made. Only from hindsight have we analyzed the objective and subjective conditions that preceded the Revolution, and then called them causes. Madero was truly an unlikely revolutionary, but he gave the discontented a national figure and symbol around which to rally. Without him, it may well be argued, the small centers of unrest would have been easily controlled by the forces available to the regime.

In its outbreak or birth the Revolution followed patterns set by other revolutions in having a symbolic act in Madero's Plan of San Luis Potosí, a decisive act of initial violence with the outbreak of revolt in Puebla, and the creation of "martyrs" in its first casualties. In the composition of its leadership in terms of age and social origins it also resembles many other revolutions; it had some fanatics but not many. Where the Mexican Revolution differs is in its stages and ideological formation. Occurring before the Russian Revolution and going beyond the liberal tenets of the French Revolution, the Mexican upheaval never proclaimed an international program or ideology. It was a home-grown revolution for Mexicans by Mexicans. It appears to be quite unique in its revival of rapid and radical social, economic, and political change after 15 years of quiescence. Unlike the French and Russian revolutions it never produced a military phase (like that of Napoleon), a phase of ideological orthodoxy (like that of Lenin), nor a draconian dictatorial phase (like that of Robespierre or Stalin). Despite the far-reaching reforms of the 1930's, these social programs were carried out with a minimum of bloodshed, virtually no exiles, and little in the way of total ruination of the landed families, reduced though they were in material resources. Moderate forces remained sufficiently powerful through all the stages of the Revolution to prevent the extremists from fully implementing their programs or ideologies. No single ideology was ever able to drive out all the rest. The result has been a conglomeration of ideas and myths that can cover almost any conceivable emphasis the Revolutionary leaders might wish to give to the direction of the country. Political leaders in Mexico today are in fact, however, restricted to minor shifts in policy. The Revolution has been "institutionalized" as indicated by the choice of a new name for the official party in 1946, the Institutional Revolutionary Party. Even the Church can claim protection from extremist measures through the compromises reached with Cárdenas and those sections of the constitution that guarantee religious freedom. The claims of all groups on the political system derive their strength from the new prosperity of the country that no major group wishes to jeopardize by reopening old conflicts and old wounds.

8

The Turkish Revolution

The impetus to reform or otherwise change the old regime in Turkey dates from at least the early eighteenth century.[1] Usually attempts at reform followed disastrous military conflicts with Western powers, but they also resulted partly from the increasing commercial and educational contacts that were made with Europe, notably with the French. Unquestionably the French Revolution at the end of the century also had its reverberations within the Ottoman Empire.[2] Nevertheless it seems useful to select (perhaps somewhat arbitrarily) as the beginning of the modern Turkish revolutionary period the deposition of the Sultan, Abdul Aziz, in 1876. The leaders of the coup, headed by Midhat Pasha, constituted the remnants of an older conspiratorial group, dedicated to the establishment of constitutional government. This coup marks the beginning of the "first Ottoman constitutional period."[3] Abdul Aziz was succeeded by Murad V, who was thought to be a supporter of constitutionalism,[4] but Murad shortly went insane, and was succeeded by Abdul Hamid II in September, 1876. Under a new constitution, proclaimed in December, Midhat became grand vizier, but in February 1877 the Sultan drove him from power and later murdered him. Nevertheless, a parliament for which the

[1] Bernard Lewis, *The Emergence of Modern Turkey* (London: Oxford University Press, 1961), p. 45. *See also* Niyazi Berkes, *The Development of Secularism in Turkey* (Montreal: McGill University Press, 1964).

[2] Bernard Lewis, *op. cit.*, p. 53. *See also* Bernard Lewis, "The Impact of the French Revolution on Turkey," *Journal of World History*, Vol. 1 (1953), pp. 105-125.

[3] *See* Robert Devereux, *The First Ottoman Constitutional Period* (Baltimore: The Johns Hopkins Press, 1963). Some suggest 1808 as the beginning of the initial constitutional period; a constitutional document was drawn up at that time and signed by the Sultan, Mahmud II.

[4] *Ibid.*, p. 33.

Constitution provided convened in March 1877, but the Sultan destroyed it, too, by a coup in February 1878. Turkey returned to absolutism.

The proponents of constitutionalism, modernism, and reformism, all of which were immiscible with the absolutism of Abdul Hamid, continued to conspire for the achievement of their goals. In 1889 the Ottoman Society for Union and Progress (OSUP) was created among students in the army; this group largely came to be made up of young military officers trained in Europe; history has labeled them the Young Turks.[5] They forced the Sultan to reinstall the old constitution in July 1908 and deposed him in April 1909. Four years later Enver Bey overthrew the constitutional government in a coup and continued to be the leading figure, at times the virtual dictator, of the Turkish government to the end of the First World War.

The war destroyed the Ottoman Empire. Parts of Turkey were occupied, and the French, British, Italians, and Greeks all made claims against its territories. Enver fled; neither the Sultan nor his government could maintain authority. At this juncture, one of Turkey's few military heroes of the war, Mustafa Kemal Pasha (later Kemal Atatürk), gathered the broken forces of Turkey together and rejuvenated the country. By an energetic display of diplomacy and military action he succeeded in expelling foreign occupation armies. Kemal formed a new revolutionary government, inaugurated a series of reforms, and fashioned a political party that was to rule Turkey for 27 years. By the time of his death (1938), these efforts had come to constitute a major social revolution; it is the Kemalist revolutionary phase that lies at the heart of the Turkish Revolution. Some authors, for example, Kemal Karpat, view the transfer of power in 1950 from the Republican People's Party (RPP) to the Democratic Party (DP) as the "second" Turkish revolution, producing as it did multiparty democracy.[6]

By 1950 Turkey had adjusted to the death of Kemal, had avoided the Second World War and had progressed to a point that permitted the first free election in the history of the Middle East. This election resulted in the ouster of the old Republican People's Party, the party of Atatürk and the vehicle of his reform program; the new Democratic Party established itself in power. The next decade witnessed an erosion of a number of the Kemalist reforms and a determined attempt by the Democrats to entrench themselves in power. In May, 1960, after increasing numbers of disturbances, the Turkish army struck against

[5] See Ernest E. Ramsaur, Jr., *The Young Turks: Prelude to the Revolution of 1908* (Princeton: Princeton University Press, 1957).

[6] Kemal Karpat, *Turkey's Politics: The Transition to a Multi-Party System* (Princeton: Princeton University Press, 1959).

the government, arrested its leaders, provided for their trial, and facilitated the re-establishment of a new civilian government more consonant with Kemalist traditions. This coup of 1960 can be thought of as a part of the continuing Turkish Revolution.[7]

The Tradition of Violence in Turkey

The stereotype of the Egyptian pictures him as docile; that held of the Turk suggests tough, warlike, violent qualities. It has not been long since Western writers were accustomed to term the Turk as "bloody," "savage," "unspeakable," and "terrible." The modern Turk is none of these things, but he possesses an early history of violence and bloodshed.

The early Turks, at first the Seljuk and later the Ottoman, were invaders from the Central Asian steppes, establishing themselves in western Asia by violence. Creating an empire by war, they geared their institutions for war and its booty. It is not surprising that life was not very secure for army commanders, governors, and minor rulers (along with their various retainers), for the landed aristocracy and the great merchants and even for the Sultan and his family. Life was considerably more secure and predictable, although hard, for the great mass of artisans and peasants. It is well to remind ourselves that political instability (and its concomitant violence) was and remains endemic to the Middle East. It is certainly possible to argue that the Ottoman Empire in consummation represented a force for stability rather than instability.

The Ottoman Empire at its height was a well-constructed political and administrative system;[8] it could not have come into being or have survived in an atmosphere of constant chaos and unadulterated cruelty and destruction. But when men were punished and held accountable, they were treated with severity.

This empire was ethnically and religiously highly heterogeneous. The Ottoman system developed to channel the loyalties of a mosaic of peoples to the Sultan and his government. In a sense, every group was a minority; the Muslims did not predominate until the nineteenth century and the ethnic Turks until the early twentieth century. The West was exercised about the plight of the Greek, Bulgarian, and

---

[7] There are thus four phases of the modern Turkish revolutionary period: the Young Turk phase, the Kemalist phase, the DP phase, and the phase ushered in by the 1960 coup.

[8] See Hamilton Gibb and Harold Bowen, *Islamic Society and the West*, Vol. I, Parts 1 and 2 (London: Oxford University Press, 1950, 1957).

Armenian minorities on more than one occasion in the nineteenth century; it is interesting that one of the charges brought against the arrested Turkish Democratic leaders after the coup of 1960 was that
they had organized riots (1955) against the Greeks. Yet it is only fair
to add that the Armenians and especially the Greeks were as savage
and brutal against the Turks when they possessed appropriate opportunities.

Neither traditional nor modern Turkey has been without its riots
and demonstrations, but significantly violence declined drastically with
the maturation of the Kemalist revolution. Kemal himself did not un-
loose bloodbaths, executing only a small number of individuals for
treasonable conspiracy. On the other hand the army junta that en-
gineered the 1960 coup insisted on several death sentences to justify
its effort;[9] this fact, some have argued, stems from the Turkish violent
character. Yet it remains a fact that modern Turkey has been generally
free from violence and capricious turbulence.

The Revolutionary Tradition

The Ottoman Empire, established in embryo form in the late thir-
teenth century, died only with the First World War. During this
period, the empire waxed and waned, as it responded to various military, dynastic, and economic pressures. The closest thing to social revolutions in this long period was the enlightened ministries of the reforming viziers, perhaps best exemplified by the career of Ahmed Köprülü
in the seventeenth century (or, of course, by that of Midhat Pasha in
the nineteenth century), or those momentous events such as the destruction of the Janissaries by Mahmud II in 1826.

But the historical record of the Ottomans is replete with many
coups, dynastic struggles, praetorian revolts, palace revolutions—to
use the many phrases that describe something short of the major social
revolution. In the earliest days of the empire the death of the Sultan
meant a contested succession, and often ambitious sons tried to anticipate their father's demise. After the sixteenth century *royal* revolts
became rare, but there never was a shortage of army commanders, successful and ambitious, who hoped to advance themselves by judicious
rebellion. The Janissaries, the once elite troops, of the Sultan, became
notorious for their rebellious behavior and ultimately demanded the
veto over the Sultan's person and policy. National minorities were often
in revolt, and Turkish garrisons in far outposts of the empire were

[9] Three were executed in 1961 and several later conspirators in 1963.

constantly compelled to defend themselves. One of the more dramatic
examples of such a revolt was that of the Serbs and their leader Kara
George in the early nineteenth century.

Much of the nineteenth century was characterized by conspiracy
against the Sultan, largely inspired by those Turks who had visited
Europe and who had been impressed by the need for modernization.
The culmination of all this was the rise of the OSUP and later its coup
in 1908, its internal coup in 1913, and its collapse with the end of the
war in 1918. Certainly Turkey possesses a revolutionary tradition. It
has had a propensity to revolt, at least in parts and fragments; seldom
has political change occurred without violence or its threat. The
Kemalist revolution was a part of a revolutionary tradition, but it was
also a *Turkish nationalist* revolution.

The Kemalist Revolution

Mustafa Kemal Pasha was born in 1881 (in Salonica) and entered
a military academy at the age of twelve.[10] His early professional life
was spent in military schools and the usual postings, but everywhere
he was involved in political conspiracy. The First World War gave him
his professional opportunities. In 1915 came the great British effort
to force the Dardanelles, at Gallipoli. Kemal's "leadership [there],
more than any other single factor, frustrated the British landings and
brought about the evacuation of the peninsula. This campaign, which
had saved Istanbul, made him a national hero, . . ."[11] For the rest
of the war he was shunted aside in an effort to blunt his popularity,
for he was feared by Enver Pasha and others in the government; yet
the war had made him the only authentic Turkish military hero.

Istanbul was occupied at the end of the war by Allied troops and
Kemal stagnated until (in April 1919) he was foolishly sent to Samsun,
in eastern Turkey, by a government embarrassed by his rebellious presence in Istanbul. Kemal used this opportunity to consolidate the
Turkish troops in the interior, to challenge publicly the vacillating government in Istanbul, to demand the end of foreign occupations in
Turkey, and to call for regional and national conferences to determine
the future of a new, nationalistic Turkey. In response to the last demand, a congress was held in Sivas in July and August, 1919; for the
next several months Kemal, in the name of the Congress, bombarded
the government in Istanbul with demands. As important as any was

[10] The definitive biography is yet to be written, but by far the best in English
is Lord Kinross, *Ataturk* (New York: William Morrow & Co., Inc., 1965).
[11] Geoffrey Lewis, *Turkey* (3rd ed.) (London: Ernest Benn, Ltd., 1965), p. 56.

the insistence on the creation of a representative national assembly and, as incredible as it may seem in retrospect, the government was frightened into resigning and its successor promised new elections for a Chamber of Deputies. Such a chamber was created (opening in January 1920), but it was to be short-lived; by March the Allied powers had interfered and forced the deportation of most of the Nationalist deputies; by mid-April the chamber was dissolved by the Sultan.

Less than two weeks later a Grand National Assembly (GNA) of Turkey was convened in Ankara with Kemal at its helm. By this time the Turks were engaged in bloody encounters with Greek occupation troops. In a remarkable series of brilliant, desperate battles, the Turks succeeded in expelling the Greeks; they also forced the other powers to recognize *de facto* the nationalist government of the GNA. The formal "capitulation" was made on October 11, 1922.

Invitations to the Lausanne Peace Conference were sent to both the nationalist government in Ankara and what was left of the Sultan's government in Istanbul. Kemal's reaction was to push the GNA into deposing the Sultan, whose subsequent flight to the safety of a British man-of-war, elicited from Kemal the statement that "we have proved that we are capable of putting an end to the comedy played by the Caliph [the Sultan] who exposed himself to humiliations of every description for the miserable object of dragging out an unworthy existence for a few days longer." [12] With the departure of the Sultan, a new Caliph was chosen by the GNA; but less than two years later, in March 1924, the GNA abolished the Caliphate itself. This act, the forerunner of the later extreme secularism of Kemal, aroused enormous protests that were never to cease.

Ismet Pasha (later Ismet Inönü) represented Turkey at the Lausanne Peace Conference that opened in November; the treaty was signed on July 24, 1923. The chief significance of the Lausanne Treaty, as Bernard Lewis has suggested,

. . . was the re-establishment of complete and undivided Turkish sovereignty in almost all the territory included in the present-day Turkish Republic. At the same time the Capitulations, long resented as a symbol of inferiority and subservience, were abolished. Thus Turkey, alone among the defeated powers of the First World War, succeeded in rising from her own ruins and, rejecting the dictated peace imposed on her by the victors, secured the acceptance of her own terms. [13]

[12] Ghazi Mustapha Kemal, *A Speech* . . . (Leipzig: K. F. Koehler, Publisher, 1929), p. 580.
[13] Bernard Lewis, *op. cit.*, p. 249.

By the fall of 1923 a definitive peace treaty had been signed, the Sultan deposed, foreign enemies expelled, the government firmly established in Ankara, and a republic proclaimed. Kemal was elected by the GNA as the first president.

To this point the Kemalist revolution was both a continuation of the Young Turk movement and also the culmination of a war of national liberation. The revolution was now to embrace major social and political reforms, many more than either the old members of the OSUP or the newer revolutionary comrades in arms might have anticipated. (As we shall learn, much the same can be said for Cuba.)

Kemal was to live until 1938, and although perhaps the most exciting of his reforms occurred in the early part of his rule, he was engaged in the task of remaking Turkey until his last years. The reforms are called Kemalist because he inspired them, but it would be a mistake to believe that he was without opposition or that what he did was enthusiastically accepted by all Turks. One does not make revolution without making enemies as well; in Turkey a number of individuals could generally be counted upon to oppose Kemal and his reforms: old religious functionaries, fragments of the Ottoman aristocracy, merchants and minorities who feared a disruption of the status quo, and the ever changing splinter groups of colleagues and associates whose ambitions and fears made them temporary opponents of this or that policy.

Both the French and Russian revolutions presented prolonged struggles for leadership. This was also somewhat true in the Mexican revolution, but it was not the case in Cuba, Egypt, or Turkey. Kemal was opposed on policy but, especially after his victory over the Greeks, there was never any serious challenge to his leadership. Even in later years when some of his most devoted supporters broke with him, there was no doubt that he was the only leader that Turkey or its people could accept.

Kemal distinguished between opposition and obstruction. The former he even fostered on occasion—his unsuccessful attempts to encourage opposition political parties are well known—but obstruction had to be destroyed. The remarkable thing was that there was so little effective opposition to the long string of reforms that eventually bore his name.

The first major reform was the abolition of the Caliphate. Religious education and religious courts were also abolished along with religious orders. In 1925 Kemal pressed for the adoption of what he called "civilized" clothing; he himself was invariably photographed in Western evening clothes. He gave particular emphasis to the hat, an emphasis that was anathema to the pious. Indeed, as Geoffrey Lewis suggests, "It is one of the ironies of history that although the Muslims of Turkey scarcely lifted a finger to preserve the Caliphate, an institution venerated by Muslims for 1,300 years, many of them fought like tigers to keep the head-dress whose introduction had outraged their ancestors' susceptibilities a century before." [14] At the same time he urged more freedom for women, including the discarding of the veil; he abolished polygamy and a mass of masculine prerogatives in 1926. By 1930 women had partially received the franchise and by 1934 all limitations on voting or running for office by women were removed.

In 1926 the Gregorian calendar was adopted. In the same year, the entire legal structure was overturned by the adoption of the Swiss Civil Code and penal and commercial codes based on European models. In 1928 the Arabic alphabet—a Semitic alphabet forced upon non-Semitic Ottoman Turkish—was jettisoned and a latinized alphabet adopted, along with other much needed language reforms. Family names became mandatory in 1935; the GNA gave the name Atatürk to Kemal, "father or preceptor of the Turks."

Kemal Atatürk was indeed the father of modern Turkey. As Geoffrey Lewis has said,

> It would be idle to pretend he was a plaster saint, when it is common knowledge that he loved drink and gambling and women. His vices were a part of him, a manifestation of his tremendous vitality. But they are irrelevant to a consideration of his achievement, . . . He forced the Turks to emerge from the crumbling ruins of the Ottoman Empire and to become a nation, at a time when many European and Asiatic peoples were lapsing into demoralization and despair amidst the wreckage of ancient empires. With an unconquerable faith in the potentialities of his people, he drove them along the road to Western civilization, which, as we read his speeches, we see that he came close to deifying. . . .
>
> His personal equipment for his task consisted of a fanatical belief in the Turks' high destiny, an over-riding strength of will, a quick wit, great powers of leadership and oratory, and the patience to bide his time. His achievement was made possible by a combination of various factors: the manifest political bankruptcy of the Sultanate, the disunity of the Allied powers; and, above all, the fact that his faith in his people was not misplaced.[15]

Aftermath: The Coup of 1960

Although Turkey did not become a belligerent, during World War II, political development was more or less arrested.[16] Atatürk's death

[14] Geoffrey Lewis, *op. cit.*, p. 94.
[15] *Ibid.*, pp. 111-112.
[16] She made the perfunctory declaration of war on the Axis in 1945, in order to attend the San Francisco Conference.

and the coming of the war were thermidorian in their effects; revolutionary fever and fervor abated as new leaders with new slogans and programs arose.

The RPP had been formed in 1923 (as the People's Party) under the dominance of Mustafa Kemal. Over the years, opposition to it had waxed and waned; Kemal himself had attempted to foster the growth of a two-party system. In 1930 he had encouraged Ali Fethi Okyar to form an opposition party, called the Liberal Republican Party, but the experiment collapsed within a few months in the face of riots between the various party supporters. With Kemal's death, the pressures for alternatives to the RPP mounted once again. The advent of the war, however, postponed the struggle between these developing political forces.

In January, 1946, the DP was formed by several dissidents from the RPP, the most prominent of whom was Celal Bayar, a long-time associate of Kemal's and former prime minister. The president of Turkey and leader of the RPP, Ismet İnönü, did not discourage the formation of this major opposition party but many of his subordinates did and, in some parts of the country, government officials hindered the establishment of the party in every possible way. Yet, in the elections of July, 1946, the Democrats gained 62 parliamentary seats out of 465.

By 1950 the political atmosphere had become more favorable to opposition parties, and revisions in the electoral laws made honest elections more likely. The result, in May 1950 was the first genuinely free election in the Middle East. The DP won 408 parliamentary seats out of 487. The RPP, permitting a peaceful transition of power to its opposition, established a landmark in Turkish history.

With the victory of the Democrats Ismet İnönü gave way to the presidency of Celal Bayar, with Adnan Menderes as prime minister. The changeover was greeted with enthusiasm. The RPP had dominated Turkish politics for more than a quarter century; even its friends were weary of tired leadership and stale slogans. Its enemies were many but none were more embittered than those for whom Islam still held meaning. The DP trumpeted the religious issue and undoubtedly gained some support from this stand, especially from the rural masses who had never been more than lukewarm supporters of the religious and other reforms. But probably any non-RPP party would have done well in 1950. Voting for the DP had been a way of protesting the many failures of the old government: the economic stagnation, the low scale of living, the continued inequities.

Initially the DP in power enjoyed considerable popularity. Unexpectedly good harvests, generous government support in the development of agriculture and industry, and acquiescence with the return of many of the outward manifestations of the old religion: all these and more warmed the hearts of countless Turks, especially the peasants. In 1954 the DP won 503 out of 541 parliamentary seats.

It was not long, however, before ominous flaws appeared in this happy picture. Economic development, while impressive, had been largely unplanned and chaotic and, moreover, accompanied by inflation, an adverse trade balance and severe shortages. Not very far abroad, the Cyprus question had already cast its pall. In addition the DP and especially the prime minister, Menderes, became unreasonably touchy about criticism and opposition. There was little that was not done to stifle opponents. Minor parties, such as the Nation Party in 1953, were suppressed. The RPP had its property confiscated, its newspapers sequestered and many of its offices closed. Inönü, its leader, was harassed, accused of treason, and on occasion physically manhandled. The press was muzzled, the universities subverted, and judges forcibly retired. In October 1957—seven years after 1950!— the DP won its election by corruption and intimidation.

By the spring of 1960 the situation had deteriorated beyond repair. In late April the Democrats made a feverish attack in the Assembly on the RPP and Inönü. A committee was created to investigate the "activities" of the RPP; and when Inönü objected to the plenary powers given to and exercised by the Committee, he was expelled from the Assembly.

Clashes between students and police occurred at both Istanbul and Ankara Universities. The universities were closed and martial law proclaimed. Further demonstrations, including one involving 1,000 military cadets on May 21, added to the difficulties of maintaining order.

On May 27 the army moved in a well-planned and efficient coup, capturing key government offices and arresting the important leaders and deputies of the DP. We now know that various army leaders had contemplated intervening against a Turkish government as early as 1946, but the strong feeling that the army should be above politics prevailed. As Dankwart Rustow has remarked, "It was the Menderes government itself, . . . which brought the army back into politics after more than three decades of civilian rule," by the injudicious use of martial law and the use of troops to perform police functions. Moreover, "Menderes had for several years attempted systematically to fill the highest military posts with officers amenable to his political directives. But the army's *esprit de corps* proved too strong to admit of effective infiltration from the top." [17]

[17] In Robert E. Ward and Dankwart A. Rustow (eds.), *Political Modernization in Japan and Turkey* (Princeton: Princeton University Press, 1964), pp. 366-367.

The army junta, called the National Unity Committee (NUC), was headed by General Cemal Gürsel, who swiftly became the *de facto* chief executive. The NUC promised a number of reforms, the punishment of those who had led the nation away from the principles of Kemal, and early elections and the re-establishment of civilian government. In the months to come the NUC guided Turkey through the trial of the ousted Democrats, the adoption of a new constitution, and the return to civilian parliamentary government.

A constitutional revision committee was almost immediately formed but quickly encountered pressure from the NUC and opposition from many other groups. "The process of evolution of the Constitution lasted just over one year and involved four different printed versions, a nationwide poll of intellectuals, a national referendum, and plenty of political dispute." [18] This open political dispute was a healthy manifestation of the political maturation that Turkey was to regain. The final constitution was approved by referendum in July, 1961, although more than a third of the votes cast were against it. The new constitution was a reaffirmation of Kemalism, although a number of the old expressions were changed or rephrased. It was also a reaffirmation of individual rights, with special emphasis on religious freedom and freedom of the press, a "reflection of the reaction to the most heavily felt abuses of the Menderes regime." [19] A Constitutional Court was established to check the operations of political parties and the constitutionality of legislation. The GNA became bicameral and a caretaker cabinet was also provided to preside during election periods. The Constitution, promulgated in the name of the people, was in many ways an imaginative effort to provide the framework for a new Turkey.

In October, 1961, four parties contested the elections that returned the government to civilian hands: the new Justice Party (JP) formed in February, 1961, by some of the supporters of the disbanded DP; the Republican Peasants Nation Party (RPNP), a reactionary religious party, formed in 1948; the New Turkey Party (NTP), at first thought to be the creature of the NUC, a heterogeneous party of liberal leanings; and the old RPP. Many observers assumed that the latter would win by a landslide. In fact, no party won a majority—the RPP received 36.7 percent of the votes; the JP, 34.8 percent; the RPNP, 14 percent; and the NTP, 13.7 percent[20]—the RPP winning a smaller percentage of the popular votes than it had in 1957. Clearly the

[18] Walter F. Weiker, *The Turkish Revolution, 1960-1961* (Washington: The Brookings Institution, 1963), p. 65. This is the best study to date of the 1960 coup and its aftermath.

[19] *Ibid.*, p. 74.

[20] *Ibid.*, p. 113.

Turkish people were not of one voice. And perhaps the most significant thing about the election was the apparent and remarkable rejuvenation of the Democrats, although under other names. Their leaders imprisoned or dead, the rank and file continued to support that "party" against which the army had mounted its coup.[21]

The election results underlined the most burning issue in Turkish politics since the 1960 coup: the fate of the former DP leaders. In order to justify its own intervention, the army junta felt compelled to hold gigantic trials of the DP leaders. The trials were carried out between October 1960 and September 1961. Weiker has given us some interesting statistics of these trials. Among others: there were 202 sessions with 150,000 spectators; there were 592 defendants along with 1,068 witnesses; the death penalty was asked 228 times, with 15 death sentences handed down and three executions; life imprisonment was meted out to 31 defendants, lesser terms to 402 others; 133 individuals were acquitted.[22]

The principal defendants were Celal Bayar, Adnan Menderes, and various of the cabinet members. The charges against them ranged from the grave and serious to the ludicrous. Among the latter were the charge against President Bayar that he had forced a Turkish zoo to purchase a dog that had been a state gift to him from the Afghan government and the charge against Prime Minister Menderes that he had fathered an illegitimate baby by an opera singer and then murdered it. On the other hand, many more serious indictments were made for the incitation of riots, destruction of newspapers, and the corruption of elections.[23]

Although 15 death sentences were announced, only three were carried out: those against Adnan Menderes, the prime minister; Rüstü Zorlu, the foreign minister; and Hasan Polatkan, the finance minister. Celal Bayar, the President, had his death sentence commuted to life imprisonment because of his age. It was not long before the question of an amnesty for the remaining imprisoned defendants became the political *cause célèbre* of the new Turkey. The demand for an amnesty became the leitmotif of the JP and aroused widespread sympathy in Turkey. In 1963 Bayar was released but the tumultuous enthusiasm with which the act was greeted caused the cautious government to

---

[21] "One hardly needs to emphasize that any party that could survive a successful military coup against it owes a great deal to the strength and adaptability of its organization" (Ergun Özbudun, *The Role of the Military in Recent Turkish Politics*, Occasional Papers in International Affairs, Number 14 [Cambridge: Center for International Affairs, Harvard University, 1966], p. 7).

[22] Weiker, *op. cit.*, p. 28.

[23] *Ibid.*, Chap. 2, *passim*.

reimprison him for a few months more. By 1966 most of the defendants had been released.

As a footnote to these developments, it is well to point out that the armed forces were never in complete or final agreement as to their objectives or the role of the NUC. There came to be a constant jockeying for power among the officer ranks, the services, and the NUC. In August 1960 the NUC forcibly retired more than 5,000 officers; in November the NUC purged itself of a third of its members; and as late as February 1962 some military elements were willing to support the abortive *coup d'état* of Colonel Talat Aydemir. Yet with all its vicissitudes the NUC guided Turkey back to civilian democracy. General Gürsel became the president only to be replaced in 1966 and to die after a lingering illness in 1967. The Justice Party achieved electoral victory in 1965 and Suleyman Demirel became the prime minister.

The RPP returned to its former role of opposition and Ismet İnönü to that of opposition leader. By 1967 the party had become badly split over the issue of how left of center it should be. A substantial number of its members have broken away, calling themselves the Reliance Party and adhering to a centralist orientation.

Leaders and Followers

Any revolution in consummation tends to realign leaders and followers. Once a revolution is successful even the defeated and dissatisfied tend to find consolation in the victorious factions. Trotsky after all was a Menshevik in his earlier days; the Red Army was well stocked with former Tsarist officers and men, and the Communist Party itself soon filled with those whose earlier affiliations had been elsewhere. In Turkey it was much the same. Those who opposed the revolution in its early stages later found it expedient to embrace, even if not fervently, the principles of Kemal and the RPP. Only the diehards, the irreconcilables, and the indifferent were left outside the fold, without power and without influence. The opposition leaders of later years were in earlier times largely active (and honored) members of the RPP.

The nineteenth-century opponents of the Sultan were likely to have been those whose contacts with the outside world had given them ideas, resources, and the opportunities for conspiracy. It is not surprising that the old Committee of Union and Progress was largely a military group, for military officers were precisely those whose training (often abroad) and sense of loyalty made them unusually sensitive to the

failings of the old regime. The CUP established itself as the *de facto*
ruling group in Turkey between 1908 and 1918 and rapidly collected
a heterogeneous group of supporters: pro-German elements, liberals
and intellectuals, military officers, merchants, and so on. But Enver
Pasha's inability to resolve the problems brought on by the war
coupled with the defeat of the Central Powers laid the basis for another shift of allegiance on the part of many Turks.

It can be argued that Mustafa Kemal was sufficiently a hero to Turks
to justify his quick rise to revolutionary leadership. But, more important, Kemal was a military hero and his early revolutionary success
in eastern Turkey (in 1919) was largely due to his ready acceptance
by Turkish army commanders. Many of his early and closest supporters—men like Ismet Pasha, Huseyin Rauf, and Ali Fuad—were
themselves military men. The military character of the first years of
the revolution could only strengthen the ties of Kemal with the military;
the revolution in its early phase was essentially a military victory. The
result was that most soldiers were fervent supporters of the revolution.[24] But Kemal was admired by many of the intellectuals—the new
writers and poets, the journalists, the academicians—although some,
like the famous writer Halide Edib, broke with him later. It is hardly
surprising that Turkish women were among his most ardent supporters, for he did much to free them from the past. But the minority
groups, obviously the Greeks and less obviously the Kurds, opposed
the revolution in varying degrees. The revolution was, after all,
Turkish and nationalistic and this could raise little enthusiasm among
the non-Turkish minority groups. At the same time, the revolution was
secular; it could be expected that the *hocas*, religious mendicants,
waqf supervisors, and the deeply religious would be opposed to the
abolition of the Caliphate and many other of Kemal's religious reforms.
Probably no opposition was as deep-seated as this; as late as 1966 a
resurgence of the Nursist movement—named after Saidi Nursi, who
had been one of Kemal's most bitter religious opponents—caused concern in the Justice Party government of Prime Minister Demirel. Also
opposing the revolution were those who were tied to the old regime in
some way or whose ambitions effectively separated them from the
revolutionary government. Many of Kemal's followers were supporters
of him alone and with his death it was not easy to keep the RPP together or the continuing revolution in high gear.

[24] "The armed forces were the most important single legacy which the Ottoman
Empire bequeathed to the Turkish Republic. . . . [Thus] fully 93 percent of
the empire's general staff officers continued their service in Turkey . . ." (Ward
and Rustow, *op. cit.*, p. 388).

The Turkish revolutionary elite has been studied in great detail.[25] Arguing that a study of the deputies of the various Grand National Assemblies will give us information about the broad scale elite, Frey has produced an incredible array of statistics.[26] Some of these follow.

Sixty-two percent of all deputies elected between 1920 and 1957 had university education and only a handful had no education.[27] During the same period more than 90 percent, on the average, of all cabinet members and top leaders had university education.[28] Of the delegates to the early nationalist Erzurum Congress (July-August 1919), 9 percent were professional, 33 percent official (including the government and the military), 28 percent were merchants, bankers, and farmers, 13 percent were labeled "religious," and 7 percent were journalists.[29] This can be compared with similar data on all deputies (1920-1957): 33 percent were official; 31 percent, professional; and 24 percent were merchants, bankers, and farmers.[30] In general there was a high rate of re-election from one assembly to another, around 60 percent.[31] The average age of the first assembly elected (1920) was 43 years—Kemal was then 39, Ismet, 36, and Celal Bayar, 37—but this average slowly crept upward; the assembly elected in 1946 had an average age of 52.8 years. This average fell slightly with the victory of the DP.[32] "Women first brightened the dark corridors of the Grand National Assembly building in Ankara in the Fifth Assembly of 1935. There were eighteen of them, some 4.1 percent of the total number of deputies." [33] But this percentage fell off: 3.4, 3.3, 2.0, 0.6, and 0.7 percent in the following assemblies.[34] Frey found, in his analyses of the ten assemblies, that the social background of the deputies changed meaningfully between 1920 and 1957 and that "the deputies have changed from being primarily a national elite group, oriented toward the tutelary development of the country, to being primarily an as-

[25] Frederick W. Frey, *The Turkish Political Elite* (Cambridge: M.I.T. Press, 1965).
[26] Because of the "high degree of governmental integration, when one examines the social backgrounds of the deputies to the Grand National Assembly, one obtains, *ipso facto*, information on the backgrounds of all the cabinets and ministers, on the formal leadership of the Assembly, and on the top political leaders as well" (Frey, *op. cit.*, p. 6).
[27] *Ibid.*, p. 44.
[28] *Ibid.*, p. 279.
[29] *Ibid.*, p. 77.
[30] *Ibid.*, p. 80.
[31] *Ibid.*, p. 164.
[32] *Ibid.*, p. 170.
[33] *Ibid.*, p. 192.
[34] *Ibid.*, p. 193.

semblage of local politicians, oriented toward more immediate local
and political advantages." [35]

The NUC has also been studied.

> Of twenty-nine members of the NUC, for whom there is social-
> background data based on newspaper interviews, most came from
> lower-middle-class or salaried middle-class families: eight were sons of
> officers, six of civil servants, six of artisans and merchants, four of pro-
> fessionals, and two of farmers. . . . None of the members appeared
> to belong to the top political or economic elite. Finally . . . only
> eleven out of the total membership of thirty-eight were born in one of
> the three large urban centers of Istanbul, Ankara, and Izmir.[36]

The average age of the so-called radical members of this group was
36.8 compared with 45.3 for those identified as moderates.[37] The
moderates ultimately became lifetime members of the Turkish Senate.

There is little evidence that the coup in 1960 altered the political
characteristics of the new assemblies (now bicameral) or the ambitions
and activities of their members. Although General Gürsel became the
new president—and after him, General Sunay—there was no great
influx of military men into the new political elite. This elite, now
virtually normalized, is educated, aging, unrevolutionary, and somewhat right of center.[38]

Turkish Revolutionary Ideology

The conditions in Turkey during the revolutionary period were
such as to encourage the growth of ideology. There was no sudden
coup d'état or easy seizure of power that neutralized those who opposed the revolution. What resulted was a war of words between the
Ankara government (of Kemal) and the Istanbul government of the
Sultan. The Ankara group denounced the Sultan and his supporters,
the Greeks and other foreigners, and all those who did not support its
program. Essentially this program called for the rejuvenation of ethnic
Turkey, that is, the Turkey of Anatolia and not that of the Ottomans,
and the expulsion of foreign occupation troops, along with such things
as Turkish control of the Straits, retention of Mosul, and the untrammeled independence of Turkey in dealing with her own minorities

[35] *Ibid.,* p. 196. The quotation was italicized in the original.
[36] Özbudun, *op. cit.,* p. 29.
[37] *Ibid.,* pp. 35-36.
[38] This is not quite true of the current leadership of the RPP.

and problems. Until the winning of the war of national independence there were only glimpses of the later Kemalist program: the antipathy toward traditional Islam, the language, legal, and political reforms, and the revolution in women's rights.

From the end of this war until Kemal's death in 1938, there was one major innovation or reform after another. Each such step required some preparation in the GNA as well as among the public. The preparation was ideological. Each step was justified and rejustified; appeals were made to national pride, to the western civilization in which, Kemal urged, Turks should participate, and to the material benefits that would flow from the modernization of Turkey.

The revolutionary ideology was built throughout these years, in the appeals, the arguments, and the justifications. It presented a slowly evolving worldview, never wholly worked out or consistent, always somewhat advanced beyond what the Turks were doing and perhaps less developed than the enthusiasms of Kemal. Kemal himself was rather specific about his principles. The RPP, in its 1931 convention, stated the six principles of Kemal explicitly, which remain the best statement of Kemalist ideology. These principles were (1) republicanism, (2) nationalism, (3) populism, (4) statism (étatism), (5) secularism, and (6) revolutionism.

In general the meaning of republicanism, nationalism, and secularism is rather apparent but the remaining three need some explanation. Statism represented the assertion that untrammeled free enterprise would not be sufficient to promote economic development. The state would need to intervene, in planning and financing. The term itself is old-fashioned; a developing state today is more apt to label itself socialist. Statism was dropped in the 1961 Turkish Constitution. Revolutionism means that the revolution is a continuing one; that it was not an event consummated but one developing. Because the nation was still in revolution, some attitudes and sacrifices, perhaps otherwise unpalatable, would have to be maintained. It is hardly surprising that modern Turkey has grown somewhat weary of revolutionism. Populism meant the destruction of privilege and the re-emphasis upon individual equality of opportunity.

Throughout Kemal's lifetime the ideology was a developing one. With his death it became frozen and as a guide to practical action it became rather remote. This was particularly true under the Democratic regime, when deep-seated and sustained attacks were made on the Kemalist programs. But attacks on the ideology (or on the memory of Kemal) were never as open or as effective as those on his programs. Moreover, the 1960 coup was undertaken, so its participants proclaimed, in order to preserve the principles of Kemal. The Kemalist ideology has reached its ultimate maturity: it is accepted, respected, and revered but it no longer completely offers a template for action.

The Impact of the Turkish Revolution

In the period immediately following World War I, the Arab Middle East was under the thumb of the British and French, and in Iran and Afghanistan the British retained considerable influence. Throughout the middle Arab belt—Iraq, Syria (including Lebanon), Palestine, and Egypt—there were abortive revolts, but it is difficult to say how much these were the product of the events in Turkey. Arabs looked on the new Turkey with interest and they were intrigued with the figure of Mustafa Kemal, but there is not much evidence that they rose in rebellion because of the Turkish example. Moreover, the new Turkey had wiped its hands of its old Ottoman interests and with the exception of the Alexandretta and Mosul irredenta, no longer concerned itself with the Arab world.

The Turkish model was noted more carefully in Iran and Afghanistan. In 1921 an army officer named Reza Khan mounted a coup in Iran, becoming Shah in 1925. In 1919 Amanullah Shah succeeded his father as the Amir of Afghanistan. Both Reza and Amanullah were very much impressed with the Kemalist revolution and both attempted to emulate many of its aspects in their countries. But their attempts were never as far-reaching and their political control never as secure. Amanullah was deposed in 1929; it was not until the 1960's that Afghanistan began to move once more toward substantial reforms. Reza Shah encountered severe opposition to his reforms in Iran; and in any case he was forced from his throne in 1941 by the British and Russians for his alleged pro-German activities. His son, the present Shah, after enduring the vicissitudes of the postwar period and the nationalist revolution of Mossadeq, has at last embarked on what he terms the "white" revolution. In both Iran and Afghanistan then the Kemalist revolution was influential and important.

Europe was impressed with the rejuvenation of Turkey and with the man who had successfully challenged the Allies. It was also concerned with the possibility of a *rapprochement* in the early twenties between the two "revolutionary" states, Turkey and Russia. Kemal was the subject of biographies in Europe and was linked with Benito Mussolini as the epitomé of the strongman in a modern state. There can be no doubt that in general the European powers respected both Kemal and his reconstructed Turkey, but as a revolution the Turkish experience had no influence on Europe. In the rest of the world, in Africa, the

Western Hemisphere, the Far East, the Turkish revolution had no influence at all.

In later years considerable interest has been generated in the Kemalist experiment. Some Egyptians refer to Nasser as a second Kemal; and as the Arabs moved into their economic and political reconstructions, they found it appropriate to re-examine the Turkish revolution. By 1960, when the coup occurred in Turkey, the world had grown so inured to coups and military takeovers that it could look on only with mild interest. The Turkish revolution is now a part of history. Its foreign influence was minimal but its impact within Turkey has been enormous and continuing.

Conclusion

In the broad sense the Turkish revolutionary movement covers the better part of the last century; in the narrower meaning it comprises the nationalist revolution led by Kemal Atatürk in the period immediately following the First World War. Turkey (the Ottoman Empire) was shattered by that war. Her possessions were largely wrested from her, much of her heartland was occupied or claimed by foreign powers, and her political institutions were paralyzed by the crises they faced.

Revolution was fed by the dissatisfaction of several generations, but it was impelled by the final burden of dismemberment which the victorious powers attempted to fasten upon a defeated Turkey. It was less the military defeat, although that was significant too, and more the ungenerous peace that spurred the Turks to react, to rebel, to revolt.

Turkey's revolution was led by Mustafa Kemal, her only authentic military hero from the war. Initially, it was intensely national in character. There was no coup nor was there any need for a coup. More and more, political allegiance drifted to Kemal and to those Turks who were fighting the invader. When the military victory was won, there remained only a Kemalist government in power. Gradually Kemal attempted to make his revolution cultural and social as well as political. He was, however, less interested in economic innovations than he was in what he termed "becoming civilized and modern." A number of reforms were instituted that had enormous repercussions in Turkey. Kemal died in 1938, and the fever of revolution abated. Perhaps thermidor can be identified with the rise of an opposition party (the Democrats) to power in the 1950's. The Democratic reaction was so severe that the Turkish army mounted a coup in 1960 to restore the principles of Kemal. Despite the army's intentions Turkey could hardly return to an earlier life. The army quickly returned the government to civilian hands, and the Turks continued to develop in modern directions, only partially consonant with earlier Kemalist intentions.

The Turkish revolution was the first modern revolution in the Middle East and until the Egyptian was the most thoroughgoing. It was an inspiration to reform in Afghanistan and Iran; it suggested military government to the officers of its neighbors, Syria and Iraq. Other than these effects, it has not been very influential in the Middle East. On the larger scene it has been only a curiosity. On the other hand, the Turkish revolution was enormously important to Turkey and was made only for Turks, who, like their leader, Mustafa Kemal Atatürk, did not want to be left behind in the twentieth century.

9

The Egyptian Revolution

The history of modern Egypt begins in the early nineteenth century
when Muhammad Ali Pasha became the semi-independent vassal of the
Sultan of Turkey. In the years that followed, Egypt was unified and her
economy was overhauled. She fought wars, winning victories and
suffering defeats. She became the prey of foreigners, who built a canal
(Suez) and attached her revenues. In 1882 the British occupied the
country. At the opening of the First World War Great Britain established a protectorate over Egypt; but by 1922, after considerable unrest and agitation, the British found it necessary to extend "independence" to the Egyptians. Despite this independence, the British maintained sufficient strength in Egypt to exacerbate the struggle between
the King—Fuad until 1936, then Farouk—and his political opponents,
and in general to muddy the waters of domestic Egyptian politics by
their presence alone.

At the end of the Second World War, the British position in the
Middle East weakened. Simultaneously with the establishment of
Israel in the midst of the Arab world, Arab nationalism rose to a peak
of intensity. The pressures produced by the external environment
sharpened the domestic political struggle. Nationalist opposition against
the British grew enormously and in the early postwar years increasingly against the King. The King was accused by many of corruption
and toadying to the British. In point of fact, his personal behavior
during this period lent some substance to the charges of his critics.
Finally he lost the confidence of the army, an army already embarrassed by its poor showing in the Palestinian war in 1948. The result
was an army coup that toppled the regime.

The Egyptian Revolution, ushered in by this coup, illustrates a
number of the points raised in the theoretical sections of this book.

157

From the viewpoint of almost any model, there existed a generous quantity of revolutionary "causation." But the social revolution which has ensued was triggered by the classic military coup. Egypt in revolution has displayed most vividly the destruction-reconstruction pattern. She has produced her budget of ideology and she has affected in an incredible number of ways the external environment of the Middle East and Africa. The Egyptian Revolution is, indeed, the most significant modern revolution in the Middle Eastern-African world.

The Coup of 1952

"Early in the summer of 1952 Egypt was oozing revolution from every pore." [1] A small body of junior army officers, under the leadership of a young, relatively unknown lieutenant colonel, Gamal Abdul Nasser, struck on the night of July 22-23, 1952. Swiftly neutralizing the garrison in Cairo and capturing most of the senior officers and the usual strategic communication points, the officer-rebels virtually had achieved success by the early morning hours. There was little resistance, only two soldiers being killed in a brief encounter outside the army General Headquarters.

But many problems had yet to be solved. Some senior commanders remained at large and the reaction of the navy and coast guard continued uncertain. Still more critical was the lack of information about the reaction of the British, who still maintained troops in the Canal Zone. The King was in Alexandria; somehow his person would have to be secured and his fate decided. The "young officers" were also uncertain as to the leadership of their own movement and what role they would all play in the postcoup period.

They had already made some tentative advances to Major General Mohammed Naguib, an officer of considerable reputation and one not unsympathetic to their aims. Although afterwards General Naguib would claim an active role in the preliminary stages of the coup, it is plain that he pledged his support only if the coup were assured of success.[2] Early in the morning of the 23rd Naguib assumed titular leadership of the movement.

At the same time the rebel leaders contacted the American and the British embassies and offered assurances that foreign lives and property would be respected and that internal order would be maintained.

[1] Jean and Simonne Lacouture, *Egypt in Transition* (London: Methuen & Co., Ltd., 1958), p. 125.

[2] *See*, for example, his account of the coup and its aftermath (Mohammed Neguib, *Egypt's Destiny* [London: Victor Gollancz, Ltd., 1955]).

Later it would be apparent that the King had looked to foreign (presumably British) intervention to save his throne for him. But when the British did nothing, the final success or failure of the *coup d'état* became a matter of purely internal Egyptian concern.

With Naguib's active participation assured it was necessary to broadcast immediately to the people what had been and what was to be done in order to calm the general public and seek its support for the revolt. At approximately 7:00 A.M. the Egyptian radio began to broadcast repeatedly the following message in the name of Naguib:

> To my brothers, the sons of the Nile:
>
> You know that our country has been living through delicate moments, and you have seen the hands of traitors at work in its affairs. These traitors dared to extend their influence to the Army, imagining that it was devoid of patriotic elements.
>
> We have therefore decided to purify ourselves, to eliminate the traitors and weaklings, and thus record a new and honourable page in the history of our country.
>
> Those who engage in destructive activities will be severely punished. The Army will co-operate with the police in maintaining order.
>
> In conclusion, I should like to reassure our brothers, the foreigners who live among us, that their interests will be respected. The Army will be fully responsible for their lives and Property.[3]

If the rebels were somewhat uncertain of their next steps in Cairo, Farouk in Alexandria was even more uncertain of his. The King had earlier demonstrated a certain facility in conspiracy and intrigue. But in this troubled hour, with his own army deserting him, he was in fact helpless. But his fate still presented delicate problems to the new military junta, which thought it prudent to move with caution against his person.

The rebels proceeded to approach Ali Mahir Pasha, a former prime minister, with the task of forming a new government and of persuading the King to abdicate.[4] Ali Mahir temporized for a few hours but on July 24 went to Alexandria to get the "permission" of the King to his formation of a new cabinet. The King gave in, although reluctantly, and thus cast the aura of legality over the coup. He had accepted the new government, including a prominent role for General Naguib—and he was still King. But he was to be King for only a matter of hours.

[3] Neguib, *op. cit.*, p. 120. Naguib claims authorship of this. There are a number of other, more elaborate, statements extant. Nasser also has claimed authorship of the statement.

[4] Lacouture, *op. cit.*, pp. 154-155.

The King's concession merely speeded up the process of his deposition. By the next day the young officers had such a powerful, and in effect legal, hold over the country, and the popularity of their action had become so overwhelmingly evident that there was no need to delay the removal of Farouk. During the night of July 25-26 the officers debated whether to exile or execute the King. The next morning they informed the King that he must abdicate and leave Egypt that evening. The anniversary of the date of his departure, July 26, continues to be celebrated in Egypt as its independence day.

Farouk had in theory abdicated in favor of his infant son, Ahmed Fuad. Egypt remained legally a kingdom under a regency. But this could hardly last. On September 7, Ali Mahir surrendered the prime ministry to General Naguib; on June 18, 1953, Egypt was proclaimed a republic.

Patterns of Violence in Egypt

The coup of July, 1952, occasioned little bloodshed, in contrast with Kassem's coup in Iraq in 1958, and did not lead to civil war as did Abdullah al-Sallal's coup in Yemen in 1962. Why? Students interested in Africa and the Middle East have often remarked how relatively nonviolent, in general, Egyptian politics have been. To be sure there have been some assassinations, a plethora of riots and demonstrations, and a narrow spectrum of violence among the peasants. Nevertheless it would be inaccurate to term modern Egyptian history as violent.

The Egyptians are in many ways politically docile. They easily accept authority; historically they have been accustomed to highly centralized government. Geography has placed severe limits on armed insurrection in that outside the Nile Valley and a handful of scattered oases there is virtually no land capable of supporting life. Egypt has no independent tribesmen to dispute its government and no enormous land over which to exercise its authority. Even a weak government can maintain itself in Egypt.

The Mamelukes who ruled Egypt in the name of the Ottoman Sultan succumbed rather quickly to Napoleon at the end of the eighteenth century. Nor did they oppose in any effective way the rise of Muhammad Ali Pasha in the wake of the French departure. Indeed, one of the few instances of political massacre in modern Egyptian history was the destruction of the leading Mamelukes by Muhammad Ali in 1811. Muhammad Ali established a dynasty, sent Egyptian armies into foreign wars, put together enormous personal land holdings with ruthlessness, but there is little evidence of widespread revolutionary violence in Egypt. The only major revolt was that of Arabi Pasha, an ambitious army officer, against Tewfik Pasha in 1880, which occasioned the occupation of Egypt by the British.

The Egyptians accepted the British occupation remarkably well—it lasted altogether until 1956—and although a great many demonstrations and riots occurred, no long-lasting bloody engagements or civil strife wracked the country. When it is remembered that Britain fought two great world wars with Egypt as her Mediterranean base without insurrection, it is a remarkable measure of the revolutionary lethargy of the Egyptians.

With the rise of the nationalist spirit, first under Mustafa Kamil (d. 1907) and later under Saad Zaghlul, who founded the Wafd (or Delegation) Party at the end of World War I, there was naturally a tendency to dramatize Egyptian opposition to foreign occupation and control through intermittent strikes, demonstrations, and other forms of unrest. Localized outbreaks of violence over the years have both contributed to and have been the result of such nationalism. One of the most notorious of these, the Denshawy incident of June 1906, produced important political repercussions. Several British officers were on a pigeon shoot when they were molested by villagers from Denshawy; in the ensuing melee some villagers were shot, a British officer killed, and another villager murdered by the British in retaliation. "This miserable tragedy, the outcome of accident and anger, provoked a state of panic among the foreign communities of Egypt, and their newspapers and the Press of Britain unleashed a violent campaign calling for examplary punishment of the guilty villagers." [5] Savage punishment was indeed meted out, but the result was a popular resentment against the British that lingered for the next half century. On January 25, 1952, an encounter between Egyptian police and British troops in the Canal Zone resulted in 43 Egyptian deaths. The next day mobs took over Cairo, burning and looting foreign shops and establishments, including the famous Shepheard's Hotel. It was the worst riot in the history of modern Egypt.

Political assassination has not been unknown in Egypt but again seems to be tied, in modern times, to the rise of nationalism. Butros Ghali Pasha was killed in 1909 largely because of his alleged weakness in opposing the new British convention on the Suez Canal. In 1924 Sir Lee Stack, the Sirdar (or commander-in-chief) of the Egyptian army, was shot on a street in Cairo. The event unloosed a veritable deluge of vengeance by the British. In 1944 two Jewish terrorists in Cairo murdered Lord Moyne, British Minister of State for the Middle

[5] Tom Little, *Egypt* (London: Ernest Benn, Ltd., 1958), p. 111.

East. The prime minister to whom their death sentences were appealed, Ahmed Mahir Pasha, was himself assassinated in 1945. In December 1948, members of the Muslim Brotherhood killed Nukrashy Pasha, the prime minister; in February 1949, the secret police in turn killed the Brotherhood's Supreme Guide, Hasan al-Banna. Abdul Nasser—who was himself involved in the terrorist attempt on the life of General Sirri Amir in 1950—has been shot at several times.

In contrast to such political violence, until very recently, minorities in Egypt have never been systematically molested, even though the great cities of Cairo and Alexandria swarmed with such groups: Greek, Italian, English, Jewish, and Armenian. During the fifties and sixties public policy encouraged such minorities to leave Egypt, but they have never been treated in such a brutal, savage way as have the Armenians and Greeks in Turkey and the Turks in Cyprus.

The political patterns of Egypt have been relatively stable. The dynasty established by Muhammad Ali lasted nearly a century and a half. The British occupation, lasting three-quarters of a century, did not result in a bloody civil war as in Algeria or Indo-China. Egypt is not a land of coups; she has had only one.[6] The Egyptian revolution has been unique in her modern history.

The Prerevolutionary Environment

Possibly most theorists of revolution could find in the Egyptian Revolution justification for their various kinds of analyses. Egypt has displayed "multiple dysfunction" in abundance, absolute misery, fluctuating periods of hope and depression, "accelerators" and "triggering" elements and, of course, without laboring the point, an *ancien régime* characterized by weakness and corruption. This *embarras de richesses* complicates our task; it is difficult to state with much confidence *why* the Egyptian Revolution occurred when it did rather than on any number of other occasions.

One fact of overwhelming importance stands out: the British presence in Egypt. Britain openly occupied the country despite the granting of "independence" in 1922 and the signing of the Anglo-Egyptian Treaty of 1936, which called for a diminution of the British presence there. Yet the outbreak of the Second World War only three years later, in the shadow of the Italians in Libya and Ethiopia, arrested any real alteration of British control over Egyptian affairs. Indeed, during the

---

[6] Tom Little has this to say of Arabi, "He was the first of his type in the history of modern Egypt to raise his voice against authority"; his attempt was abortive (*ibid.*, p. 85).

war in a rather famous incident (1942), the British ambassador forced King Farouk—by surrounding his palace with British tanks—to dismiss one government and form another. After the war the British forces gradually retired to the Suez Canal Zone, but even there they hung like the blade of Damocles over the head of every Egyptian government. This meant that until the coup of 1952 virtually any revolutionary act would have had to have been directed at the British. The result would have been a war of national independence. Since the British exercised strong and effective control, and the geography of Egypt inhibits guerrilla warfare, the British presence effectively retarded revolution.

At the same time the British presence encouraged revolutionary fervor. No foreign occupation is loved; that of the British in Egypt was detested. Although the burgeoning Egyptian nationalism was the product of many factors, surely its chief impetus was the almost universal detestation of the British who occupied Egypt. But it was a nationalism that seemed forever frustrated. The Egyptians could not understand how the British occupation could be justified in the face of the then current Wilsonian platitudes of self-determination. They asked for the opportunity to present their case at the Peace Conference in Paris after the First World War. Although the British successfully sidetracked this reasonable request, their action resulted in the almost instant growth of the Wafd Party, the first genuinely popular political party in Middle Eastern history. The Wafd won elections, won ministerial posts for its leaders and sometimes the empty symbols of government, but it was never successful in obtaining untrammeled authority for running Egyptian affairs. The great object of its and all nationalist doctrine, the departure of the British and the hordes of foreign entrepreneurs who controlled so much of the Egyptian economy, was precisely what it could not accomplish. The Wafd ended in corruption and indignity; nationalism—simply Egyptian and not yet Arab—continued to exist and grow, but uncontrolled and leaderless.[7]

For some Egyptians these frustrations forced an inward reorientation and a resurrection of religious totalitarianism. In 1927 Hasan al-Banna founded the Muslim Brotherhood, which preached the return to the Islam of the Prophet's day, a purification of the Egyptian way of life, and a rejection of the entire spectrum of the corrupting, debilitating foreign influences in Egypt. The Muslim Brotherhood became much more than a religious movement; by the end of the Second World War it had assumed the proportions of a major political force. Organized in cells, with an active, authoritarian leadership, and

[7] This period is well covered in Mahmud Y. Zayid, *Egypt's Struggle for Independence* (Beirut: Khayats, 1965).

permeating all ranks of Egyptian life, the Brotherhood offered an alternative to those who could not cope with the British or with the internal problems of Egypt.

Egypt was and is a land of great misery. The standard of living of its peasantry has ranked among the lowest in the world. Its ever burgeoning population—9,000,000 in 1897, 31,000,000 in 1966—has frustrated enormous efforts, including the massive irrigation scheme associated with the Aswan High Dam, to raise substantially its living standards. Although manufacturing has existed in Egypt for years— certainly it antedates the revolution—Egypt remains essentially an agricultural land. The bulk of its inhabitants continues to labor with primitive implements on land watered almost entirely by irrigation and partially subject still to the vagaries of the Nile flow. In the past it was land not his own on which the Egyptian peasant, the *fellah*, labored —in 1952, 94 percent of the landowners possessed but 36 percent of the land [8]—and the rent he paid was often exorbitant. His crops were ravaged by insects as he himself was by a myriad of diseases. He was constantly in debt, uniformly exploited, debilitated by disease and a subsistence diet. His only luxury was sex, his only hope was the surcease of an early death.

The fellah's counterpart, the urban worker, had little more. He and his companions had flocked to the city to escape the hopelessness of the countryside but he brought with him few skills or talents. He found little employment, which in any event paid him very little, and he lived in squalid and miserable conditions. All too often he turned to crime and hashish. In company with others he formed a part of the Cairo (or Alexandria) "street," that amorphous mass of humanity that lends substance to every riot or demonstration.

Such were the conditions of life for the rural and "urban" peasantry. Their lives, in Hobbes's classic phrase, were "solitary, poor, nasty, brutish and short." Although they did not make revolution by themselves, they were a living reminder of the failure of the old regime; and when the revolution did come, it was made in their name.

In stark contrast to the miserable conditions of the great mass of Egyptians, there existed in vast splendor a very small group of "exploiters." Essentially these consisted of the landowners, many of them absentee; they were the multitudinous members of the royal family, or their favorites, the remnants of the Mamelukes (the aristocrats of the past) and the newly rich, the new industrialists who insured their

[8] Charles Issawi, *Egypt in Revolution* (London: Oxford University Press, 1963), p. 156. In 1948 nearly 2 million peasants owned an average of 0.4 acre each (Henry H. Ayrout, *The Egyptian Peasant* [Boston: Beacon Press, 1963], p. 57).

status and wealth by investing in land. But all led lives astronomically removed from those of the masses. The gap between the rich and the poor, literally to understate the case, was very great in Egypt. And there seemed no way to redress this difference short of revolution.

Egypt has always been a land where corruption pervades every walk of life. Although no one doubts the honesty of Nasser and his immediate entourage, it can hardly be said that the revolution has altered this very much. When the police of Cairo earn only £E10 per month, it would be incredible to expect that they would be above accepting bribes for minor favors. Traditionally their superiors accepted bribes for major favors. People had little faith or trust in government; everyone assumed that virtually all bureaucrats were corrupt. Nevertheless the Egyptian public was shocked by two examples of corruption in the prerevolutionary period. The financial scandals surrounding Nahas Pasha, his wife, and other leaders of the once popular, nationalist Wafd Party represented a blow from which neither the Wafd nor popular democracy could recover. And in the disgraceful aftermath of the Palestinian War (1948) it was alleged that even the King was implicated in the corruption surrounding the army stores; if this were true the King had treasonably hamstrung the military efforts against the Zionists. It was to be a vital factor in driving the army to revolt.

Much has been made of the spectacle of King Farouk in the postwar period. Crowned King as a boy in 1936, he had been then handsome and immensely popular in a land that had long known kings. His private life, however, soon became entangled in alcohol and women; he grew enormously obese; the scandals surrounding his divorce of his popular Queen Farida and his subsequent marriage to Narriman Fadaq ate away at what was left of the respect that Egyptians felt for him. His public life never survived his unsuccessful confrontation with the British in 1942; and although he possessed political shrewdness, he seemed unable to fathom the groundswell of popular dissatisfaction that surrounded him. He wanted to be named Caliph (technically, the successor to the Prophet, Muhammad, and in effect spiritual head of the Muslims) but the suggestion seemed ludicrous to most Middle Easterners; he proclaimed himself King of the Sudan, but this seemed to impress no one in the Sudan or elsewhere. In 1948 he threw his prestige behind the war in Palestine; with the ignominious defeat of the Egyptian army there the King's position suffered a grievous blow.

Undoubtedly the Palestinian War constituted a major conditioning factor for the revolution of 1952. Israel, proclaimed a state in May 1948, immediately engaged in hostilities with armies of several of the Arab states. Arab military efforts in general were unsuccessful but those of Egypt incredibly inept. Although the largest Arab state, its

army was miserably equipped and badly led. Nasser has told rather
eloquently of his experience in Palestine and how much the younger
officers resented both the irresponsible leadership of their superiors
and the lack of governmental support for the army. The army had been
defeated in the field; it had been disgraced; its younger officers felt
this keenly. The 1952 coup enabled them to rehabilitate the honor of
the army.

Obviously a variety of other conditions made up the prerevolutionary environment. Nevertheless it seems likely that the most significant
parts of this environment included the xenophobic hatred of the
British and their occupation—and their exploitation of Egypt and its
resources—for example, the Suez Canal—only a minute fraction of
whose revenues became Egypt's; the continued exploitation by the
immense foreign community in Egypt; the enormous gap between the
small number of very rich and the immense number of very poor; the
continued corruption and public fraud that contaminated the King
and even the Wafd Party itself; the pitiful figure of a king who could
no longer lead; and the national disgrace of the military defeat in
Palestine.

Egypt in 1952 was a land of misery with an old regime that offered
no hope and an army that had suffered humiliation. The coup took
place during the phasing out of the British presence; prior to that it
could have been directed only against the British. The masses of
Egyptians—the weak, the poor, the exploited—did not make the coup
of 1952. But they supported it with their enthusiasm, producing the
most popular government Egypt has had in centuries. It was this support that permitted the coup to develop into a social revolution.

The Revolution and Its Aftermath

The young officers apparently believed that, with the King and the
worst of the old politicians out of the way, the Egyptian polity would
somehow right itself; they did not expect to have to assume the permanent burden of maintaining a government. But this was not to be.
Nasser himself has described, in his *Philosophy of the Revolution,* how
difficult it was to find selfless, honest Egyptians to accept governmental
and political responsibility. At any event the officer junta was immersed in political crises from the very outset; it never had an opportunity to disengage.

Ali Mahir was named Prime Minister and General Naguib Minister of War. Naguib also served nominally as the leader of the junta (and so the world believed), but the dozen members of the Committee of Free Officers had minds of their own. Without doubt Gamal Abdul Nasser exercised leadership over this committee but he did so by a combination of energy, articulate persuasion, and charm (of which he still retains an unusual measure). Decisions were collegiate in the early days of the coup, and it is significant, that even a decade later, many members of the original Committee still occupied governmental positions of consequence.

Initial and continuing problems of leadership and direction plagued the junta in the aftermath of the coup. There was, as we know, early disagreement as to what the fate of Farouk should be. Some argued for retention of the monarchy. Both the Muslim Brotherhood and the Communists claimed to have inspired the coup and some officers were sympathetic to these groups. It was natural that Naguib would grow restive under the restraints of the younger officers; indeed, he "soon came to see himself as the saviour of Egypt with a popular mandate to lead the country." [9] It was equally natural for Nasser, after years of planning and struggle, to want to be more than a first-among-equals in the junta. Moreover, he was determined to see that the fruits of the revolt were not lost because of inadequate leadership. The very nature of the struggle by the various dissident groups within the junta and by its later collective struggle against Naguib made army disengagement impossible. Once Naguib had been proclaimed "leader" there was no way that he could step down in the tumultuous popularity of the coup; once Nasser had turned against Naguib for backsliding, there could be no abdication from a role that likely he had never envisaged.

The conflict between Nasser and Naguib is instructive of the ways of revolutionary power struggles. Ali Mahir had been named Prime Minister because he was the least unattractive of the old politicians. But once the officers had decided to embark on land reform in the summer of 1952, there was no longer any remote possibility that any remnant of the old regime could head up the government. By early September Ali Mahir was dropped, Naguib assuming the prime ministry. With the proclamation of the republic in June, 1953, Naguib became President as well as Prime Minister, Nasser receiving the deputy prime ministry and the ministry of interior. At this point the members of the Revolutionary Command Council (RCC), as the junta

[9] Peter Mansfield, *Nasser's Egypt* (Baltimore: Penguin Books, Inc., 1965), p. 44. Despite its modest size and price, this is one of the very best books on contemporary Egypt.

was now called, began "to regret that they had ever given so much power to Naguib, while Naguib himself seems to have felt that he did not have enough." [10] Naguib came to be more cautious and less revolutionary while at the same time more jealous of his position. He was challenged in a number of minor ways by Nasser, who did not always consult his superior. The final break came in February, 1954, when Nasser banned the Muslim Brotherhood without informing the President; Naguib resigned on February 23. The RCC accepted his resignation, announcing that he had aspired to dictatorship. A wave of resentment swept Egypt, fanned into flame by every opponent of the revolution, who viewed Naguib as a brake on the radical RCC. Elements within the army, largely among the cavalry officers expressed their dissatisfaction; Nasser, although he himself became Prime Minister, was forced to acquiesce in the restoration of Naguib to the presidency.

This restoration was popular but short-lived. Nasser feverishly set about arresting as many of Naguib's supporters as he could, while simultaneously building support for himself in the Liberation Rally (the revolutionary "party") and in the labor unions. On March 9 he himself resigned in favor of Naguib, relaxing at the same time all of the multitudinous restrictions that the revolution had imposed. In effect he was saddling Naguib with the responsibility "for restoring the discredited political system which the revolt had been carried out to destroy." [11] The situation proved impossible for Naguib; on April 17 he surrendered the prime ministry once again to Nasser—who, with army support, reimposed the authoritarian rule of the RCC—and a few months later he was out of the presidency as well. Only a few weeks had been needed by Nasser to destroy Naguib's support and to enable him to drop Naguib permanently. With the departure of Naguib there was no one to challenge the personal ascendency of Gamal Abdul Nasser.

The left has never posed a serious challenge to the revolution. The well-publicized incident at Kafr el-Dawar in August, 1952, in which two workers were hanged for leading a wildcat strike at a spinning mill, did not ingratiate the junta with the political left. The Communist and socialist movements in Egypt have had little strength; moreover Nasser found it convenient to jail many of their leaders. As the revolution itself drifted to "socialist" positions in subsequent years, the old left found its position undermined by Nasserist reforms.

[10] *Ibid.,* p. 48.
[11] *Ibid.,* p. 51.

The right presented a much greater danger in Egypt. This danger did not emanate from the great landlords or industrialists, for although they obstructed the revolution until they were broken by arrest and sequestration, they were organized to resist effectively only in the fairly open parliamentary system of the old regime. Had there been free elections, however, in 1954, the junta would have been hard put to have competed with the variety of parties that would have sprung back into existence, including the Wafd. The primary danger lay in the extremist Muslim Brotherhood, with its conspiratorial organization and its willingness to use violence. At first some members of the junta sympathized with the Brotherhood but when, in the showdown between Nasser and Naguib, it chose increasingly to support Naguib, the junta members recognized that its challenge would have to be met. Nasser banned it in February, 1954. On October 26 the Brotherhood attempted Nasser's assassination in Alexandria; as a consequence, six Brothers were hanged and Hasan al-Hudaibi, the Supreme Guide and Hasan al-Banna's successor, imprisoned for life. The power of the Brotherhood seemed broken forever, but we know now that the organizational network continued to exist. The Brothers became the implacable enemies of Nasser and his regime, and made several more attempts on his life; as late as the summer of 1966, several Muslim Brothers were hanged for these attempts.

By the end of 1954 Nasser had established sway over the army, relegated Naguib to oblivion, smashed the Muslim Brotherhood, and won for himself incredible personal popularity. He had also succeeded in negotiating the British out of Egypt—they agreed to leave by the spring of 1956. In April, 1955, he went to the Bandung Conference in Indonesia, where he found exciting inspiration for a host of new ideas, including neutralism and what was to become Arab socialism. Three months later he shocked the Western world by trading Egyptian cotton for Russian weapons. Earlier in the same year he had spurned the Baghdad Pact; in May of 1956 he extended recognition to Communist China. In August, 1956, after the United States and Great Britain had refused to aid in the construction of the Aswan High Dam, he nationalized the Suez Canal! The international repercussions from these activities were immense, but he emerged from all of them victorious. In October, 1956, Great Britain, France, and Israel, in concert with one another, attacked Egypt. In spite of early military success, they were forced to retire. Throughout these trials both the army and the people remained steadfastly loyal to Nasser. (Even after the disastrous conflict with Israel in the summer of 1967, Nasser was able to maintain much of his popularity and control.) All this represented considerable achievement—revolutionary achievement. But it was also part of the reconstruction that we must now examine.

Revolutionary Reconstruction

It is difficult to pinpoint very exactly when the destructiveness of a revolution subsides to be replaced by reconstruction. A revolution progresses to the degree that it can eliminate opposition and obstructionary groups. In Egypt the revolutionaries resolved their own leadership problems rather quickly while at the same time they eliminated the monarchy, hamstrung the great landowning class, and neutralized the British. They suspended parliamentary government and elections and banned political parties; that is to say, the natural vehicles through which the old ruling elite had exercised its dominance were denied them. The extremist groups such as the Communists and the Muslim Brotherhood were successfully contained. The constitution was of course abrogated and the dependence upon the British nullified. Had there been only this destruction, the coup would have made a staggering impact upon Egypt, but in the 16 years since it took place, much of the fabric of Egyptian society has been changed.

In 1952 the most urgent piece of reconstruction, the revolutionary leaders believed, was land reform; in September a decree limited individual landholdings to roughly 200 acres (with an additional 100 for children). Land rents were also reduced for tenants. Excess land was taken by the government, with little compensation, and redistributed among the fellahin in small parcels. In 1961 the total holdings permitted any one family were reduced to 100 acres.[12]

The land reform has successfully destroyed the economic base of the old ruling class but it has not revitalized Egyptian agriculture or rescued the fellah from perennial poverty. At first bureaucratic bungling and corruption permitted the actual redistribution to lag, and only the reservoir of the royal estates permitted immediate distribution of land. In any event, the amount of land given to the fellah, less than five acres, was barely enough to support a family. Moreover, the fellah was expected to pay for his land; and although the government as creditor was much more generous and understanding than the old landlord had been, the payment remained a considerable burden. The redistribution of land does not always result in increased agricultural production; sometimes production is lowered by the fragmentation of farms. Ulti-

---

[12] See Issawi, op. cit., for a discussion of the impact of the land reform. See also Patrick O'Brien, The Revolution in Egypt's Economic System (London: Oxford University Press, 1966).

mately the Egyptians attempted to solve this problem by the formation of cooperative farms, which reinstalled the advantages (and some of the pains) of landlordism. But psychologically land reform was a major step toward rebuilding a new Egyptian sense of self-esteem. Even those who shared its benefits only vicariously became enthusiastic; the effects of land reform were felt at all levels of Egyptian society.

Land reclamation has been of great importance. Fully 95 percent of the land in Egypt is barren, much of it simply because of the lack of water. The Nile river remains the most obvious source of water, but it is not inexhaustible. But something more could be done with the river than had been done. The High Dam at Aswan, Nasser's vision and dream, is expected with its completion to add an additional 1,000,000 arable acres to Egypt's agricultural soil. Deep-well drilling, the re-designing of crop cycles and irrigation facilities, the increased use of fertilizers: all these will result, it is hoped, in a marked increase in the cultivated land and its harvest. One project, that of Liberation Province —a large area of reclaimed land, with modern homes and equipment and specially chosen, literate farmers—has not succeeded as was hoped. But the effort in general to reclaim land has been modestly successful.

As a consequence of these activities, the fellah is somewhat better off today than he was in 1952; he has better medical facilities; he is more likely to be treated fairly by landlord and government; he receives succor during crop failures and famine; and his children are increasingly being educated.

In the early 1960's the Egyptian government began a massive effort to introduce birth control and family planning as a part of a studied effort to better the status of Egyptian women. Increasingly education and job opportunities are opening for them—in 1963 the first woman minister in history, Hekmat Abu Zaid, was appointed—and their husbands are finding it more difficult to divorce them whimsically. Religious opposition to this, as to many other things that Nasser has done, has not been inconsiderable. Nasser, though not antireligious, has not brooked much opposition from the most tendentious of the shaikhs and religious leaders. He has insisted upon the modernization of Al-Azhar University; he has confiscated the *waqfs* (religious endowments); and he has pushed ahead with a variety of reforms, such as those on marriage and divorce, which have been anathema to the conservatively religious. Of course, women in the lower economic classes and in the villages have not yet shared so much in these rights.

Nasser nationalized the Suez Canal in August, 1956. It was generally believed then that the Egyptians could not successfully operate the Canal. The gloomy predictions not only proved false but the Canal became a showpiece of efficiency and productive operation. Until the unfortunate events of the summer of 1967, it was a great earner of foreign exchange.

"When the Free officers seized power in July, 1952, they were without an economic ideology, and apart from land reform not even the most general ideas relating to economic organization had formed part of their pre-revolution discussions on the future of Egypt." [13] Patrick O'Brien argues very strongly that until 1956 "the Free Officers attempted to achieve development by employing traditional methods and techniques"; he calls the period the "free-enterprise phase of the Egyptian Revolution." [14] He suggests also that an intermediate phase followed, that of "guided capitalism," [15] in which entrepreneurs were free so long as they respected the public interest and accepted government guidance for this responsibility. By the late 1950's, however, the Nasser government began to intervene in the domestic economy more energetically. The French-British-Israeli aggression that followed the nationalization of the Suez Canal permitted a widescale sequestration of French and British properties. These properties became the kernel of the public sector of industrial and commercial enterprise. The exodus of foreign residents that also occurred at this time resulted in an increased Egyptianization of additional enterprise. In early 1957 most insurance companies and foreign banks were forced under Egyptian control. In February, 1960, the National Bank of Egypt and the Bank Misr were nationalized. This action inaugurated a broad spectrum of nationalization: in June all of the newspapers, buses, and tramways were taken. A year later "the government took over the entire import trade of the country and a large part of the export trade including cotton"; altogether "about 300 industrial and trading establishments were taken over either wholly or partly by the State." [16] Between October, 1961, and February, 1962, about 600 wealthy Egyptian families, many of them non-Muslim, had their properties sequestered.[17] In August, 1963, a further nationalization of some 300 companies took place, and in March, 1964, a smaller number occurred. As a result of these nationalizations and sequestrations the overwhelming bulk of the Egyptian economy became public. Not everything was nationalized —and, indeed, some small companies have been returned to their

[13] O'Brien, *op. cit.*, p. 68.
[14] *Ibid.*, p. 84.
[15] *Ibid.*, p. 85 and Chap. 4, *passim*.
[16] Mansfield, *op. cit.*, p. 137.
[17] *Ibid.*, p. 138. It has been suggested that the old ruling families had approached Field Marshal Abdul Hakim Amer to mount a coup against Nasser (as a result of the breakup of the UAR in September, 1961). See O'Brien, *op. cit.*, pp. 131-132.

original owners—but the core of Egyptian industry and commerce now resides in governmental hands.

Along with the nationalization of industrial enterprise came the inevitable crash programs: the five-year plans. In the decade 1960-1970 the national income was to have been doubled! Such plans and hopes must obviously be revised in the light of the recent Israeli war. Even prior to 1967 considerable disagreement existed as to what strides were being made in the attainment of these goals, but the government regularly issued statistics to suggest that the goals would be reached. Its political stake in these goals was readily apparent.

A part of the Nasserite reorientation of Egyptian society consisted of wage floors and income ceilings. The government enacted a rigorous income tax scheme to eliminate the great incomes (roughly, those above $10,000) and decreed minimum wages, along with the beginnings of social security. ("Public expenditure on social services . . . has risen by 70 percent since 1952. . . . [The proportion of GNP] devoted to social services has risen from 8.1 to 12.5 percent. . . .")[18] But the great leveling of all Egyptians has not come about. The very poor still labor for very little and inflation continues to eat away at what economic gains they have been able to make; the wealthy not only survive but their education and background make them the most suitable for managerial benefits. Nevertheless, the scope of Nasser's economic program has become evident: he intends to guarantee to all Egyptians a modest standard of living, along with education, national service, and new opportunities in occupational and social mobility. He has termed this program Arab Socialism.

Nasser's plans have usually been applauded in Egypt but their results have at times been sharply criticized. His economic reforms have been matched by a determined, but somewhat less than successful, attempt to mobilize the mass behind the revolution. What was needed was a new political system. No one regretted the fall of the monarchy or the establishment of the republic but many resented the banning of political parties and the authoritarian insistence on a single path to progress. Nasser scrapped western parliamentary democracy on the ground that the country could tolerate no system that would permit those who had dominated politics in the past to take hold once more. Any free election a decade ago in Egypt would have brought to the fore these very elements, for they were the only ones that had sufficient resources and organization to exploit such elections. Nasser did not need to be reminded that these individuals largely had vested interests in the past and would seek to obstruct any basic change in Egyptian

[18] O'Brien, op. cit., pp. 297-298.

society. He obviously believed that the political system would have to be changed, or at least suspended, until a new electorate with new leaders, more in tune with the revolution, could be formed.

While Naguib was still on the scene the young revolutionaries took the first step toward the formation of a national revolutionary party: the Liberation Rally. It proved abortive, since without parliament or elections its only tasks were propaganda and revolutionary popularization. In early 1956 the regime adopted a new constitution, and Nasser stood for the first time as a presidential candidate. The new constitution provided for a National Union (NU) to replace the Liberation Rally. The NU was officially created in May, 1957, and when the United Arab Republic (UAR) was proclaimed in February, 1958, the NU was extended to the Syrian sector as well. Its organization was perforce more elaborate and refined than the Liberation Rally, for with the creation of a national assembly, elections would have to be held. The NU had as its primary functions, however, the mobilization of mass support, political recruitment, and the communication of discontent (which to some degree it succeeded in doing). Yet it too proved a failure. Nasser himself said, "Reaction managed to infiltrate into the National Union to paralyse its revolutionary potentialities and turn [it] into a mere organizational façade unstirred by the forces of the masses and their genuine demands."[19] Apparently important elements of the NU could not agree on the goals for Egypt, let alone for Syria. And, in any case, Nasser found it necessary to explain away failures of programs and dreams—the breakup of the UAR, for example, in 1961— and the NU became an obvious target for his ire.

With the breakup of the UAR Nasser set about a further reorganization of his Egyptian political system. In May, 1962, he convened a National Congress of Popular Powers (of nearly 2,000 members) to consider his proposed National Charter, in effect the ideological base for a new constitution. The Congress accepted the charter without alteration in June, 1962; it provided for the NU's successor, the Arab Socialist Union (ASU). The ASU, similar to the old NU, constitutes a tiered representative organization of farmers, workers, soldiers, and other groups. Its very complications permit considerable control from above. Its fate is yet uncertain particularly because it has not yet been fully implemented. More than a dozen years after Nasser's consolidation of power over Naguib, he has failed to build a popular revolutionary force that can be left to its own devices. Nevertheless with the creation of the ASU, whose organization is presumably immune to reaction, Nasser felt that it was safe to produce a National Assembly

[19] Quoted in Peter Mansfield, *op. cit.*, p. 197.

as well, first convening it in March, 1964. Although the Assembly has not been a complete nullity, free representative government in Egypt remains to be achieved. And, of course, the events of 1967 make the future of parties and assemblies even more uncertain.

Revolutionary Leaders and Followers

The coup of 1952 was an army coup; the men who led it were young middle-grade officers, whose social background was middle class. P. J. Vatikiotis has pointed out that the founding committee of the conspiratorial army group consisted entirely of graduates (1938-1940) of the Egyptian Military Academy. Eight out of the 11 members of this group had entered the Academy in 1936, the first year in which entrance to the Academy had been popularly broadened.[20] Vatikiotis goes on to say,

> The average age of the members of the Revolutionary Council in 1952 was thirty-three years. Only three of them had higher education other than military training. With one exception all had seen active service in the Palestinian War. Excluding General Muhammad Naguib, all had been involved in some kind of political activity earlier in their careers.

The bulk of the officers came from the lower middle class and had been educated in the larger towns and cities.[21]

There were of course officers whose economic and social background was above the group as a whole. But the remarkable thing was the common experience of the Egyptian Military Academy. Moreover, these officers shared an extreme interest in politics and an intense and patriotic concern for the welfare of their country. The group, secret and conspiratorial, built up its comradery in the early days of planning and talking, and its unity survived remarkably well for a generation. Vatikiotis has argued, rather persuasively, that organizationally the Free Officers came into being only in 1949 (in the aftermath of the Palestinian debacle) and that before that time "any cohesion among these officers was based . . . entirely on their personal relations and contacts." [22]

After the coup the group found it necessary to recruit additional

[20] P. J. Vatikiotis, *The Egyptian Army in Politics: Pattern for New Nations?* (Bloomington: Indiana University Press, 1961), p. 45.
  [21] *Ibid.*, p. 46.
  [22] *Ibid.*, p. 56.

leadership, particularly as the scope of its responsibility widened. The most natural source of many of the new recruits continued to be the armed forces, the crucial personal factor now being the posture adopted by the individual during the coup itself. Over the years a very large number of responsible, important positions have been entrusted to military officers who until 1967 formed a significant segment of the Egyptian political elite. Since the Israeli War the army as a whole has been discredited and officers forced out of certain key positions.

Recruitment could not, however, be entirely restricted to the military. As it turned out, most of the old bureaucracy had to be used (there was hardly an immediate alternative) and a number of professionally trained individuals of high competence became available, for instance, Mahmoud Fawzi, long-time foreign minister. The influence of the "civilians" has undoubtedly increased over the years. Loyalty to the regime has not been a major problem and the Egyptian universities and training institutes themselves have turned out increasing numbers of competent, loyal young men whom the government has employed. Until 1967 they certainly did not occupy in any numbers the front rank of decision-makers.

The political elite must also include certain nonofficial but influential individuals such as Muhammad Husainin Heykal, often identified as "Nasser's unofficial spokesman." As editor of the government-controlled al-Ahram, one of the great newspapers of Egypt, Heykal has sent up trial political balloons and editorialized on a variety of vital political and social issues. The revolution has also pushed into prominence a new political elite based on attachment to the ideals of the revolution and possession of the skills necessary in the period of modernization: technical, literary, engineering, military, and similar skills. The old bases of the elite—wealth, family, and social position—have greatly declined in significance.

The success of the 1952 coup depended not so much on large numbers of followers as on simple acquiescence. The Egyptian masses adhered to their habit of obedience and produced little trouble for the revolutionary regime. Shortly thereafter they became its enthusiastic supporters. If the revolution did not bring much economic prosperity, it brought a variety of attempts to level the classes and raise the standard of living. Socialism became the ideology; the word "people" became commonplace in the description of revolutionary goals and objectives. Land reform took place, educational levels were raised, key prices were fixed, various features of social welfare were introduced. The loyalty to the regime of the great mass of Egyptian lower and lower-middle-class elements has never wavered, even in 1967; challenges have been the enervating costs of the Yemen and Israeli wars.

The new middle class in Egypt—the professional men, the newly trained bureaucrats, the managers—have warmly supported the revolution in consummation, although not uniformly in all programs or goals. But the old middle class, primarily the merchants, have quite naturally been unhappy with the consequences of the revolution. Although they have had no normal way to express their discontent, most have acquiesced with feigned enthusiasm. It goes without saying that the minority groups in Egypt—the Greeks, Italians, Jews, and even the Copts—have been only lukewarm in supporting this strongly nationalist revolution.

Revolutionary Ideology

For centuries Cairo has been the literary center of the Arab world. Since the 1952 coup it has produced an enormous amount of literature, radio and television broadcasting, and motion picture films. Much of this has extolled the virtues of the revolution. Except for his short essay on the revolution, Nasser has not written his memoirs. A few others have—for example, Naguib and Anwar al-Sadat—but none has achieved a wide audience. Nasser's speeches (and to a lesser degree those of his lieutenants), the monitored records of Egyptian broadcasts, and the enormous body of newspaper and pamphlet commentary have provided the most important sources of an ideology. We also have such official documents as the *National Charter*, which suggests an ideological finality.

Every revolutionary ideology alters in time. Immediately after the coup the ideological emphasis had to be on *justification* and *explanation*. Promises had to be vague and considerable attention had to be paid to *denunciation* of easily identifiable enemies and dangers. Between 1952 and 1954 a certain confusion resulted from the power struggle within the officer group, but as Nasser emerged as the sole leader ideological targets became more consistently displayed. The regime went through several phases in its attitudes toward the economy and the private sector; all of these attitudes were buttressed by appropriate ideology. There always has been a strong *negative* coloration to this revolutionary ideology; as late as 1968 Nasser continued to berate the United States, Israel, and others for the difficulties besetting the Egyptians.

The *National Charter*, an official résumé of revolutionary principles and goals, serves as a convenient source of present-day Egyptian ideol-

ogy.[23] It begins by reciting the "principles" for which the revolution in
1952 was mounted: "Destruction of imperialism and its stooges among
Egyptian traitors"; "Ending of feudalism"; "Ending monopoly and the
domination of capital over the Government"; "Establishment of social
justice"; "Building of a powerful national army"; "Establishment of a
sound democratic system." [24]

The Charter emphasizes that it was possible to implement these
"principles" because the national struggle had produced:

1. "A will for revolutionary change which rejects all restrictions and
limitations on the rights and needs of the masses."

2. "A revolutionary vanguard which the will for revolutionary change
has enabled to seize power in the state and channel this power from
the service of existing interests to the service of those who are le-
gitimately entitled to it, namely, the masses."

3. "A deep consciousness of history and its effect on contemporary
man on the one hand, and of the ability of man in turn to influence history, on the others."

4. "A mind open to all human experiences, from which it benefits
and to which it contributes with no fanaticism or complex."

5. "Unshakable faith in God, His Prophets and His sacred messages
which He passed on to man as a guide to justice and righteousness." [25]

All of these aspects of popular will and determination, it is argued,
produced the revolution. The *National Charter* goes on to state the
inexorable need of revolution[26] and the attachment to Arab nationalism,
which has as its goals "freedom, socialism and unity." [27] But a "revolution . . . by its very nature, signifies progress";[28] socialism is a measure
of this progress,[29] democracy of its popularity.[30] "Socialism is the way to
social freedom." [31] Socialism means nationalization, the expansion of
the public sector, and the redistribution of land: "The revolutionary
solution to the problem of land in Egypt by increasing the number of

[23] The Information Department, United Arab Republic, *The Charter* (no place
or date of publication listed). All page references are to this edition. An analysis
of this document and its enveloping ideology can be found in Baha Abu-Laban,
"The National Character in the Egyptian Revolution," *The Journal of Developing
Areas*, Vol. 1 (1967), pp. 179-198. *See also* O'Brien, *op. cit.*, pp. 199-214.
[24] *Ibid.*, pp. 6-7.
[25] *Ibid.*, pp. 10-11.
[26] *Ibid.*, p. 13.
[27] *Ibid.*, p. 14.
[28] *Ibid.*, p. 35.
[29] *Ibid.*, p. 36.
[30] *Ibid.*, p. 35.
[31] *Ibid.*, p. 49.

landowners." [32] It also means the "doubling of the national income every ten years." [33] The United Arab Republic continues the "War on imperialism and domination"; it labors "to consolidate peace"; and it seeks "international cooperation for the sake of prosperity." [34] Amidst all these programs and goals, history is recast and the proper homilies reiterated: "Human labor is the only key to progress." [35] "The people are the leaders of the revolution." [36]

Although few scholars are impressed with its "new history" and few economists with its recipe for "doubling income every decade" [37] the Charter was produced as a myth to win popular support and to rationalize action in the name of the people.

Revolutionary Impact on the International Environment

In his *Philosophy of the Revolution,* Nasser reminded Egyptians of their Arab, African, and Mediterranean responsibilities; he has himself pushed Egypt into the world arena. Farouk and his Egypt counted for relatively little either in the Arab world or outside it. No one now can deny the energetic role that Egypt (as the UAR) has tried to play everywhere in the world. If the significance of a revolution is measured by its exportability and its impact abroad, then the Egyptian revolution has been a very significant one.

Within the Arab world the impact has been immense. Many Arabs had earlier spoken vaguely of Arab unity but it was Nasser who gave current Arab nationalism *élan* and drive. In spite of his setback in 1967, he towers above all other Arabs as a charismatic leader. His successes have given pride to all Arabs; his programs within Egypt have become the dreams of many Arabs in other lands. Since he proclaimed himself as a radical democratic ruler, all traditional rulers have become suspect and weakened. He encouraged and fostered revolution—in Algeria, in Yemen, in Iraq. He propagandized his views everywhere in the Arab world and became almost its *de facto* leader. The amalgamation of Syria and Egypt in 1958 as the United Arab Republic, though it failed, appeared to be the first concrete step toward the unity of all Arab states.

[32] *Ibid.,* p. 61.
[33] *Ibid.,* p. 59.
[34] *Ibid.,* p. 93.
[35] *Ibid.,* p. 78.
[36] *Ibid.,* p. 85.
[37] *See,* for example, Issawi, *op. cit., passim.*

His star among the Arabs, however, has tarnished somewhat in later years. Even before 1967 many Palestinian Arabs had grown weary of what they termed his unfulfilled promises on the destruction of Israel; today most Arabs have become disillusioned with his leadership in the light of his military defeat. His war in Yemen had to be abandoned, with the consequent loss of influence throughout South Arabia. The UAR after all did break up in 1961 and attempts to resuscitate it have been futile. Many of his enemies in the Arab world still survive— Bourguiba in Tunisia, Faisal in Saudi Arabia—and some of his friends —Ben Bella in Algeria, Abdul Salam Aref of Iraq, Abdullah al-Sallal of Yemen—have disappeared. The novelty of some of his programs has worn thin; the freshness of his image has suffered from overexposure. Nevertheless he remains the most popular and dynamic Arab leader in several centuries. Moreover, as a revolutionary, the repercussions of his leadership, in one way or another, have spread everywhere in the Middle East.

It is more difficult to assess the influence of the Egyptian revolution on subsaharan Africa. Indirectly any revolution against colonialism or an old regime, especially one within the African continent, will encourage further revolution. The Egyptian Revolution has exerted such influence. Nasser has attempted, however, to be more than just an influence. He has constantly urged rebellion against the "exploiters" in subsahara; he has made Cairo a training center for would-be African revolutionists and a home for a variety of governments-in-exile. He has helped organize African summit conferences and organizations, of which the Casablanca Group is a good example, and he has continued to participate in every African activity as a full-fledged member of the subsaharan community. On occasion, as with the Congo Stanleyville government, he has shipped arms and equipment to those who seemed to espouse his kind of socialism; he has offered credits and economic aid to a number of African states.

Yet this picture again is not without its flaws. Nasser is after all not black, and Egypt has never been much of a factor south of the Sahara. Arabs, as slave traders in the past and merchants in the present, have been hated in many parts of Africa. Although Islam is spreading in the continent, Arab influence has not grown concomitantly. Some of Nasser's friends have become less consequential—Nkrumah and Tourè, for example—and the new breed of African rulers, men like Mobutu in the Congo, are hardly under Nasser's enchantment. Israel, too, has succeeded in building some influence in Africa, by judicious technical assistance, astute diplomacy, and now by the example of military victory. Africa remains in revolutionary travail but the continuing revolution is not quite Nasser's.

In the Mediterranean area, outside the Arab territories, Nasser's influence has been minimal. Anger over Turkish recognition of Israel inspired Nasser to support the Greeks in the Cyprus dispute, yet confiscations of Greek property within Egypt has destroyed the benefit of this earlier posture. Only in Yugoslavia has Nasser found a congenial reception, but here he has been the disciple of Tito, rather than his teacher.

But in the world as a whole Nasser and the Egyptian Revolution have made their mark. The original coup occurred at the height of the cold war; Nasser became a founding member of the ensuing club of neutralists and one of its most articulate spokesmen. He became, in the mixed company of Tito, Nehru, Sukarno, and Nkrumah, an influential leader of yet another world force. He challenged the West and to a lesser degree the East; he rode out the Suez crisis; as the Arab's most natural leader he had to be listened to during the long moment in which the West has been dependent upon Arab oil. He has attempted to muddy the waters of revolution everywhere, if not often very successfully. Thus, his well-publicized friendship for Castro.

A dozen and more years after Nasser's rise to power in Egypt one can raise a number of significant questions. What material benefits have accrued to the Egyptian people? How has the cause of political freedom prospered in Egypt or in the Arab world? Has Arab unity become more likely? Has the plight of the Palestinian refugees been ameliorated or the issues with Israel resolved? Has Nasser, the statesman, contributed much to the solution of African, Asian, or world problems? Although these questions can generally be answered negatively, there can hardly be much dispute that the Egyptian Revolution has lifted its people from stagnation. Nasser became, for a time at least, a world figure of influence; and Egypt found a new dignity and pride. Yet today, in the wake of his disastrous Israeli adventure, one can only conclude that he has thrown away most of his achievements.

Conclusion

The Egyptian Revolution stemmed from all the traditional dysfunctions, but was set off by the classic coup. In 1952, the Egyptians possessed an old regime which had done little to solve the nation's problems. The King was irresponsible, the greater share of the population lived in great poverty, a foreign occupation army still maintained its hold, and the Egyptian army itself was humiliated by its experience during the first Israeli war of 1948. All these dysfunctions, and others, served as a backdrop to revolution when it came.

Probably no factor was more significant than the malaise of the Egyptian military, and the frustrations that the middle grade officers had to endure in the period after 1948. This period saw increased violence, the apogee being reached in January 1952. When it became apparent, in the spring of that year, that the King would attempt to retire or remove many of the disgruntled officers, the vague conspiracies within the armed forces were quickly channeled, triggered off, as it were, into a *coup d'état* in July.

The insurgents had little idea of social revolution in the summer of 1952. After nearly two years of internal struggle the mantle of leadership finally fell to Gamal Abdul Nasser. Because of a number of early and dramatic successes Nasser quickly found himself not only the popular leader of Egypt but also the leading political figure in the Arab world. As he faced various crises over the years, his internal program gradually became more radical. Termed "Arab Socialism," it entailed the nationalism of industry, the distribution of agricultural land, the sequestration of capital, the regimentation of labor. By the 1960's, the Egyptian Revolution had become genuinely social in character and had become the model for radical aspirations everywhere in the Arab world.

Nasser and his revolution have come to grief over foreign adventures. Twice he has become entangled with the Israelis (in 1956 and 1967), and both conflicts occasioned military defeat for the Egyptians. In 1956 he escaped with his reputation largely untarnished; in 1967, although by year's end he continued to cling to power, he had lost territory and prestige to the Israelis, his country's economy was in shambles, his attempts to win Yemen and South Arabia were in collapse, and he had become, in a sense, a caretaker for the remnants of a once burgeoning revolution.

Among the Arabs the Egyptian Revolution has been the most significant one in the modern age. It has been enormously influential in the Middle East; elsewhere its impact has been pronounced. But by 1968 the Revolution was in stagnation, and its prognosis was uncertain.

10

The Cuban Revolution

On December 2, 1956, eighty-two armed rebels, led by a little known young lawyer and politician, Fidel Castro, landed on a remote and rugged section of the southeastern coast of Cuba in Oriente Province. The government of General Fulgencio Batista that had come to power as a result of a barracks coup four years before seemed firmly entrenched; its forces reacting vigorously killed or captured all but a handful of the attackers in the first few days. As the year ended the government confidently predicted the collapse of the rebellion; virtually all observers, foreign and domestic, were inclined to agree.

But the rebellion did not collapse. The survivors successfully eluded government forces, slowly recruited a few more followers, and eventually began to strike back. Stalemate followed the government's inability to suppress the Castro band, and by mid-1958 the dictatorship began to lose support rapidly. When the military wavered, the end appeared. Batista flew into exile and Castro assumed power in January, 1959.

Force, Violence, and Terror in Cuban Politics

Like most of Latin America, Cuba has experienced widespread use of force and violence in its political life. Long-simmering discontent with Spanish rule erupted into civil war between 1868 and 1878 with an estimated 200,000 casualties and extensive property damage.[1] Spanish arms eventually crushed the revolt, and quickly suppressed a renewed effort in 1880. After 15 years of uneasy truce, economic dis-

[1] Charles E. Chapman, *A History of the Cuban Republic: A Study in Hispanic American Politics* (New York: The Macmillan Company, 1927), p. 43.

locations, and broken promises of political reform, the independence movement revived in 1895 when a small band of revolutionaries from Florida landed in eastern Cuba. Although the United States drove Spain out of Cuba in 1898, the island did not gain its independence until 1902, when the United States military regime turned over the government to Tomás Estrada Palma, Cuba's newly elected first president.

Independence, however, brought no peace to Cuban politics. The next election, held under purely Cuban auspices, resulted in armed rebellion and renewed intervention from the United States. Armed revolt occurred again following the 1916 elections, and a threatened third rebellion in 1920 was averted only by pressure from the United States. The elections of 1924 came off peacefully enough, but when Gerardo Machado extended his term of office and tried to silence the opposition, violence was renewed. From 1930 to 1933 running battles between Machado and his opponents, centering in the University of Havana, became frequent occurrences. Hundreds of suspects were murdered by Machado's agents, and reprisals followed. Machado fled in 1933 when the United States showed its displeasure and the army withdrew its support.[2]

The revolution of 1933 brought to power a new group of political leaders. The dominant sectors consisted of reform-minded nationalists who advocated government action to raise the cultural, social, and economic levels of the people. Critical of the United States and foreign business interests, these young revolutionaries assailed foreign influences in Cuban life as threats to the nation's honor, dignity, and economic well-being. The revolutionaries, however, quarreled bitterly among themselves; in the midst of the political squabbling, an army sergeant, Fulgencio Batista, successfully led a sergeants' revolt against their officers, most of whom had supported Machado. Although he dominated the civilian governments that held office between 1933 and 1940, he supported Cuba's first labor legislation, the extension of rural education, and a mobile health program. These measures and many other social and economic guarantees were written into a new constitution promulgated in 1940. Their implementation, however, remained sporadic.

Batista regularized his position by running for and winning the presidency in 1940. He permitted open elections in 1944 and retired temporarily from the country. His successor repeated the pattern in 1948, and in national politics at least, during these 12 years violence notably declined. As the 1952 elections approached, Batista declared

[2] Wyatt MacGaffey and Clifford R. Barnett, *Cuba: Its People, Its Society, Its Culture* (New Haven: HRAF Press, 1962), p. 20.

his candidacy once more. When it became apparent that he could not possibly win, Batista declared that the outgoing president was preparing a fraudulent election and in March overthrew the government. Most of the population remained apathetic in the face of the coup, but several politicians, among them Fidel Castro, challenged the dictator in the courts. Failing in this maneuver Castro gathered about him some like-minded young men and on July 26, 1953, launched an attack on the Moncada Barracks in Santiago. Many of his followers were killed in the attack or later, but Castro himself was captured and imprisoned. Released in 1955, he left for Mexico, where he prepared his second and successful armed attack on the regime.

Upon assuming power Castro has ruled both by suppression and by persuasion. As his reform programs proceeded in directions not anticipated by some of his early supporters, opposition began to form and some of his lieutenants voiced their criticism. Castro swiftly silenced some of these opponents; others fled into exile and still others attempted open revolt. Promises of elections never materialized, and large mass organizations were mobilized to report disloyalty to the new regime. By 1962 Castro had successfully eliminated all dangers to his government, and had mobilized a large body of Cubans as his active supporters.

To sum up, violence has been ever present in Cuban politics. Although Cuba escaped the church-state disputes and the federalist-centralist quarrels that plagued the rest of Latin America, her elitist Liberals and Conservatives fought bitterly for personal power. Few coups occurred, but government frequently rested on force. The revolution of 1933 admitted to the political arena new parties speaking for new groups, particularly urban labor and the professionals. As a social revolution, however, the upheaval of 1933 was aborted. Captured by the middle class, it spewed forth much socialist ideology, which it incorporated into the Constitution of 1940. Most of the promises were never fulfilled, and the unsatisfied demands of the newly awakened lower classes contributed to an unsettled political atmosphere. Most of the new political leaders after 1933 were content with finding places for themselves beside the old elite, and the two groups soon meshed comfortably together. Although the three administrations between 1940 and 1952 appeared to receive broad support, society itself was badly fragmented. Party factions, labor unions, and university groups all resorted to violence during these years as a normal part of their political activities. Shootings and assassinations were fairly common, and on one occasion an armed band broke into the Havana Court House to destroy incriminating records. Some students and faculty members of the University of Havana regularly carried guns, and organized armed bands "shot it out" on the streets of the capital.[3] Castro, with his social revolution, has attempted to eliminate all substantial opposition in order to create a unified polity and society.

Finally, the patterns of violence and force include little outright and systematic terror. The word "terror" has been used occasionally to describe gang warfare on the island, but there appears to have been little effort made to subjugate large sectors of the population through fear, horror, or despair to support one side or the other in civil conflict. On the other hand, burning the cane fields during the war for independence, and the indiscriminate shootings by Machado and Batista may be characterized as "terror." Castro, too, for a brief period in the spring of 1959 resorted to something similar to terrorist actions by the public trials and executions of supporters of the previous regime, and by the draconian measures he meted out to his own followers who criticized his reform programs. All of these terrorist phases were short-lived and none seem to have become a fixed feature of Cuban political violence.

Causes of the Cuban Revolution

The "multiple sources of dysfunction" that are commonly the background of modern revolutions existed in pre-Castro Cuba: a small depressed peasantry, particularly in Oriente Province; an underemployed rural labor force in the cane growing areas; a large urban lower class on the margin of existence; unstable, insecure, and violence-prone middle classes that sought to imitate upper-class modes of life; and middle and upper classes tied in with foreign interests that seemed almost totally oblivious of lower-class problems. Government was dictatorial and corruption-ridden, education and health programs were elite-oriented, and many of the vital sectors of the economy were owned or controlled by foreigners. By Latin American standards, however, Cuba was well off, and although political violence was predictable, the revolution of 1933 and its aftermath seemed to indicate that only limited changes might be expected. How then do we explain the success and the direction of the Cuban Revolution? Before we attempt to answer that question, let us examine more carefully some of the major sources of unrest and discontent in the country in the pre-Castro years.

Cuban intellectuals, including university students, and many political leaders have resented the predominance exercised by the United

[3] William S. Stokes, "National and Local Violence in Cuban Politics," *The Southwestern Social Science Quarterly*, Vol. 34 (1953), p. 62.

States over the affairs of the island since it attained its independence. Some became so bitter over this role in Cuba that they attempted to denigrate the participation of the United States in the independence movement, and preferred to view United States interests solely in economic terms. The several interventions in the island, expanding control over the island's economy, even the preferential market for Cuban sugar, all became sources of bitter criticism and discontent. Not only did these critics condemn specific practices by the United States and its citizens, they simply deplored the resulting domination. Many insisted that Cuba had only substituted an economic for a political colonialism. Much of this discontent was siphoned off or silenced as the angry young men matured and became absorbed into the economic and political structures of the country. For many the choice was simply to accept the situation and find their places within it, or become outcasts with all the penalties implied. The vast majority opted to work within the system and grumbled occasionally, particularly if they did not obtain their expected rewards.

When Cubans spoke or thought of foreign economic controls, they meant the United States. "United States businessmen dominated the field of foreign investment" although their share of sugar production had dropped from a high of 55 percent in the 1930's to less than 40 percent in 1958. Nevertheless, United States entrepreneurs owned

> . . . over 90 percent of the telephone and electric services, one-half of the public service railways, one-fourth of all bank deposits, . . . and much of the mining, oil production and cattle ranching. . . . The major American companies were closely knit, both by interlocking directorates and by common interest; business was conducted and decisions made with reference to their mutual interest.[4]

In addition, the commercial policy of pre-Castro Cuba, which favored the United States in return for a preferential sugar price and import quotas, discriminated against third-country exporters and prevented the Cubans from establishing tariffs to protect new industries. With good reason some sectors of the Cuban economy, nationalist intellectuals, and a number of political leaders became increasingly critical of United States policies toward Cuba, particularly in times of economic difficulties.

During the Second World War the Cuban economy boomed, but after the war relative stagnation set in. Economists, both foreign and domestic, called for diversification, reduction of graft, and better distribution of national resources. In all probability the discontent gener-

[4] MacGaffey and Barnett, *op. cit.*, p. 177.

ated by such criticisms did not contribute directly to anti-Batista attitudes, since it was directed as much to previous democratically elected regimes. Obviously, the peasants of Oriente did not flock to Castro's banner, no rival leader arose to proclaim agrarian reform, and no labor battalions organized to fight. Castro's call for a general strike in 1958 remained unanswered, in part because of the opposition of Communist labor leaders, and most businesses carried on as usual. And yet economic problems were worrisome. A widespread belief prevailed that political leadership and political institutions had failed the Cuban people. It is quite possible that some of the business support that accrued to Castro was predicated upon the belief that he would tackle some of these pressing economic problems. After all, he had demonstrated considerable concern with such matters in his Moncada defense.[5]

Although there existed widespread disapproval of Batista's coup in 1952, no one attempted armed resistance. With a promise here and a concession there Batista soon won the acquiescence of most major interest groups, political parties, and factions. The major exception to the general pattern manifested itself in Castro's attack on the Moncada Barracks in Santiago the following year. His impassioned plea before the court that tried him made something of a temporary sensation, but most Cuban political and economic leaders quickly forgot the affair. Batista's political opponents, divided among themselves, geared for the general elections promised for 1953. As the scheduled date approached, it became clear that Batista was not prepared to hold free and open elections. The primary opposition candidate withdrew from the race, and Batista duly proclaimed himself elected. Some of the disgruntled politicians went into exile, but most again acquiesced. One could detect little revolutionary sentiment on the island except for that generated by a few students and intellectuals who at most sporadically and ineffectually set off bombs.[6]

Outside of a few young lower-level leaders and aspirants to power, virtually none of the first-rank leaders entertained ideas of basically restructuring Cuban society. The violence and struggles that ensued were carried out to improve individual positions or the status of their groups in the existing framework. Complaints and criticisms were directed largely at correcting "inequities," however these may have been defined. The most substantial changes advocated involved the nature of Cuban-U.S. relations, but even here few anticipated a switch from an alliance with the United States to one with the Soviet Union. Many Cubans knew what they did not like in these arrangements, but few

[5] James O'Connor, "On Cuban Political Economy," *Political Science Quarterly,* Vol. 79 (1964), pp. 236-239.

[6] MacGaffey and Barnett, *op. cit.,* pp. 26-27.

had any clear notions of alternatives. Even Castro worked within the structure in his first ventures into politics and only the coup of 1952 led him to the path of revolution. At the time of the Moncada attack and even at the landing in Oriente in 1956, Castro's actions constituted the serious disaffection of a very small part of the elite, hardly its disintegration. True, other elements of the elite were discontented and dissatisfied with the Batista dictatorship, but most were simply apathetic. It was only in 1958 when Batista, in desperation at the failure of his efforts to suppress the Castro revolt, turned to wanton murder and terror that a widespread disintegration of the elite began. Normally conservative businessmen and middle-class groups began to supply the Castro forces with men, material, and information. As Batista's terrorist campaign mounted, disgust and horror grew apace. And with civilian support for Castro increased, the loyalty of the army toward the regime began to waver and finally collapsed. At that point the end was reached, not only through rebel military victories and the popular appeal of Castro, but more important, through the withdrawal of support for the regime by its own military when the citizenry lost its apathy and began to support the opposition. When all is said and done, the success of this Revolution must be ascribed to the will and determination of Fidel Castro and his close lieutenants who drove the dictator to desperation. Once in power Castro made full use of his charisma to mobilize mass support to carry out far-reaching programs of social and economic reform in the face of middle- and upper-class opposition, at the same time alienating many of his original followers.

Stages of the Revolution

The Cuban Revolution is still too young to permit us to speak confidently of its stages. We do not yet know where it will end or how or when it will become institutionalized. What we may now regard as important turning points may well prove to be blind alleys or temporary detours from the main highway of its progress. Lack of perspective also makes it difficult to tie together the different aspects of the revolution—for example, economic experiments, domestic political arrangements, and international relations. We do know now precisely when it began, but at the moment of its birth few would have predicted its survival; in fact, to many it first appeared stillborn.

Throughout 1956 Castro was preparing for an invasion of Cuba. Former President Prío Socorrás and other exiles in the United States supplied funds with which the rebels bought an old yacht, the *Granma*. Slipping away from the Mexican authorities on November 25 with 82 men, the ship made slow progress. Not knowing that the Castro group was still at sea on November 30, the date of their scheduled landing, armed partisans rose in revolt in Santiago and students struck the University of Havana. Contrary to expectations, no general revolt or even widespread protests accompanied these actions. The rebels in Santiago were quickly rounded up and Batista closed the university; it remained closed until Castro's victory. Forewarned, military units spotted the *Granma* off the Oriente coast, killing or capturing all but "twelve" of the original complement.

This remnant from the *Granma* for the first few weeks sought simply to survive in the rugged mountainous and isolated terrain of eastern Cuba. Under the indomitable leadership of Fidel, seconded by his brother Raúl and his close associate Che Guevara, the little band slowly grew, attracted some local support, and eventually began to counterattack government forces in a guerrilla campaign. As the rebels proved their staying power, allied resistance forces in the cities again became active in hit-and-run attacks on the regime, in propaganda distribution, and in organized work among students, workers, and young people in general. These rebellious organizations never developed, however, into mass movements. Except toward the very end, Castro commanded only about 1,000 men, and although his support in the cities could be reckoned in the thousands, the vast majority of the population kept aloof from the struggle until it was virtually over.

Political confusion and uncertainty prevailed during the first few weeks after the fall of the old regime. Castro, at first, assumed no official position except commander of the armed forces, while provisional president Manuel Urrutia appointed a civilian cabinet composed predominantly of the older and more experienced political opponents of Batista. Throughout Cuba, however, real power at the local level lay with the youthful commanders of the rebel army. Castro, the great national hero, continued his speech-making, in the course of which he often announced major public policies without prior consultation with the cabinet. In an attempt to bridge this gap between the theoretical and the actual holders of power, Prime Minister Miró Cardona resigned in favor of Castro in mid-February.

At the same time, a virtual clean sweep was made of Batista supporters in the bureaucracy and thousands of sinecures were eliminated. Some of the more notorious of the Batista officials, military and civilian, were brought to trial before Revolutionary Tribunals, and hundreds were executed summarily. The regime discontinued these trials in the face of criticism both at home and abroad in May 1959, but continued to confiscate the property of supporters and collaborators of the former dictator.

The legal basis of the new regime became the Constitution of 1940 as amended by the Fundamental Law of February 1959. In effect the social and economic provisions of the Constitution remained in force, but its political sections were "temporarily" set aside to take recognition of the revolutionary situation prevailing. Castro announced, however, in early 1959, as he had done during the fighting, that he intended to hold general elections and to restore the Constitution of 1940.

By the end of May this first and moderate stage of the Revolution gave way to a transitional period of increasing radicalization in both economic and political policies. In the next six months, the Agrarian Reform Law was enacted, the Communist People's Socialist Party (PSP) emerged as the only legal political party, the labor union leadership was purged and replaced by Communists, and the 26th of July Movement was downgraded because of the strength of moderate and anti-Communist forces within it. In the process Castro forced Manuel Urrutia from the presidency, and all of the moderates in the cabinet were replaced by men of the radical left and of unquestioning loyalty to Castro. Several were or had been members of the PSP. Raúl became minister of the armed forces, and Guevara president of the National Bank and, in effect, czar of the national economy. This phase was completed by the end of the year.

The third stage of political development marked the forging of ever tighter bonds between Fidel Castro and his personal followers on the one hand and the old-line leaders of the PSP on the other. Castro turned rather naturally to the PSP, since it accepted his leadership of the revolution with complete loyalty, proclaimed an identity of interests with the specific reforms he advocated, presented him with a trained and organized apparatus to carry out the program, and offered him a theoretical foundation for his revolution. On all these points the PSP compared favorably with the 26th of July Movement, Castro's original organization. The party established mass organizations like the Committees for the Defense of the Revolution, and in late 1961 set up the Integrated Revolutionary Organization, the protoparty that evolved first into the United Party of the Cuban Socialist Revolution and finally into the Communist Party of Cuba.

The Communists, however, overplayed their hand. On March 26, 1962, Fidel Castro reasserted his leadership of the revolution. He exiled one of the more prominent PSP leaders, censured the others, and reshuffled his political organization from top to bottom. Thus was ushered in the last and present stage of political development in Cuba. In the past six years the old-line Communists have been gradually downgraded. Only a very few are included in the 100-member central committee of the party and only two are on the six-man secretariat. Castro is indisputably in political control. He has not broken with the old-line Communists, but seems to rely more on persons loyal to himself than on PSP militants.

One of the most significant achievements of the revolution is the virtual elimination of illiteracy. Academic training at all levels is accompanied, however, by ideological indoctrination, and has been restricted in quality by the flight of technical and professional people inimical to the regime. The next stage of education now that the breadth of the program has been completed is to improve its quality and to produce a greater number of technical people needed in economic development programs. This second stage has barely begun.

In its economic policies, the Castro regime has progressed through three distinct stages. Its first two years were marked by a vast and rapid redistribution of the national wealth. Beginning with the Agrarian Reform Law of June, 1959, land was progressively nationalized and organized into state collective farms. At the same time most domestic and foreign-owned industries and businesses were expropriated. Some low-income housing was constructed, and peasants and unskilled urban workers received increases in real income although skilled organized workers suffered some losses. The cattle herds were literally eaten up and breeding stock thereby badly depleted.[7] Except for what they possessed in foreign holdings the upper classes were wiped out and middle-class families lost all their income-producing property. Homes of the wealthy were used as "housing for students, as nurseries or as clubs for workers."[8]

The second period lasted for three years, 1961-1963. Planning, industrialization, and agricultural diversification became the watchwords of the regime. A minimum 10 percent annual increase in the GNP was set as the goal for the four-year period 1962 to 1965. Near disaster ensued. Few of the factories materialized, but the greatest disaster resulted from declines in agriculture. Sugar lands converted to other uses led to spectacular drops in sugar production, the main earner of foreign currencies, without leading to substantial increases in production of other crops. In fact, food production declined. Prices climbed steadily, the black market flourished, and rationing had to be introduced first in the cities and then in the rural areas.[9]

The third stage began in late 1963 with retrenchment from the am-

[7] David D. Burks, "Cuba Seven Years After," *Current History*, Vol. 50 (1966), p. 40.
[8] David D. Burks, *Cuba Under Castro* (New York: Foreign Policy Association, 1964), p. 18.
[9] *Ibid.*, p. 23.

bitious industrial program. Sugar regained its primacy in the Cuban economy, but the rapid improvements in living standards in the first stage and the decline in sugar production in the second drew many experienced cane cutters from the sugar-growing areas. They became difficult to recruit, and Castro has had to rely on relatively inexperienced "volunteer" labor or high-cost hired workers. Soviet cane combines have been imported, but they have not proved entirely satisfactory. Furthermore, the increased Cuban sugar production since 1964 has depressed the world price. The next step in Cuba's process of economic development cannot be determined.

The foreign relations of the Castro regime also fall into three distinct periods. From the seizure of power in January 1959 to May of that same year, Castro attempted to declare his "independence" from U.S. domination, but sought at the same time to maintain some normal relationships. Castro turned down tentative offers of aid when he visited the United States in April, but declared that Cuba stood with the West in the Cold War and would honor its commitments in the Inter-American Mutual Defense Pacts.

Some tensions began to arise between the two countries as a result of the summary trials and executions of Batista's supporters, but the serious decline began in June with the promulgation of the Agrarian Reform Law. From that date to the missile crisis in October 1962, Cuban foreign relations were in a transitional stage in which hostility between Cuba and the United States grew apace with Cuban-Soviet *rapprochement*. Cuban confiscation of foreign property, U.S. abolition of the Cuban sugar quota, the renewal of Cuban-Soviet diplomatic relations and the inauguration of trade agreements, the break in diplomatic relations with the United States, and the Bay of Pigs battle were all stages in the shift of Cuba's alignments from the United States to the Soviet Union. In the process Castro got caught up in the Sino-Soviet quarrel, but in this stage succeeded in remaining on good terms with both. Also during this period Castro began to assert the international character of his revolution. In 1960 he called for an "anti-imperialist" revolution in all of Latin America with his now famous remark about converting "the Cordillera of the Andes into the Sierra Maestra of the American continent." [10] To support this line, Cuban money, arms, and propaganda were distributed in various parts of Latin America to foment revolution, and Cuba itself operated training schools for guerrillas.

Castro, encouraged by his successes, and the Russians, perhaps misinterpreting U.S. caution as weakness, began to install Russian inter-

[10] MacGaffey and Barnett, *op. cit.*, p. 332.

---

mediate range missiles in Cuba in the fall of 1962. The Kennedy administration reacted with such vigor and determination that the Russians withdrew these missiles. Castro suffered an immediate loss of prestige, as it appeared that Cuba was not the "first free territory of the Americas" as he proclaimed but a pawn in the power struggle between the Soviet Union and the United States. In the long run Castro may have gained more benefit than loss from the event in that, now safe from U.S. invasion, he has more freedom in conducting domestic policies. Although "United States–Cuban relations have remained in a state of frozen hostility" [11] since the missile crisis, Soviet-Cuban relations have remained, in a sense, frozen too. Castro has a free hand in Cuban political affairs, but on economic matters he must take some degree of Russian advice since he depends so heavily on Russian markets and subsidies.

In foreign affairs Cuba has played a complex role. Although the Cubans have never signed the nuclear test ban treaty, and have continued to advocate armed rebellion as the means to social change, and have tried to explain to the Chinese why they support the Russians on some issues, the Chinese still consider Castro as a member of the Moscow bloc. During the Tricontinental Conference of January 1966, in which Castro attempted to play a role in Asian and African Communist movements, Cuban-Chinese relations began to deteriorate with the announced Chinese cut in rice shipments. At the same time the Russians and the Cubans have disagreed seriously on the proper means of achieving socialism. The Russians and their supporters in the Communist Parties of Latin America generally oppose violence, while Castro advocates national liberation movements, citing Vietnam as an example. Finally in March, 1967, Castro virtually read the Russians out of the Communist movement in Latin America. The Russians can do little about the matter because their prestige is so heavily committed to the continuation of a viable revolutionary regime in Cuba.[12]

The first period of the revolution from January through May 1959 was marked by a heady intoxication with victory and gropings toward economic and political policies, both domestic and international. By June, Castro appeared determined to break Cuba's dependence on the United States, to seek extrahemisphere support, and to restructure the Cuban economy and society. The second period is characterized by all

[11] Burks, *Cuba Under Castro*, p. 56.
[12] David D. Burks, "Soviet Policy for Castro's Cuba," in John J. TePaske and Sydney N. Fisher (eds.), *Explosive Forces in Latin America* (Columbus: Ohio State University Press, 1964), pp. 22-23.

sorts of experiments to implement these policies. It is difficult to be precise about the terminal date of the second period. By the spring of 1962 Castro had reasserted his personal authority after a heavy reliance on old-line Communist leadership; by mid-1963 he had shifted economic policy back to primary reliance on sugar after a disastrous attempt at agricultural diversification. Cuba's present international posture was pretty well set by the missile crisis of October, 1962. No real thermidor has appeared. In the political sphere, no definitive institutional arrangements have yet jelled to the point where one can foresee future developments with any certainty.

Revolutionary Leaders and Followers

In pre-Castro Cuba, intellectual protest did not imply an alienation of the intellectuals from their society. Some middle-class intellectuals adopted "Marxist historical and economic determinism" to advocate an anticapitalist and anti-imperialist revolution, but few Cubans seriously planned such a revolution until the advent of Fidel Castro. Most, like the literary revolutionist Jorge Mañach, shifted "from radical leftist beginnings toward conservatism," as they advanced up the social scale. Mañach left Cuba in 1960.[13] Some politicians made a racist appeal by identifying Cuban cultural achievements as of mestizo origin in contrast to the parasitism of the white elite. A number of university professors, such as Raúl Roa, Castro's foreign minister, "prompted by chronic underemployment and political frustration" engaged in studies of their societies, but found themselves too ill-equipped "by their anti-empirical training to be effective." [14]

Batista's coup of 1952 introduced a minor change in the pattern. Fidel Castro, a member of one of the reform parties, became convinced that necessary changes could take place only by a violent overthrow of the dictatorship. Born of a provincial upper-class landed family, university educated, gifted as an orator, he entered the political arena in Havana by joining the Ortodoxo Party and standing as one of its candidates for the abortive 1952 elections. In his first revolutionary effort in 1953 he attracted a following of some 170 young men, many of whom came from the lower-middle or even lower classes, but included some like himself of middle-class or provincial upper-class origin. His following in Mexico in 1955 and 1956 came apparently from the same social sectors, and included, of course, his brother Raúl

[13] MacGaffey and Barnett, *op. cit.*, p. 220.
[14] *Ibid.*

and Che Guevara, a young Argentine medical doctor and the son of an architect.[15]

In March, 1957, some 58 recruits from Santiago joined the remnants of the original landing party. These were primarily middle-class students or recent graduates. To maintain himself in the mountains, Castro needed the support of the local peasantry and to this end began to champion its cause. A few recruits continued to come from the urban middle classes but by 1958 the majority of the small fighting force consisted of peasants from Oriente under the leadership of urban middle-class intellectuals and students.[16]

Because of the paucity of his forces, Castro long regarded the struggle in the cities against Batista as the key to victory. This force too was "overwhelmingly middle class in composition," and youthful except for some of the old-line political opponents of Batista. But this middle-class following alone proved unable to overthrow the regime. Its weaknesses became evident in the students' failures to assassinate Batista and more strikingly in its inability to carry off the strike called by Castro in the spring of 1958. At that time, it is apparent, the organized urban workers still supported Batista, the Communists still regarded Castro as a "bourgeois putschist," and the mass of the urban and rural lower classes remained unorganized and probably ignorant of the issues in conflict.

When the Castro forces assumed power in January 1959, the old tradition of middle-class politics seemed assured of reinstatement. The older and more experienced leaders among the opponents of the dictator predominated in the Cabinet, Castro had given repeated assurances of free elections and the restoration of the Constitution of 1940, and many of his followers in the 26th of July Movement, while reformers, were known to be moderate in outlook. Within two months the picture began to change and by the summer of 1959 it became clear that the more conservative and moderate elements of the revolution, regardless of age or previous alignments, were being systematically eliminated, and more radical leaders both young and old were taking control. Throughout the process ultimate power as distinguished from titles and office holdings rested in Fidel Castro, the new hero of the masses. The new men coming to prominence behind him represented first of all the leaders and organizers of the PSP and secondly

[15] Theodore Draper, *Castro's Revolution: Myths and Realities* (New York: Frederick A. Praeger, Inc., 1962), p. 11; Hugh Thomas, "Middle-Class Politics and the Cuban Revolution," in Claudio Véliz (ed.), *The Politics of Conformity in Latin America* (London: Oxford University Press, 1967), pp. 259-260.
[16] Theodore Draper, *Castroism: Theory and Practice* (New York: Frederick A. Praeger, Inc., 1965), p. 60.

the more radical leaders of the 26th of July Movement. The older generation of political leaders were forced out of politics and their political parties forbidden. Only the PSP legally operated.

This line-up persisted until the Escalante crisis of March, 1962, when Castro asserted his personal authority over the revolution in the face of PSP attempts to undermine his position. Aníbal Escalante, something of a scapegoat, went into exile, and Castro castigated the whole leadership of the PSP. Shortly thereafter, Castro reorganized his political apparatus to favor followers loyal to himself rather than to the PSP. The leadership changes made in the spring of 1962 have persisted with some exceptions to the present. Che Guevara disappeared from Cuban political life early in 1965, and the PSP leaders have further declined in numbers and prestige in the directing ranks of the revolution. Castro continues as the supreme leader, Raúl is second in command, and lieutenants personally loyal to the Castros hold most of the top positions. Castro has not eliminated the old PSP leaders, but they are now of secondary rank in the leadership hierarchy.[17]

Who are the rank and file supporters of Castro, and how numerous are they? With the overthrow of Batista, Castro enjoyed universal support except for a few thousand close supporters of the former dictator. By the spring of 1959 this support had begun to erode among some middle- and upper-class elements who were becoming fearful of his increasing radicalism. Nonetheless a sample survey of urban and semi-urban populations in the spring of 1960 indicated that 86 percent of the people supported the regime, and if one considers that Castro's support in the rural areas (constituting 40 percent of the population) was always higher than in the cities, his popular support was still over 90 percent.[18] Further erosions took place as we know from the flow of exiles and Castro's own speeches. Castro's ideological swing to the left, enforced educational indoctrination, political repression, expropriation of property, and attacks on the Church all contributed to a loss of following. "Furthermore, pervasive shortages of food, clothing and services compounded popular discontent."[19] There is no way of knowing the exact support for Castro today. In all probability half or more of the population simply accepts the regime as they have accepted stable regimes in the past, and a plausible estimate would divide the remaining percentage about evenly among active supporters and opponents. His strongest support comes from students and young

[17] Burks, "Cuba Seven Years After," pp. 38-39.
[18] Richard R. Fagan, "Mass Mobilization in Cuba: The Symbolism of Struggle," *Journal of International Affairs*, Vol. 20 (1966), p. 268.
[19] *Ibid.*

people across class lines, and among the poorest inhabitants including the Negroes, across age lines.[20] It has been pointed out, however, that "at least one out of every two adult Cubans now participates directly in mass activity under the revolutionary banner." [21] The result of mass mobilization such as this combined with indoctrination of school-age children (practically all of whom now attend school) may well be the creation in the next generation of a more homogeneous population in terms of political outlook and socioeconomic orientation.

In sum the early phases of the revolution were made by leaders of middle-class origin with support drawn from all classes. Within six months of his assumption of power, however, Castro and his lieutenants began systematically to alienate and eliminate much of his middle-class and all of his upper-class support. Theodore Draper has pointed out that despite its leadership "this was not a revolution of the middle class." First of all the middle sectors were too divided to be designated revolutionary or counterrevolutionary. The generational division, with bourgeois young people destroying their own class in the name of nationalism and socialism, constituted only the most serious split in the class. But if the revolution is not middle class, neither is it a peasant nor proletarian revolution. Rather it is a classless revolution whose leaders "have used one class or another, or a combination of classes, for different purposes at different times." In other words, the Cuban Revolution is a "déclassé revolution." [22]

The Ideology of the Cuban Revolution

Castroism has been described as "a leader in search of a movement, a movement in search of power, and power in search of an ideology." [23] Castro's first programmatic statement with ideological implications was his now famous speech "History Will Absolve Me" delivered at his defense trial in October, 1953. As later published, the speech called for the restoration of the Constitution of 1940, general elections, restrictions on the size of land holdings, and nationalization of some foreign-owned utilities. This list of specifics contained nothing that had not constituted standard fare of leftist (but non-Communist) political leaders since the early 1930's.[24]

During the period of armed struggle, followers of Castro published

---

[20] Burks, *Cuba Under Castro*, p. 14.
[21] Fagan, *op. cit.*, p. 261.
[22] Draper, *Castroism*, pp. 132–133.
[23] *Ibid.*, pp. 48-49.
[24] *Ibid.*, p. 21.

various statements about the movement's programs and aspirations; probably the most significant was the "Manifesto of the Sierra Maestra." Basically a plea for unity among the divergent elements opposing Batista, it repeated the democratic political goals of the trial speech and called for land distribution with prior indemnity, industrialization, and campaigns against illiteracy and unemployment. Other documents of the period do not diverge greatly from the trial speech and the manifesto, but they do demonstrate an increasingly moderate tone.

The shift in tone probably represented a tactical move designed to attract broad support. David Burks states flatly that as Castro struggled in the mountains "he became in fact increasingly committed to a more radical kind of program." [25] His actions after the seizure of power support this interpretation. During his first few months in power, Castro gave every indication of undergoing a personal internal struggle. He accepted the support of the PSP and on occasion he said that to be anti-Communist was to be antirevolutionary; on several other occasions, however, he forcefully rejected the Communist way as Cuba's road to reform.[26] As late as May 1959, he condemned Communist doctrine for suppressing liberties and sacrificing man as pitilessly as capitalism.[27] Attempting to find a position between capitalism and Communism, Castro adopted the term "humanism" to describe his movement, and defined "humanism" as "liberty with bread." One section of the 26th of July Movement picked up the slogan, but when PSP leader Escalante in late June condemned it as "ideological confusion," Castro dropped it and never used it again.

During the summer of 1959 *Castristas* and Communists became firm allies. Elections were postponed indefinitely, talk of restoring the Constitution subsided, and anti-Communists were removed from positions of authority and responsibility. For about a year the Revolution had no defined ideological position, although Marxists and Communists clearly dominated political and economic actvities. Thus in July 1960 Che Guevara defined Castro's movement as "applied Marxism." [28] By the end of the year the "alliance" between *Castristas* and Communists was transformed into a "fusion" when provision was made for the founding of a single party and Communists placed in charge of the schools for the training of party cadres.[29] Ideological development moved rapidly thereafter. In April 1961, Castro announced that the

[25] Burks, *Cuba Under Castro*, p. 28.

[26] Loree Wilkerson, *Fidel Castro's Political Programs from Reformism to Marxism-Leninism* (Gainesville: University of Florida Press, 1965), pp. 55-56.

[27] Draper, *Castroism*, p. 37.

[28] Quoted in Wilkerson, *op. cit.*, p. 67, n. 26.

[29] Draper, *Castroism*, p. 35.

Revolution was "socialist." Escalante of the PSP said that the move into the socialist stage meant that the Revolution had taken a decisive step on the road to Communism. This ideological phase reached its high point with Castro's declaration of adherence to "Marxism-Leninism" in his speech of December 2-3, 1961. In this same speech he admitted his ideological deficiencies with respect to Marxism-Leninism; he promised to remedy them by further study; and he declared his intention of shifting power from himself to the revolutionary party.[30]

Escalante apparently took Castro's promise of party leadership too literally, and suffered for his temerity. Forced by circumstances to rely on Soviet support, Castro has not strayed too far from the orthodox Communist line. Despite his pique at the withdrawal of Soviet missiles in October 1962, he eventually took the Russian side in the Sino-Soviet dispute, and dubbed his party the Communist Party of Cuba. Castro on the other hand has asserted "his individuality within the world Communist movement." [31] He maintains that the "objective conditions" for revolution now exist in Latin America, and only the lack of revolutionary determination on the part of the local Communists impedes it. In a speech in January 1963, Castro maintained that while the masses make history, revolutionary leaders and organizations must launch them as they did in Cuba. He also maintained that while the peaceful road to socialism is theoretically possible, there is no single case to substantiate the theory. Armed struggle, he insisted, must be the road for Latin America.[32] This view, held by the Cubans and rejected by most of the Communists in Latin America, created further tensions in the world Communist movement and have not yet been resolved despite some attempts at compromise and reconciliation. Castro continues to regard himself as the model, and hopefully the leader, of social change in Latin America. At the moment the exact mix cannot be determined, but a reasonable estimate would be that in the long run the primary sources of the revolution will prove to be the domestic rather than the foreign.

International Repercussions
of the Cuban Revolution

The Cuban Revolution has involved the world's two superpowers in one major confrontation and an on-going rivalry in the Caribbean

[30] Draper, *Castro's Revolution,* pp. 147-149.
[31] Draper, *Castroism,* p. 40.
[32] *Ibid.,* p. 41.

area. After the Second World War the Soviet Union, by then one of the world's great powers, began to interest herself in Latin America. Guatemalan revolutionaries appealed for East Bloc assistance in the face of growing U.S. hostility in the early 1950's, and a few years later the Soviet Union announced its own trade offensive throughout Latin America. It was but natural then that Fidel Castro, schooled in a vague kind of Marxism and bitterly hostile toward the United States, should seek aid from the Soviet Union in an attempt to free Cuba from dependence on the United States. One may demonstrate that the U.S. government acted imprudently and injudiciously on several occasions prior to the rupture of diplomatic relations in January 1961, but the weight of evidence seems to indicate that Castro and his chief advisers were convinced that revolutionary Cuba could not do business with its economic overlord without surrendering some of its revolutionary goals. To make this break the Cubans needed massive outside support and could find this only in the Soviet Union. Cuban Marxists had no qualms ideologically about cooperating with the Soviet Union, and the latter occupied a power position from which it could offer economic and some types of military assistance.

A second factor that contributed to Cuba's success in soliciting outside aid resides in the rising nationalism and anticolonialism of so much of the world since the Second World War. These sentiments have deeply affected Latin Americans, even those who have little sympathy with Communism. As a result, the U.S. government believes that it can no longer brandish the big stick as it did in earlier years for fear of harming U.S. interests in other areas of the globe. Obviously, when the government believes major security problems are involved, or the administration believes that its popular support is seriously endangered by events in Latin America, U.S. power is brought directly to bear on the situation. The hesitation and half-way measures of the Bay of Pigs attack demonstrates the problem of balancing interests, while the missile confrontation in Cuba and the intervention into the Dominican Republic demonstrate the concerns with security matters and the power of public opinion in intervention policy. Both the latter moves clearly indicated circumstances in which the U.S. government would brook no interference, actual or potential, from outside the hemisphere. The Soviet Union has apparently accepted these conditions, and no other powers can remotely hope to challenge them. Since the missile crisis, relations between the United States and the Soviet Union with respect to Cuba have settled down into predictable patterns. The United States has embargoed virtually all trade with Cuba and pressures its allies to limit their commercial exchanges, while the Soviet Union, under "strong obligation to ensure the survival of Castroism," continues as the island's primary trading partner and supplier of equipment, including military assistance.[33]

Castro and his lieutenants have seen their revolution as a harbinger of similar upheavals throughout the hemisphere. These sentiments have been expressed through Castro's famous statements designating Cuba as the "first free territory of the Americas" and predicting that the Andes will become the Sierra Maestra of South America. They have been translated into action by the establishment in Cuba of training centers for would-be Latin American revolutionaries, the dissemination of written and oral propaganda throughout the hemisphere, and the equipping of revolutionary elements with weapons and money especially in the circum-Caribbean area. As Castro identified his movement, at least verbally, more and more with international Communism of the Moscow variety, he began to lay claim to Communist leadership throughout Latin America. Most of the old-guard leaders resented this intrusion but, at least during the first few years of Castro's rule, Communists and young Castroites cooperated rather well. Following the missile crisis of 1962, however, many of the old-guard Communists found Castro something of an embarrassment because of his insistence upon violence as the road to socialism in Latin America.[34] This divergence of views has not been settled despite attempts at compromise at international meetings of Latin American Communist parties.

Castro's general support in Latin America has also declined from the earlier years. Almost universally popular in 1959 with Latin American peoples and governments, he lost much of his following as he moved progressively to the left in domestic policies and toward the Soviet Union in foreign policies. The trials of "war criminals," suppression of free speech, the invasion of the University of Havana, the attack on the labor movement, all alienated some sectors of his support. His dictatorial political regime and his attacks on Latin American liberals such as Betancourt and Figueres contributed to the break in diplomatic relations with democratic regimes such as those of Venezuela and Costa Rica. The missile crisis produced the gravest setback for Castro in Latin America, however, because it demonstrated that Cuba was not the first free territory of the Americas, but had merely exchanged one master for another. Today Castro still enjoys some support in Latin America, but it is restricted to a minority of politicians, intellectuals, and students, isolated from the main streams of political development.[35]

[33] Burks, "Soviet Policy for Castro's Cuba," p. 22.
[34] Burks, *Cuba Under Castro*, pp. 44-45.
[35] *Ibid.*, pp. 46-47.

Conclusion

In many respects Cuba fits the generalizations made about revolutions. There existed "multiple dysfunctions" in the old regime: frustrations and anxieties among important sectors of the population, economic dislocations, and alienation among intellectuals. There also appeared the man of words to prepare the way for change, the man of action to plot conspiracy and carry out rebellion, and the man of administration to consolidate the gains once the old regime was overthrown and that man has been Fidel Castro. The revolution also produced leaders in age and background that fit most norms, proceeded through stages of enthusiasm and disappointments, and produced programs, slogans, and ideology to justify and rationalize its activities. Like the French and Russian revolutions, the Cuban has also attempted to carry its message of salvation to its benighted neighbors. But the Cuban Revolution also diverges from suggested norms, and proceeds on its own way to add something to revolutionary theory. Perhaps in no other modern revolution has a single leader loomed so large. Without Castro there would have been no social revolution in Cuba. At most the political and economic upper and middle classes of Cuba wanted an end to the dictatorship and a restoration of the *status quo ante* Batista. The lower classes gave no indication of revolutionary inclinations even after Castro began his struggle in the mountains. Castro and a handful of close counselors made the Cuban Revolution what it is by mobilizing the masses after their victory against the old regime, by turning against their former supporters, and by carrying out radical changes not in response to popular demands but in response to their own understanding of what the demands should be. The Cuban Revolution is also unique in that the same top leadership group with the exception of Guevara has maintained itself at the head of the revolutionary movement from its earliest beginnings as a protest movement, to military victory, to the beginnings of institutionalization. At the same time there has been a substantial turnover in second- and third-echelon personnel. Thirdly, no true thermidor has yet taken place nine and a half years after victory; politically the regime still appears to be largely a one-man operation with the development of no more than a primitive political apparatus. The latter appears to be a deliberate policy that assures Fidel Castro of ease of control over the revolution. Finally, the Cuban Revolution produced a variety of slogans and ideological positions, although only one predominated at any one time. There never was a compromise of ideologies or a blending of ideologies forced by contending power groups. The ideology at any given moment has been what Castro says it is, and during the course of the revolution he has changed his mind, at least publicly, several times. These changes have not been mere tactical maneuvers, as in Russia under Lenin, but substantial shifts in basic doctrines. Where the revolution will eventually stabilize politically, no one can predict, but Cuba will never again return to pre-1959 conditions.

11

Modern Revolutions:
Comparisons and Prospects

How Representative Are These Case Studies?

Our four cases of twentieth-century revolution drawn from Latin America and the Middle East may not be representative of all modern revolution, for revolution may well occur in areas which are no longer in the developing stage. But, how representative are they of their own regional areas and also of the broad underdeveloped world at large?

The Mexican and Cuban revolutions resemble the French and Russian revolutions far more than they do any other revolution in Latin America except perhaps the Bolivian upheaval of 1952. No study of Latin American revolution can be complete without giving consideration to the Mexican and Cuban examples, although they are not at all the barracks-revolt, coup-oriented type so common in Latin American history. Far more typical is Batista's takeover in Cuba in 1952, or Onganía's seizure of power in Argentina in 1966. Yet however untypical our examples may be of Latin American revolutions, they remain by far the most important because of their obvious connection with the world revolutionary movement, social in character and now nearly two centuries old.

Most of the army officers and others who mount their coups in Latin America are not such thoroughgoing revolutionaries as to look to Mexico or Cuba for their model. Few want really to reform or alter very substantially the social and economic structures of their countries. In most cases a Latin American revolution does not even displace the ruling elite but merely redistributes offices and rewards among that elite. How different the Mexican and Cuban revolutions!

After the great struggles for national independence a century and a half ago Latin America developed a kind of revolutionary isolationism. To be sure, palace revolts have been common to Latin American history and a successful coup in one country has at times stimulated a similar effort in a neighboring state. *Revolucionismo* in fact conjures up, in the common mind at least, the very essence of Latin American politics. In this context the Mexican and Cuban revolutions have not been emulated in Latin America; neither have they been particularly influential, perhaps because of a general fear of what ultimately happened in both countries. Until the success of Castro in Cuba, Latin American revolutionaries rarely received their training or their inspiration from other Latin American revolutionary experiences; Bolivia is again the exception. This is not to say that revolution in Latin America is not commonplace, but rather that it is not directly interconnected. Very rarely have *caudillos* or presidents attempted to export their revolutions to their neighbors, Castro of course excepted.

The Mexican and Cuban revolutions are by no means carbon copies of one another. Mexico produced no single leader of the stature of Fidel Castro in terms of charisma, influence, and overriding domination. Indeed, in many ways the Cuban revolution is Castro. Without his leadership, drive, and will, it is unlikely that the revolution would have occurred when it did and highly unlikely that it would have been as thoroughgoing. The Mexican revolution was the product of many leaders and forces, none of whom dominated the movement so thoroughly. Furthermore, while Castro has looked upon his revolution as the model for all of his continent and is eager to export it, the Mexicans regarded their revolution as strictly for home consumption.

Just as revolution has characterized Latin American politics, coups and violent upheavals have been commonplace in the Middle East. In recent years such upheavals have occurred in Algeria, Egypt, Sudan, Yemen, Lebanon, Syria, Turkey, Iraq, Iran, and Pakistan. Many of the governments established by such revolutions have been short-lived and few have embarked on any widescale overhaul of their societies. The two most far-reaching revolutions in the Middle East in the twentieth century—although not typical of the many coups and military takeovers in the area—are the Egyptian and Turkish revolutions. The Turkish revolution is important for what was accomplished within Turkey, the Egyptian revolution for the inspiration that it has given potential Arab revolutionary leaders throughout the Middle East. The Turkish revolution was relatively uninfluential abroad but more or less successful in achieving its internal goals; the Egyptian revolution, although its "success" can still be questioned, has been of tremendous influence throughout the Middle East and in Asia and Africa as well. Both of these revolutions were led by military officers and in this they were very much like all revolutions in the Middle East.

One, the Egyptian, came into being by the classic coup; the other, the Turkish, was the product of a national uprising coupled with successful military action against foreign invaders. Of the two, the Egyptian revolution has embraced much more reform in the economic sphere than has the Turkish. Whatever can be said of Egypt, one cannot argue that its current economic organization and structure bear much resemblance to those of the Egypt before 1952. In Turkey, on the other hand, there is a great economic continuity with the past and the economic class structure has not been greatly altered. The great impact of the Turkish revolution was social and cultural; surprisingly enough, there has been less change in this respect in Egypt.

Comparison with the Classic Revolutions

We have referred to the French and Russian revolutions as the classic examples of revolution, embodying as they do in rich detail the many facets of the revolutionary process. It is inviting to measure the case studies against these examples. That they can be compared in this way at all is a measure of their significance.

One of the most striking features of both the French and Russian revolutions was the existence of an *ancien régime*. Among our cases, only in Turkey can one find an *ancien régime* that was really old, and there the drive for revolution was primarily the product of the disaster of World War I and the detestation aroused by foreign intervention into Turkish affairs. In short, the Turkish revolution was nationalist in origin, destroying the Sultanate and Caliphate as the revolution unfolded. Egypt also had an *ancien régime;* at least it possessed a dynasty more than a century old. The Egyptian monarchy, like the Turkish, had deteriorated, and was increasingly blamed for the miseries and failures of Egyptian life. In Mexico and Cuba there were no *anciens régimes* of this sort. The Spanish monarchy had been driven from Mexico in 1821 and from Cuba in 1898. Despite the overthrow of the *ancien régime* politically, social and economic structures in both countries had been little altered when their revolutions broke out. A few reforms effected in mid-nineteenth-century Mexico had been largely vitiated by 1910 and a would-be social revolution of the 1930's in Cuba proved abortive. When the revolutions broke out, both countries were controlled by dictators bent upon preserving the status quo The existence of an *ancien régime* almost always encourages revolution; but its absence does not guarantee stability.

All four revolutions can be called middle-class affairs in the sense that they were led primarily by members of the middle classes. Mexico is an outstanding example of the middle-class revolution despite large-scale participation of the peasantry in the period of violence. Middle-class leaders, however, never lost control of the conflict nor sight of their personal and group interests. Not all these revolutions, however, have incorporated middle-class values or redounded to the benefit of these classes. In Cuba a middle-class-led revolution was ultimately turned against that class by a high command that did not identify with the class of its origins. The Turkish revolution resembles the Mexican in the persistence of middle-class values and orientation, while the Egyptian military leaders of the 1952 revolution, although middle class by definition, built a great deal of their support on the peasantry and urban working class. Why our examples developed along their respective class lines cannot be explained with our current knowledge of revolution.

In Egypt and Turkey, the revolutions were led by officers of the regular military, while in Cuba and Mexico the officer corps at least initially opposed the revolutions. The Latin American examples thus more clearly resembled the classic cases in which the officer corps played either a passive or a negative role. Although the success of these latter examples negates the proposition that revolution can only take place with the blessing of the military, it seems altogether likely that most modern revolution will involve the military.

The misery and economic disasters of the prerevolutionary environment in France and Russia have been exaggerated. There was misery to spare in Turkey in 1919—she was exhausted from the First World War, yet was still opposing the invader—but it was almost certainly not the economic distress of Turkey that spawned the revolution. Indeed, misery alone, although no less prevalent in the case studies than in the classic examples, cannot explain the outbreak of these revolutions. There was certainly misery in Mexico in 1910 and undoubtedly the revolution fed on it, but it was not the *causa revolutionis*. The misery of the Egyptian fellah in 1952 could hardly have been exaggerated, but it was really army disenchantment and humiliation (over Palestine) that precipitated the revolution. The material well-being of the Mexican and Egyptian peasant has not improved markedly since their revolutions, but their continued misery does not in itself presage much more revolutionary turmoil. In Cuba, there was a considerable veneer of prosperity in 1956 but just as considerable lack of enthusiasm for the Batista regime. In Cuba, indeed, one might argue that the Castro triumph was won by default. There was no widespread enthusiasm for him, but neither was there a deep-felt commitment to the Batista dictatorship.

If poverty, hunger, and suffering do not cause revolutions, what factors do? It appears that a variety of interacting forces, similar but never precisely the same, produce revolutions. Loss of confidence by the ruling elite in themselves, in their institutions, and in their ability to produce, if not solutions, substantial amelioration for the problems of their society appear in our cases as well as in the classic models. The Mexican elite like the French did not seriously oppose the overthrow of the government, but fought long and hard after the victory of the revolution to preserve at least part of its wealth; the Cuban, like the Russian, collapsed quickly. The Turkish elite never had its socio-economic position seriously challenged, while the Egyptian came to terms with the new order and preserved a portion of its economic base. The point is, however, that none fought to preserve the regime intact when the revolt began.

A second and related factor is the presence of widespread discontent, frustration, and alienation among numerous sectors of the population. Among our cases and the classic models, for a variety of reasons, millions of people were ready to welcome a change of regime, by force if necessary. In Turkey, like Russia, the disasters of a foreign war, the presence of foreign troops and the fear of an uncertain future, while in Cuba and Mexico economic dislocations, the magnitude of foreign investments, the fraud and corruption of dictatorial rule, all led to the refusal of popular support for the government. In Egypt, the disaster of the first Arab-Israeli war in 1948 (in which the army was defeated), the continued British presence, the open and brazen exploitation by foreign nationals, and the sullied symbol of the King contributed to the same end.

And, finally, the proper leadership had to appear, that is, a leader or leaders had to come forward to touch the right chords of discontent, to unify the sources of alienation, and to direct them against the incumbent rulers. In this respect the Mexican revolution resembled the French, except that a symbol of unity appeared briefly in Madero. Behind Madero, however, was a variety of leaders whose basic antagonisms blossomed once the dictator vanished. In Turkey, Cuba, and Egypt, however, one leader clearly predominated, held the revolution together, and gave it direction and ideology, as Lenin did in Russia after October 1917. As a consequence, not only did the Mexican revolution try to incorporate often divergent ideologies and points of view but dragged on in bloody civil war for nearly ten years, moving in fits and jerks the fulfillment of proclaimed goals for another 20 years. On the contrary, the other three were carried out with much less bloodshed, far shorter struggles, and more unified leadership and sense of direction.

The classic revolutions were well known for terror. There was almost no terror in the Turkish example, some in the Cuban revolution, but relatively little in Egypt—at least until the uncertain events of 1967—and Mexico, despite the bloody struggles of almost ten years in the latter. None of the cases possesses terror to the degree that characterized either the Russian or French revolutions. Perhaps a factor in this is that in none of our cases were the revolutionaries threatened by an emigré group plotting with foreign invaders to overturn the revolution and reinstall the *ancien régime*.

The French and Russian revolutions were distinguished by their production of ideology and their attempt to export revolution to their neighbors. The Cuban and Egyptian revolutions most resemble the classic models in that their leaders have been anxious to inspire revolution abroad; the Turkish and Mexican revolutions, on the other hand, have been noteworthy in their almost total disinterest in foreign revolution. Modern-day revolutionary leaders as different from each other as Nkrumah and Boumédienne all find themselves in an international context that encourages them to play supranational roles. This situation developed in the last 40 years, in part from the internationalization of ideology and in part from technological advances in communication and transportation. Nasser and Castro both find themselves in this new tradition.

Both the Turkish and the Mexican revolutions—coming as they did a half-century ago—occurred before the Russian revolution could make its full impact abroad. In fact, the Mexican revolution preceded the Russian while the Turkish was nearly contemporaneous with it. Consequently, in neither country was Communism, organized or otherwise, of any significance. Both revolutions were nationalist and both pointed to the social rejuvenation of their peoples. The Mexican revolution was strongly influenced by early twentieth-century socialist doctrines as well as by older French revolutionary ideas. Like Mexico, Turkey was influenced by nationalist ideologies emanating from the French revolution; but unlike Mexico she borrowed little from Marxism. At the same time both of these revolutions fed on themselves and were to some degree *sui generis*. Castro, on the other hand, has loudly proclaimed his doctrinal identification with Communism. Yet he has insisted on the maintenance of his personal power, while using and exploiting the party cadres for their organizational and ideological skills. Nasser has just as forcibly denied his Communist attachment and has punctuated this denial by the wholesale arrest of Communist activists; yet his domestic programs and his postures abroad have proved miscible with ideological Communism. Nasser and Castro have on occasion proclaimed their brotherhood and identity of goals.

The classic cases were "great" revolutions in that the entire social fabric was challenged and altered. This is largely true in our cases although it is somewhat early to foresee the *dénouement des aventures* in Cuba and Egypt. In Cuba, destruction of the old order has outrun reconstruction of a new order. The old political system has been destroyed but a new one has not yet been created, and the revolution remains closely tied to the personality of Fidel Castro. In the same way the old social and economic structures have been overturned, but the final forms of the new institutions to replace them remain obscure. Much the same can be said of Egypt. After a slow beginning Nasser has, in the last decade, attempted to destroy virtually all of the old economic and political systems. Reconstruction has not yet matured; Egyptian military disaster in the summer of 1967 has not, quite obviously, contributed to stability. In Turkey there was great reform, much of which has lasted. Although many have viewed the Democratic Party interlude in the 1950's as a setback to the Kemalist revolution, in truth it was hardly so significant. Revolutionary reconstruction has gone a long way in Turkey; today she possesses considerable political stability. This is certainly true of Mexico as well. Over 25 years have passed since the last great changes were made there. A stable political system has emerged, new patterns of land holdings have developed, and in urban areas a strong modernizing trend predominates. Although neither Turkey nor Mexico fully measures up to the classic examples in the sense described, in the context of their areas they have been noteworthy for the amount of cultural and social change brought about.

Can thermidor be found in the case studies? In both the Mexican and Turkish revolutions—possibly because they are older—there are such inflection points: in Turkey with the rise of the Democratic Party in the 1940's and in Mexico almost simultaneously. There are periods that can be called revolutionary plateaus in Cuba and Egypt but it does not seem appropriate to term them thermidorian, because we lack perspective.

Although there are of course many differences not only between these cases and the classic examples but also among the case studies themselves, there are sufficient similarities in essentials to underline the importance of these revolutions. They also substantiate a conclusion drawn earlier: there is no single (or simple) model of revolution. In practice revolution assumes a multitude of forms.

The Future of Revolution

Is revolution any more prevalent today than it has been over the last two centuries? Has the emergence of many newly independent

countries assuaged the thirst for revolutionary change? Has the awareness of what one does not have in comparison with what others have—
the results of the incredible changes in communication—produced
expectations that cannot be fulfilled and frustrations that lead to revolution?

Even a cursory view of recent history forces an acknowledgment
that we are living in a new era of revolution. Fragmented societies
have always been subject to revolutionary turmoil, and will continue
to be. However, the collapse of the old imperial system following the
Second World War ushered in a new revolutionary round: a worldwide movement of national independence against colonial powers, in
both economic and political terms. The euphoria of independence in
some areas (and hard currency accumulated as a result of the Second
World War in others) produced an interregnum of stability, but in
most cases the internal problems and external ambitions created new
strains within these countries. The inevitable result has been continuing revolution.

Although the last third of the twentieth century promises to be a
period of almost constant revolutionary turmoil, these violent upheavals are not equally likely everywhere. They seem less likely to
occur in Western Europe and North America (and in such areas as
Australia and the Soviet Union). In these places a high level of political and social consensus can be discerned. However, revolution may
occur in even the most mature, prosperous, and literate area. Thus in
the France of 1958 the struggle over Algeria bitterly divided the
populace and brought France to the brink of revolution. The difficulties
of specific and detailed prognostication in such cases, however, are
immense.

It is easier to believe that revolution will continue to characterize
Latin America, Asia, and Africa. These areas are the developing ones
—their economies, their political systems, and their social structures—
and the stresses and strains of development are such as to encourage
the short-circuiting of constitutional processes. It is probable that
relatively few of these revolutions will be *social* in character, although
the men who guide such violent alterations will continue to argue and
justify their efforts on the grounds of social and economic metamorphoses. Although the experience of France and Bolivia suggests the
contrary, one can argue that once social revolution has been consummated, further violent systematic alterations become less likely. There
is, certainly, no reason to believe that the contemporary political, economic, and social patterns of Latin America and the Middle East will
continue to exist unaltered and unthreatened by change. It is in these
areas that further revolutions can be expected, but generally revolu-

tion that will at most introduce incremental changes into their societies and frequently only changes in governing personnel.

In the underdeveloped areas, and specifically in Latin America and the Middle East, the leadership of revolution, at least in its early stages, will fall generally to the military. In these societies, recently improved educational facilities and foreign travel have considerably broadened the understanding, quickened the interest, and increased the self-confidence of military officers in political affairs. Furthermore, their virtual monopoly of heavy weapons, their possession of superior hierarchy and discipline, and their high level of agreement on at least what they oppose make them a key factor in any coup attempt whether instigated by civilian or military leaders. A few guerrilla operations today challenge the regular military. Although guerrillas have been active in many parts of Latin America during the past decade, they have generally not been able to expand their operations into a full-scale revolution, and nowhere do they appear to have much chance for success. Cuba, because of unique characteristics and circumstances, appears to be the outstanding exception. Mass outbursts like the kind which overthrew Mexican and Bolivian regimes (including the regular military) in 1910 and 1952 respectively do not appear to be in the cards for any country in Latin America today. In the Middle East, guerrilla warfare was a real factor in the Algerian struggle for independence from the French. In Iraq the regular military forces have been unable to put down the Kurdish rebellion in the north, and in Yemen a large body of Egyptian troops found it impossible to destroy the tribal followers of Imam Muhammad al-Badr. In contrast to Latin America all of these examples are struggles primarily for political independence or autonomy, against "outsiders" or "foreigners," rather than purely internal struggles for power. The Middle East, like Latin America, makes its revolutions through the military and it is highly unlikely that internal struggles for power that have reached the stage of violence will not involve the military. The unique exception was the Lebanese revolution of 1958, when the army played the role of referee between contending revolutionary forces; it is noteworthy that the revolution there was a stand-off.

Our case studies perhaps indicate how political revolt may turn into social revolution. All of our examples but one originated as coups or revolts with limited political aims. The one exception, Cuba, appears to have been conceived by Castro as a social revolution, but the evidence is not clear that he foresaw from the beginning how deeply changes would be introduced into Cuban life. Moreover, many of his lieutenants believed that only minor alterations would be made, and broke with Castro when the scope of his operations began to unfold.

Generally, the leaders of the other three revolutions—Atatürk is somewhat an exception—wanted to restore former or to improve upon existing structures, but discovered that once embarked upon, reforms in
one area led to changes in others. Our case studies also seem to indicate
that once some basic adjustments have been made in the social and
economic structures of a country, revolutionary zeal begins to abate
and older cultural habits and traits reassert themselves.

Finally, what can we say about the predictability of revolution as to
time and place and form? Will Nasser be replaced within the year in
Egypt? Will Mexico undergo another round of unconstitutional and
perhaps violent reform within five years? Will the military seize power
in Turkey again? Will Castro be overthrown in the next ten years?
Most experts on these areas could answer "possibly" with little hesitation, "probably" with serious qualifications, and "surely" only by setting
up such detailed hypothetical situations as to make prediction value-
less. In other words, except perhaps in the case of Mexico, no one
would be greatly surprised if revolution of some type should occur in
these countries, but no one can at present speak with authority on the
likelihood or improbability of revolution anywhere at any given time,
much less the course that a revolution might take. The complexity
of the circumstances and the role of individual will and determination,
not to speak of chance events, involved in revolution pose too many
and too indeterminate factors for precise predictability of revolutionary action.

In the Middle East, revolutionary turbulence can well be expected
in Algeria, Libya, Egypt, Sudan, Jordan, Saudi Arabia, Aden and
south Arabia, the Oman conglomerate, Iraq, and Syria. Such turbulence
will occur for a galaxy of reasons. But expectations of this kind certainly
do not preclude revolution in other areas, such as Afghanistan and
Tunisia, whose current stability is above that of the area as a whole.
The Middle East is highly unstable and almost certainly will continue to generate revolution. In Latin America, Mexico, Costa Rica,
Uruguay, and Chile seem the most likely to avoid revolutionary upheavals. Haiti at the other extreme appears to be on the point of explosion. A few countries like Venezuela and El Salvador have achieved
at least temporary settlements of internal political quarrels and can be
expected to maintain their regimes constitutionally for the moment.
Others, like Cuba, Paraguay, and Nicaragua, will avoid serious trouble
through iron control by police and military forces. The remainder
demonstrate various degrees of instability resulting from serious internal conflicts. Revolution has been endemic in the area and with the
exception of a few countries will so continue to be. But precise predictions will remain difficult to make.

In summary we can say that:

1. The fever of revolution will not abate in the last third of the twentieth century.

2. Continuing revolution is very likely to occur in the underdeveloped areas, certainly in Latin America and the Middle East.

3. In most instances such revolution is likely to be a coup or a limited political revolt.

4. Such revolution will frequently be led or supported by the military, who have the weapons, the organization and discipline, and an increasing political awareness and interest.

5. In any particular area, revolutionary upheavals will continue until substantial social adjustments have been made.

6. Revolution is not really precisely predictable as to time and place.

Bibliography

Adams, Brooks. *The Theory of Social Revolutions.* New York: The Macmillan Company, 1913.

Aktan, Reşat. "Problems of Land Reform in Turkey," *The Middle East Journal,* Vol. 20 (1966), pp. 317-334.

Amann, Peter H. "Revolution: A Redefinition," *Political Science Quarterly,* Vol. 77 (1962), pp. 36-53.

Arciniegas, Germán. "What's Behind Our Revolutions?" *Américas,* Vol. 1 (1949), pp. 22-24, 48.

Apter, David E. (ed.). *Ideology and Discontent.* New York: The Free Press, 1964.

Arendt, Hannah. *On Revolution.* New York: The Viking Press, Inc., 1963.

————. "Totalitarian Imperialism: Reflections on the Hungarian Revolution," *The Journal of Politics,* Vol. 20 (1958), pp. 5-43.

Arnade, Kurt Conrad. "The Technique of *Coup d'État* in Latin America," *United Nations World,* Vol. 4 (1950), pp. 21-25.

Artz, Frederick B. *Reaction and Revolution, 1814-1832.* New York: Harper & Row, Publishers, 1934.

Baron, S. H. "First Decade of Russian Marxism," *American Slavic and East European Review,* Vol. 14 (1955), pp. 315-330.

Becker, Frances Bennett. "Lenin's Application of Marx's Theory of Revolutionary Tactics," *American Sociological Review,* Vol. 2 (1937), pp. 353-364.

Bell, Daniel. *The End of Theology.* New York: The Free Press, 1960.

Beloff, Max. *Public Order and Popular Disturbances, 1660-1714.* London: Oxford University Press, 1938.

Berkes, Niyazi. *The Development of Secularism in Turkey.* Montreal: McGill University Press, 1964.

Billington, James H. "Six Views of the Russian Revolution," *World Politics*, Vol. 18 (1966), pp. 452-473.

Binder, Leonard. *The Ideological Revolution in the Middle East*. New York: John Wiley & Sons, Inc., 1964.

Black, Cyril E., and Thomas P. Thornton (eds.). *Communism and Revolution: The Strategic Uses of Political Violence*. Princeton: Princeton University Press., 1964.

Blasier, Cole. "Studies of Social Revolution: Origins in Mexico, Bolivia, and Cuba," *Latin American Research Review*, Vol. 2 (1967), pp. 28-64.

Borkenau, Franz. *World Communism: A History of the Communist International*. New York: W. W. Norton & Company, Inc., 1939.

Brandenburg, Frank R. *The Making of Modern Mexico*. Englewood Cliffs, N.J.: Prentice-Hall, Inc., 1964.

Brinkmann, Carl. *Soziologische Theorie der Revolution*. Göttingen: Vandenhoeck & Ruprecht, 1948.

Brinton, Crane. *The Anatomy of Revolution*. New York: Vintage Books, 1956.

————. *The Jacobins: An Essay in the New History*. New York: The Macmillan Company, 1930.

————. "The Manipulation of Economic Unrest," *The Journal of Economic History*, Sup. 8 (1948), pp. 21-31.

Brogan, Denis W. *The Price of Revolution*. New York: Harper & Row, Publishers, 1952.

Brown, Lyle C. "General Lázaro Cárdenas and Mexican Presidential Politics, 1933-1940; A Study in the Acquisition and Manipulation of Political Power." University of Texas: Unpublished Ph.D. Dissertation, 1964.

Bruce, Robert V. *1877: Year of Violence*. Indianapolis: The Bobbs-Merrill Co., Inc., 1959.

Bunzel, John H. "The Appeal of Revolution: The Liberal's Quandary," *The Antioch Review*, Vol. 21 (1961), pp. 319-327.

Burks, David D. "Cuba Seven Years After," *Current History*, Vol. 50 (1966), pp. 38-44.

————. *Cuba Under Castro*. New York: Foreign Policy Association, 1964.

————. "Soviet Policy for Castro's Cuba," in John J. TePaske and Sydney N. Fisher (eds.), *Explosive Forces in Latin America*. Columbus: Ohio State University Press, 1964.

Burns, C. D. *The Principles of Revolution: A Study in Ideals*. London: George Allen & Unwin, Ltd., 1920.

Burr, Robert N. (ed.). *Latin America's Nationalistic Revolutions. The Annals of the American Academy of Political and Social Science*, Vol. 334 (1961).

Calvert, P. A. R. "Revolution: The Politics of Violence," *Political Studies,* Vol. 15 (1967), pp. 1-11.

Canetti, Elias. *Crowds and Power.* New York: The Viking Press, Inc., 1962.

Carr, Edward Hallett. *The Bolshevik Revolution: 1917-1923.* 3 vols. London: Macmillan & Co., Ltd., 1950-1953.

――――. *Studies in Revolution.* New York: Grosset & Dunlap, Inc., 1964.

Castro Ruz, Fidel. *History Will Absolve Me.* New York: Lyle Stuart, 1961.

Chamberlin, William Henry. *The Russian Revolution, 1917-1921.* 2 vols. New York: The Macmillan Company, 1952.

Chapman, Charles E. *A History of the Cuban Republic: A Study in Hispanic American Politics.* New York: The Macmillan Company, 1927.

Chorley, Katharine. *Armies and the Art of Revolution.* London: Faber & Faber, Ltd., 1943.

Clark, Marjorie R. *Organized Labor in Mexico.* Chapel Hill: University of North Carolina Press, 1934.

Cline, Howard F. *The United States and Mexico* (rev. ed.). New York: Atheneum Publishers, 1963.

Cobban, Alfred. "Age of Revolutionary Wars: An Historical Parallel," *Review of Politics,* Vol. 13 (1951), pp. 131-141.

――――. *The Social Interpretation of the French Revolution.* London: Cambridge University Press, 1964.

Cockcroft, James D. "Intellectuals in the Mexican Revolution. The San Luis Potosí Group and the Partido Liberal Mexicano, 1900-1913." Stanford University: Unpublished Ph.D. Dissertation, 1966.

Cohn, Norman. *The Pursuit of the Millennium.* Fair Lawn, N.J.: Essential Books, Inc., 1957.

Coser, Lewis A. *The Functions of Social Conflict.* New York: The Free Press, 1956.

――――. "The Myth of a Peasant Revolt," *Dissent,* Vol. 13 (1966), pp. 298-303.

Cosío Villegas, Daniel (ed.). *Historia moderna de México.* 7 vols. Mexico City: Editorial Hermes, 1955-1965.

Crozier, Brian. *The Rebels: A Study of Post-War Insurrections.* London: Chatto & Windus, Ltd., 1960.

Da Cunha, Euclides. *Rebellion in the Backlands,* trans. by Samuel Putnam. Chicago: University of Chicago Press, 1944.

Dahl, Robert A. (ed.). *Political Oppositions in Western Democracies.* New Haven: Yale University Press, 1966.

Dahrendorf, Ralf. *Class and Class Conflict in Industrial Society.* Stanford: Stanford University Press, 1959.

Daniels, Robert V. "The State and Revolution: A Case Study in the Genesis and Transformation of Communist Ideology," *The American Slavic and East European Review*, Vol. 12 (1953), pp. 22-43.

Davies, James C. "Toward a Theory of Revolution," *American Sociological Review*, Vol. 27 (1962), pp. 5-19.

Debray, Regis. *Revolution in the Revolution.* New York: Monthly Review Press, 1967.

de Grazia, Sebastian. *The Political Community: A Study of Anomie.* Chicago: University of Chicago Press, 1963.

Devereux, Robert. *The First Ottoman Constitutional Period: A Study of the Midhat Constitution and Parliament.* Baltimore: Johns Hopkins University Press, 1963.

Draper, Theodore. *Castroism: Theory and Practice.* New York: Frederick A. Praeger, Inc., 1965.

————.*Castro's Revolution: Myths and Realities.* New York: Frederick A. Praeger, Inc., 1962.

Dumont, Jean (ed.). *Les Coups d'état.* Paris: Librairie Hachette, 1963.

Eastman, Max. *Marx, Lenin and the Science of Revolution.* London: George Allen & Unwin, Ltd., 1926.

Eckstein, Harry (ed.). *Internal War, Problems and Approaches.* New York: The Free Press, 1964.

————. "On the Etiology of Internal Wars," *History and Theory,* Vol. 4 (1965), pp. 133-163.

Edwards, Lyford P. *The Natural History of Revolution.* Chicago: University of Chicago Press, 1927.

Ellwood, Charles A. "A Psychological Theory of Revolutions," *The American Journal of Sociology,* Vol. 11 (1905-1906), pp. 49-59.

Elton, Godfrey. *The Revolutionary Idea in France, 1789-1871.* New York: Longmans, Green & Co., Inc., 1923.

Fagan, Richard R. "Mass Mobilization in Cuba: The Symbolism of Struggle," *Journal of International Affairs,* Vol. 20 (1966), pp. 254-271.

Faÿ, Bernard. *L'Esprit révolutionnaire en France et aux États-Unis à la fin du XVIIIᵉ siècle.* Paris: Librairie Ancienne Éduard Champion, 1925.

Feierabend, K. Ivo, and Rosalind L. Feierabend. "Aggressive Behaviors Within Polities, 1948-1962: A Cross-National Study," *Journal of Conflict Resolution,* Vol. 10 (1966), pp. 249-271.

Ferguson, J. Halcro. "The Cuban Revolution and Latin America," *International Affairs,* Vol. 37 (1961), pp. 285-292.

Finer, S. E. *The Man on Horseback: The Role of the Military in Politics.* New York: Frederick A. Praeger, Inc., 1962.

Fischer-Galati, Stephen. "The Peasantry as a Revolutionary Force in the Balkans," *Journal of Central European Affairs,* Vol. 23 (1963), pp. 12-22.

Fitzgibbon, Russell H. "Revolutions: Western Hemisphere," *The South Atlantic Quarterly*, Vol. 55 (1956), pp. 263-279.

Fluharty, Vernon Lee. *Dance of the Millions: Military Rule and the Social Revolution in Colombia, 1930-1956*. Pittsburgh: University of Pittsburgh Press, 1957.

Frey, Frederick W. *The Turkish Political Elite*. Cambridge: The M.I.T. Press, 1965.

Friedrich, Carl J. (ed.). *Revolution* (Nomos VIII). New York: Atherton Press, 1966.

Gadalla, Saad M. *Land Reform in Relation to Social Development in Egypt*. Columbia: University of Missouri Press, 1962.

Galula, David. *Counterinsurgency Warfare: Theory and Practice*. New York: Frederick A. Praeger, Inc., 1964.

Garthoff, Raymond L. "Unconventional Warfare in Communist Strategy," *Foreign Affairs*, Vol. 40 (1962), pp. 566-575.

Gerhart, John D. "Africa's New Revolutionaries: Three Profiles," *The Harvard Review*, Vol. 4 (1966), pp. 25-34.

Gershoy, Leo. *The French Revolution and Napoleon*. New York: Appleton-Century-Crofts, 1964.

Gillespie, Joan. *Algeria: Rebellion and Revolution*. New York: Frederick A. Praeger, Inc., 1961.

Giritli, Ismet. "Some Aspects of the New Turkish Constitution," *The Middle East Journal*, Vol. 16 (1962), pp. 1-17.

Glade, William P., and Charles Anderson. *The Political Economy of Mexico*. Madison: University of Wisconsin Press, 1963.

Godechot, Jacques. *France and the Atlantic Revolution of the Eighteenth Century, 1770-1799*, trans. by Herbert H. Rowen. New York: The Free Press, 1965.

Goldenberg, Boris. *The Cuban Revolution and Latin America*. New York: Frederick A. Praeger, Inc., 1965.

Goodspeed, D. J. *The Conspirators: A Study of the Coup d'État*. London: Macmillan & Co., Ltd., 1962.

Gottschalk, Louis. "Causes of Revolution," *The American Journal of Sociology*, Vol. 50 (1944), pp. 1-8.

Greer, Donald. *The Incidence of the Terror During the French Revolution: A Statistical Interpretation*. Cambridge: Harvard University Press, 1935.

Groth, Alexander. *Revolution and Elite Access: Some Hypotheses on Aspects of Political Change*. Davis: Institute of Governmental Affairs, University of California, 1966.

Guevara, Che. *On Guerrilla Warfare*. New York: Frederick A. Praeger, Inc., 1961.

Halpern, Manfred. *The Politics of Social Change in the Middle East and North Africa.* Princeton: Princeton University Press, 1963.

Hamill, Hugh M., Jr. (ed.). *Dictatorship in Spanish America.* New York: Alfred A. Knopf., Inc., 1965.

Hammers, O. J. "Spectre of Communism in the 1840's," *Journal of the History of Ideas,* Vol. 14 (1953), pp. 404-420.

Hampson, Norman. *A Social History of the French Revolution.* London: Routledge & Kegan Paul, Ltd., 1963.

Hansen, Bent, and Marzouk, Girgis A. *Development and Economic Policy in the UAR (Egypt).* Amsterdam: North-Holland Publishing Company, 1965.

Harris, Christina Phelps. *Nationalism and Revolution in Egypt: The Role of the Muslim Brotherhood.* The Hague: Mouton and Co., 1964.

Harris, George S. "The Role of the Military in Turkish Politics," Parts I, II, *The Middle East Journal,* Vol. 19 (1965), pp. 54-66, 169-176.

Harris, Richard. *Independence and After: Revolution in Underdeveloped Countries.* London: Oxford University Press, 1962.

Hatto, Arthur. " 'Revolution': An Enquiry into the Usefulness of an Historical Term," *Mind,* Vol. 58 (1949), pp. 495-517.

Heilbrunn, Otto. *Partisan Warfare.* New York: Frederick A. Praeger, Inc., 1962.

Heyd, Uriel. *Foundations of Turkish Nationalism: The Life and Teachings of Ziya Gökalp.* London: Luzac and Co., Ltd., 1950.

Hill, Christopher. *Intellectual Origins of the English Revolution.* Oxford: The Clarendon Press, 1965.

Hobsbawm, E. J. *The Age of Revolution: 1789-1848.* Cleveland: World Publishing Co., 1962.

————. *Primitive Rebels: Studies in Archaic Forms of Social Movement in the 19th and 20th Centuries.* New York: Frederick A. Praeger, Inc., 1963.

Hoffer, Eric. *The True Believer: Thoughts on the Nature of Mass Movements.* New York: New American Library, 1958.

Hook, Sidney. *The Paradoxes of Freedom.* Berkeley: University of California Press, 1962.

Hoover, Calvin B. "Revolutions and Tyranny," *The Virginia Quarterly Review,* Vol. 36 (1960), pp. 182-194.

Hopper, Rex D. "The Revolutionary Process: A Frame of Reference for the Study of Revolutionary Movements," *Social Forces,* Vol. 28 (1950), pp. 270-279.

Howard, Michael (ed.). *Soldiers and Governments: Nine Studies in Civil-Military Relations.* London: Eyre & Spottiswoode, Ltd., 1957.

Huntington, Samuel P. (ed.). *Changing Patterns of Military Politics.* New York: The Free Press, 1962.

Isaacs, Harold R. *The Tragedy of the Chinese Revolution* (rev. ed.). Stanford: Stanford University Press, 1951.

Issawi, Charles P. *Egypt in Revolution.* London: Oxford University Press, 1963.

Janos, Andrew C. "Unconventional Warfare: Framework and Analysis," *World Politics,* Vol. 15 (1963), pp. 636-646.

Janowitz, Morris. *The Military in the Political Development of New Nations: An Essay in Comparative Analysis.* Chicago: University of Chicago Press, 1964.

Jaszi, Oscar, and John D. Lewis. *Against the Tyrant: The Tradition and Theory of Tyrannicide.* New York: The Free Press, 1957.

Jellinek, Frank. *The Paris Commune of 1871.* London: Victor Gollancz, Ltd., 1937.

Johnson, Chalmers A. *Peasant Nationalism and Communist Power: The Emergence of Revolutionary China.* Stanford: Stanford University Press, 1962.

———. *Revolution and the Social System.* Hoover Institution Studies No. 3. Stanford: Hoover Institution, 1964.

———. *Revolutionary Change.* Boston: Little, Brown & Co., 1966.

Johnson, John J. *The Military and Society in Latin America.* Stanford: Stanford University Press, 1964.

———. *Political Change in Latin America: The Emergence of the Middle Sectors.* Stanford: Stanford University Press, 1958.

Karpat, Kemal H. *Turkey's Politics: The Transition to a Multi-Party System.* Princeton: Princeton University Press, 1959.

Kautsky, John H. (ed.). *Political Change in Underdeveloped Countries: Nationalism and Communism.* New York: John Wiley & Sons, Inc., 1962.

Kazamias, Andreas M. *Education and the Quest for Modernity in Turkey.* Chicago: University of Chicago Press, 1966.

Khadduri, Majid. "The Role of the Military in Middle East Politics," *The American Political Science Review,* Vol. 47 (1953), pp. 511-524.

Kiernan, V. G. *The Revolution of 1854 in Spanish History.* Oxford: The Clarendon Press, 1966.

Kinross, Lord. *Ataturk: A Biography of Mustafa Kemal, Father of Modern Turkey.* New York: William Morrow & Co., Inc., 1965.

Kirchheimer, Otto. "Confining Conditions and Revolutionary Break-throughs," *The American Political Science Review,* Vol. 59 (1965), pp. 964-974.

—————. *Political Justice: The Use of Legal Procedure for Political Ends.* Princeton: Princeton University Press, 1961.

Kirkpatrick, Ivone. *Mussolini: A Study in Power.* New York: Hawthorn Books, Inc., 1964.

Kling, Merle. "Towards a Theory of Power and Political Instability in Latin America," *The Western Political Quarterly*, Vol. 9 (1956), pp. 21-35.

Knollenberg, Bernhard. *Origin of the American Revolution: 1759-1766.* New York: The Macmillan Company, 1960.

Koehan, Lionel. *Russia in Revolution, 1890-1918.* New York: New American Library, 1967.

Koenigsberger, H. G. "Organization of Revolutionary Parties in France and the Netherlands During the Sixteenth Century," *Journal of Modern History*, Vol. 27 (1955), pp. 335-351.

Lacouture, Jean, and Simonne Lacouture. *Egypt in Transition.* London: Methuen & Co., Ltd., 1958.

Lacy, Dan. *The Meaning of the American Revolution.* New York: New American Library, 1966.

Lasswell, Harold D., and Daniel Lerner (ed.). *World Revolutionary Elites: Studies in Coercive Ideological Movements.* Cambridge: The M.I.T. Press, 1965.

Latham, R. C. "English Revolutionary Thought," *History*, N.S., Vol. 30 (1945), pp. 38-59.

Lauterpacht, H. "Revolutionary Activities by Private Persons Against Foreign States," *The American Journal of International Law*, Vol. 22 (1928), pp. 105-130.

LeBon, Gustave. *The Psychology of Revolution.* New York: G. P. Putnam's Sons, 1913.

Lefebvre, Georges. *The French Revolution from Its Origins to 1793*, trans. by Elizabeth M. Evanson. New York: Columbia University Press, 1962.

—————. *The French Revolution: From 1793 to 1799*, trans. by John Hall Stewart and James Friguglietti. New York: Columbia University Press, 1964.

Leflon, Jean. *La Crise révolutionnaire, 1789-1846.* (*Histoire de l'église*, Vol. 20.) Paris: Blond & Gay, 1949.

Lehning, Arthur. "Buonarroti and His International Secret Societies," *International Review of Social History*, Vol. 1 (1956), pp. 112-140.

Lenin, Vladimir Ilich. *State and Revolution.* New York: International Publishers, 1932.

Lewis, Bernard. *The Emergence of Modern Turkey.* New York: Oxford University Press, 1961.

————. "The Impact of the French Revolution on Turkey," *Journal of World History*, Vol. 1 (1953), pp. 105-125.

Lewis, Geoffrey. *Turkey* (3rd ed.). London: Ernest Benn, Ltd., 1965.

Lewis, J. D. (ed.). "Marxism, Revolution, and Democracy: 1848 and 1948," *Journal of Politics*, Vol. 11 (1949), pp. 518-565.

Lofchie, Michael F. *Zanzibar: Background to Revolution*. Princeton: Princeton University Press, 1965.

Loomis, Stanley. *Paris in the Terror, June 1793-July 1794*. Philadelphia: J. B. Lippincott Co., 1964.

Lubasz, Heinz (ed.). *Revolutions in Modern European History*. New York: The Macmillan Company, 1966.

MacGaffey, Wyatt, and Clifford R. Barnett. *Cuba: Its People, Its Society, Its Culture*. New Haven: HRAF Press, 1962.

Madelin, Louis. *La Contrerévolution sous la révolution 1789-1815*. Paris: Librairie Plon, 1935.

Maguire, James Joseph. *The Philosophy of Modern Revolution*. Washington: The Catholic University of America Press, 1943.

Majdalany, Fred. *State of Emergency: The Full Story of Mau Mau*. Boston: Houghton Mifflin Company, 1963.

Malaparte, Curzio. *Coup d'État: The Technique of Revolution*. New York: E. P. Dutton & Co., Inc., 1932.

Mann, F. K. "Fiscal Component of Revolution: An Essay in Fiscal Sociology," *Review of Politics*, Vol. 9 (1947), pp. 331-349.

Mansfield, Peter. *Nasser's Egypt*. Baltimore: Penguin Books, Inc., 1965.

Mao Tse-tung. *On Guerrilla Warfare*. New York: Frederick A. Praeger, Inc., 1961.

Markov, Walter (ed.). *Jakobiner und Sansculotten, Beiträge zur Geschichte der französischen Revolutionregierung, 1793-1794*. Berlin: Rütten und Loening, 1956.

Mason, Henry L. *Mass Demonstrations Against Foreign Regimes: A Study of Five Crises*. New Orleans: Tulane University, 1966.

Mathiez, Albert. *After Robespierre: The Thermidorian Reaction*. New York: Alfred A. Knopf, Inc., 1931.

————. *The French Revolution*. New York: Grosset & Dunlap, Inc., 1964.

Mazour, Anatole G. *The First Russian Revolution, 1825: The Decembrist Movement, Its Origins, Development, and Significance*. Stanford: Stanford University Press, 1961.

McNeely, John H. "Origins of the Zapata Revolt in Morelos," *The Hispanic American Historical Review*, Vol. 46 (1966), pp. 153-169.

Meisel, James H. *Counterrevolution: How Revolutions Die*. New York: Atherton Press, 1966.

226   Bibliography

Merleau-Ponty, M. *Humanisme et terreur: Essai sur le problème communiste.* Paris: Éditions Gallimard, 1947.

Mészáros, János. "On the Eve of a Revolution," *Journal of Central European Affairs,* Vol. 18 (1958), pp. 48-68.

Michelet, Jules. *History of the French Revolution.* University Park: Penn State University Press, 1967.

Miller, John C. *Origins of the American Revolution.* Boston: Little, Brown & Co., 1943

Mitchell, Allan. *Revolution in Bavaria, 1918-1919: The Eisner Regime and the Soviet Republic.* Princeton: Princeton University Press, 1965.

Moore, Barrington, Jr. *Social Origins of Dictatorship and Democracy: Lord and Peasant in the Making of the Modern World.* Boston: Beacon Press, 1966.

———. *Terror and Progress USSR: Some Sources of Change and Stability in the Soviet Dictatorship.* Cambridge: Harvard University Press, 1954.

Moore, Stanley. *Three Tactics: The Background in Marx.* New York: Monthly Review Press, 1963.

Morton, Ward M. *Castro as Charismatic Hero.* Lawrence: Center of Latin American Studies, University of Kansas, 1965.

Myers, Robert C. "Anti-Communist Mob Action: A Case Study," *Public Opinion Quarterly,* Vol. 12 (1948), pp. 57-67.

Namier, L. B. *1848: The Revolution of the Intellectuals.* London: Geoffrey Cumberlege, 1944.

Neumann, Sigmund. "The Structure and Strategy of Revolution: 1848 and 1948," *The Journal of Politics,* Vol. 11 (1949), pp. 532-544.

Nieburg, H. L. "The Threat of Violence and Social Change," *The American Political Science Review,* Vol. 56 (1962), pp. 865-873.

Nollau, Günther. *International Communism and World Revolution: History and Methods.* London: Hollis & Carter, Ltd., 1961.

Nomad, Max. *Apostles of Revolution.* Boston: Little, Brown and Co., 1939.

———. *Aspects of Revolt.* New York: Bookman Associates, 1959.

———. *Dreamers, Dynamiters and Demagogues: Reminiscences.* New York: Waldon Press, Inc., 1964.

———. *Rebels and Renegades.* New York: The Macmillan Company, 1932).

Obinani, F. Chukwuma. "The Roots and Direction of the Nigerian Revolution," *The Harvard Review,* Vol. 4 (1966), pp. 12-24.

O'Brien, Patrick. *The Revolution in Egypt's Economic System.* New York: Oxford University Press, 1966.

O'Connor, James. "On Cuban Political Economy," *Political Science Quarterly,* Vol. 79 (1964), pp. 233-247.

Osanka, Franklin Mark (ed.). *Modern Guerrilla Warfare: Fighting Communist Guerrilla Movements, 1941-1962.* New York: The Free Press, 1962.

Özbudun, Ergun. *The Role of the Military in Recent Turkish Politics.* (Occasional Papers in International Affairs, Number 14.) Cambridge: Center for International Affairs, Harvard University, 1966.

Padgett, L. Vincent. *The Mexican Political System.* Boston: Houghton Mifflin Co., 1966.

Palmer, R. R. *The Age of the Democratic Revolution: A Political History of Europe and America, 1760-1800,* Vol. I, *The Challenge.* Princeton: Princeton University Press, 1959.

———. *The Age of the Democratic Revolution: A Political History of Europe and America, 1760-1800,* Vol. II, *The Struggle.* Princeton: Princeton University Press, 1964.

———. *Twelve Who Ruled: The Committee of Public Safety During the Terror.* Princeton: Princeton University Press, 1941.

———. "World Revolution of the West: 1763-1801," *Political Science Quarterly,* Vol. 69 (1954), pp. 1-14.

Paret, Peter. *French Revolutionary Warfare from Indochina to Algeria.* New York: Frederick A. Praeger, Inc., 1964.

Payne, P. S. Robert. *The Terrorists: The Story of the Forerunners of Stalin.* New York: Funk & Wagnalls, Co., Inc., 1957.

Payne, Stanley G. *Falange: A History of Spanish Fascism.* Stanford: Stanford University Press, 1961.

Pennar, Jaan. "Moscow and Socialism in Egypt," *Problems of Communism,* Vol. 15 (1966), pp. 41-47.

Peretz, Don. "Democracy and the Revolution in Egypt," *The Middle East Journal,* Vol. 13 (1959), pp. 26-40.

Pettee, George Sawyer. *The Process of Revolution.* New York: Harper & Row, Publishers, 1938.

Pierremont, E. (trans.). *Tche-Ka: Matériaux et documents sur la Terreur bolcheviste: Recueilles par le Bureau Central du Parti Socialiste Révolutionnaire Russe.* Paris: J. Povalozky & Cie, 1922.

Pletcher, David M. *Rails, Mines, and Progress: Seven American Promoters in Mexico, 1867-1911.* Ithaca: Cornell University Press, 1958.

Postgate, R. W. *Revolution from 1789 to 1906.* London: Grant Richards, Ltd., 1920.

Pye, Lucian W. *Guerrilla Communism in Malaya: Its Social and Political Meaning.* Princeton: Princeton University Press, 1956.

Qubain, Fahim I. *Crisis in Lebanon.* Washington: The Middle East Institute, 1961.

Quintana, Segundo V. Linares. "The Etiology of Revolutions in Latin America," *The Western Political Quarterly*, Vol. 4 (1951), pp. 254-267.

Quirk, Robert E. *An Affair of Honor: Woodrow Wilson and the Occupation of Veracruz*. New York: McGraw-Hill Book Company, 1964.

————. *The Mexican Revolution, 1914-1915: The Convention of Aguascalientes*. Bloomington: Indiana University Press, 1960.

Radkey, Oliver Henry. *The Sickle Under the Hammer: The Russian Socialist Revolutionaries in the Early Months of Soviet Rule*. New York: Columbia University Press, 1963.

Ramsaur, Ernest Edmondson, Jr. *The Young Turks: Prelude to the Revolution of 1908*. Princeton: Princeton University Press, 1957.

Reich, Jerome R. *Leisler's Rebellion: A Study of Democracy in New York, 1664-1720*. Chicago: University of Chicago Press, 1953.

Resnick, Daniel P. *The White Terror and the Political Reaction after Waterloo*. Cambridge: Harvard University Press, 1966.

Riezler, Kurt. "On the Psychology of the Modern Revolution," *Social Research*, Vol. 10 (1943), pp. 320-336.

Ristic, Dragisa N. *Yugoslavia's Revolution of 1941*. University Park: Penn State University Press, 1966.

Robertson, Priscilla. *Revolutions of 1848: A Social History*. New York: Harper & Row, Publishers, 1960.

Robinson, Richard D. *The First Turkish Republic: A Case Study in National Development*. Cambridge: Harvard University Press, 1963.

Rose, R. B. *The Enragés: Socialists of the French Revolution?* New York: Cambridge University Press, 1965.

Rosenau, James N. (ed.). *International Aspects of Civil Strife*. Princeton: Princeton University Press, 1964.

Rosenstock-Huessy, Eugen. *Out of Revolution: Autobiography of Western Man*. New York:' William Morrow & Co., Inc., 1938.

Ross, Stanley R. *Francisco I. Madero, Apostle of Democracy*. New York: Columbia University Press, 1955.

Rothschild, Joseph. *Pilsudski's Coup d'État*. New York: Columbia University Press, 1966.

Roucek, Joseph S. "Sociological Elements of a Theory of Terror and Violence," *The American Journal of Economics and Sociology*, Vol. 21 (1962), pp. 165-172.

Rudé, George. *The Crowd in the French Revolution*. Oxford: The Clarendon Press, 1959.

————. *The Crowd in History; A Study in Popular Disturbances in France and England, 1730-1848*. New York: John Wiley & Sons, Inc., c. 1964.

Rue, John E. *Mao Tse-tung in Opposition, 1927-1935.* Stanford: Stanford University Press, 1966.

Russett, Bruce M. "Inequality and Instability: The Relation of Land Tenure to Politics," *World Politics,* Vol. 16 (1964), pp. 442-454.

Safran, Nadav. *Egypt in Search of Political Community: An Analysis of the Intellectual and Political Evolution of Egypt, 1804-1952.* Cambridge: Harvard University Press, 1961.

Sanders, Ralph. "Mass Support and Communist Insurrection," *Orbis,* Vol. 9 (1965), pp. 214-231.

Scalapino, Robert A. (ed.). *The Communist Revolution in Asia: Tactics, Goals, and Achievements.* Englewood Cliffs, N.J.: Prentice-Hall, Inc., 1965.

Schwarz, Solomon M. *The Russian Revolution of 1905: The Workers' Movement and the Formation of Bolshevism and Menshevism.* University Park: Penn State University Press, 1967.

Scott, Robert E. *Mexican Government in Transition.* Urbana: University of Illinois Press, 1959.

Seers, E. Dudley (ed.). *Cuba: The Economic and Social Revolution.* Chapel Hill: University of North Carolina Press, 1964.

Selznick, Philip. *The Organizational Weapon: A Study of Bolshevik Strategy and Tactics.* New York: The Free Press, 1960.

Seton-Watson, H. "Twentieth Century Revolutions," *Political Quarterly,* Vol. 22 (1951), pp. 251-265.

Sharabi, Hisham B. *Nationalism and Revolution in the Arab World.* Princeton: D. Van Nostrand Co., Inc., 1966.

Sharp, Gene. "The Meanings of Non-Violence: A Typology (revised)," *The Journal of Conflict Resolution,* Vol. 3 (1959), pp. 41-66.

Sigmund, Paul E., Jr. (ed.). *The Ideologies of the Developing Nations.* New York: Frederick A. Praeger, Inc., 1963.

Simpson, Dwight J. "Development as a Process: The Menderes Phase in Turkey," *The Middle East Journal,* Vol. 19 (1965), pp. 141-152.

Smelser, Neil J. *Theory of Collective Behavior.* New York: The Free Press, 1963.

Smith, Elaine Diana. *Turkey: Origins of the Kemalist Movement and the Government of the Grand National Assembly, 1919-1923.* Washington: Privately printed, 1959.

Smith, Robert F. *The United States and Cuba: Business and Diplomacy, 1917-1960.* New York: Bookman Associates, 1961.

Sorel, Georges. *Reflections on Violence.* New York: The Free Press, 1950.

Stokes, William S. "National and Local Violence in Cuban Politics," *The Southwestern Social Science Quarterly*, Vol. 34 (1953), pp. 57-63.

———. "Violence as a Power Factor in Latin-American Politics," *The Western Political Quarterly*, Vol. 5 (1952), pp. 445-468.

Stone, Lawrence. *Social Change and Revolution in England, 1540-1640*. New York: Oxford University Press, 1966.

———. "Theories of Revolution," *World Politics*, Vol. 18 (1966), pp. 159-176.

Suárez, Andrés. *Cuba: Castroism and Communism*. Cambridge: The M.I.T. Press, 1967.

Swarup, Shanti. *A Study of the Chinese Communist Movement*. Oxford: The Clarendon Press, 1966.

Sydenham, M. J. *The French Revolution*. New York: G. P. Putnam's Sons, 1965.

Sydnor, Charles S. *American Revolutionaries in the Making: Political Practice in Washington's Virginia*. New York: The Free Press, 1965.

Szyliowicz, Joseph S. "The Political Dynamics of Rural Turkey," *The Middle East Journal*, Vol. 16 (1962), pp. 430-442.

———. "The Turkish Elections: 1965," *The Middle East Journal*, Vol. 20 (1966), pp. 473-494.

Tannenbaum, Frank. "On Political Stability," *Political Science Quarterly*, Vol. 75 (1960), pp. 161-180.

Tanter, Raymond, and Manus Midlarsky. "A Theory of Revolution," *The Journal of Conflict Resolution*, Vol. 11 (1967), pp. 264-280.

Thomas, Hugh. *The Spanish Civil War*. New York: Harper & Row, Publishers, 1961.

———. "Middle-Class Politics and the Cuban Revolution," in Claudio Vélez (ed.). *The Politics of Conformity in Latin America*. London: Oxford University Press, 1967, pp. 249-277.

Thompson, J. M. *Robespierre and the French Revolution*. London: English Universities Press, Ltd., 1952.

Tilly, Charles. *The Vendée*. Cambridge: Harvard University Press, 1964.

Timashef, Nicholas S. *War and Revolution*. New York: Sheed & Ward, 1965.

Tischendorf, Alfred. "The Assassination of Chief Executives in Latin America," *The South Atlantic Quarterly*, Vol. 60 (1961), pp. 80-88.

Tocqueville, Alexis de. *The Old Régime and the French Revolution*. Garden City: Doubleday & Company, Inc., 1955.

Trotsky, Leon. *The History of the Russian Revolution*. 3 vols. New York: Simon and Schuster, Inc., 1932.

Ulam, Adam B. *The Bolsheviks: The Intellectual and Political History of the Triumph of Communism in Russia*. New York: The Macmillan Company, 1965.

Ulman, A. Haluk, and Frank Tachan. "Turkish Politics: The Attempt to Reconcile Rapid Modernization with Democracy," *The Middle East Journal*, Vol. 19 (1965), pp. 153-168.

Vagts, Alfred. *A History of Militarism: Civilian and Military* (rev. ed.). New York: Meridian Books, Inc., 1959.

Vali, Ferenc A. *Rift and Revolt in Hungary: Nationalism versus Communism*. Cambridge: Harvard University Press, 1961.

Van Duzer, Charles Hunter. *Contribution of the Ideologues to French Revolutionary Thought*. Baltimore: Johns Hopkins University Press, 1935.

Vatikiotis, P. J. "Dilemmas of Political Leadership in the Arab Middle East: The Case of the U.A.R.," *International Affairs*, Vol. 37 (1961), pp. 189-202.

———. "Egypt 1966: The Assessment of a Revolution. An Interpretive Essay," *The World Today*, Vol. 22 (1966), pp. 242-251.

———. *The Egyptian Army in Politics: Pattern for New Nations?* Bloomington: Indiana University Press, 1961.

Venturi, Franco. *Roots of Revolution*. New York: Grosset & Dunlap, Inc., 1966.

Verba, Sydney, and Gabriel A. Almond. "National Revolutions and Political Commitment," [Mexico] in Harry Eckstein (ed.), *Internal War: Problems and Approaches*. New York: The Free Press, 1964.

Voegelin, Eric. "The Formation of the Marxian Revolutionary Idea," *The Review of Politics*, Vol. 12 (1950), pp. 275-302.

"Voices of Revolution," *The Harvard Review*, Vol. 4 (1966), pp. 115-131.

Vucinich, Wayne S. "Marxian Interpretations of the First Serbian Revolution," *Journal of Central European Affairs*, Vol. 21 (1961), pp. 3-14.

Wada, George, and James C. Davies. "Riots and Rioters," *The Western Political Quarterly*, Vol. 10 (1957), pp. 864-874.

Walter, E. V. "Power and Violence," *The American Political Science Review*, Vol. 58 (1964), pp. 350-360.

Walzer, Michael. "Revolutionary Ideology: The Case of the Marian Exiles," *The American Political Science Review*, Vol. 57 (1963), pp. 643-654.

Ward, Robert E., and Dankwart A. Rustow (eds.). *Political Modernization in Japan and Turkey*. Princeton: Princeton University Press, 1964.

Weiker, Walter F. *The Turkish Revolution: 1960-1961; Aspects of Military Politics*. Washington: The Brookings Institution, 1963.

Weiner, Peter H. "Guatemala: The Aborted Revolution," *The Harvard Review*, Vol. 4 (1966), pp. 35-48.

Wheelock, Keith. *Nasser's New Egypt: A Critical Analysis.* New York: Frederick A. Praeger, Inc., 1960.

White, Theodore H. "The Battle of Athens, Tennessee," *Harper's Magazine,* Vol. 194 (1947), pp. 54-61.

Wildman, Allan K. *The Making of a Workers' Revolution.* University Park: Penn State University Press, 1967.

Wilkerson, Loree. *Fidel Castro's Political Programs from Reformism to Marxism-Leninism.* Gainesville: University of Florida Press, 1965.

Willer, David, and George K. Zollschan. "Prolegomena to a Theory of Revolutions," in George K. Zollschan and Walter Hirsch (eds.), *Explorations in Social Change.* Boston: Houghton Mifflin Company, 1964, pp. 125-151.

Wittfogel, Karl A. "The Marxist View of Russian Society and Revolution," *World Politics,* Vol. 12 (1960), pp. 487-508.

Wolfe, Bertram D. " 'War Is the Womb of Revolution': Lenin 'Consults' Hegel," *The Antioch Review,* Vol. 16 (1956), pp. 190-197.

Wolpert, J. F. "Myth of Revolution," *Ethics,* Vol. 58 (1948), pp. 245-255.

Woodcock, George. *Anarchism: A History of Libertarian Ideas and Movements.* London: Penguin Books, Ltd., 1963.

Wright, Quincy. "Subversive Intervention," *The American Journal of International Law,* Vol. 54 (1960), pp. 521-535.

Wriston, Henry M. "The Age of Revolution," *Foreign Affairs,* Vol. 39 (1961), pp. 533-548.

Yoder, Dale. "Current Definitions of Revolution," *The American Journal of Sociology,* Vol. 32 (1926), pp. 433-441.

Zayid, Mahmud Y. *Egypt's Struggle for Independence.* Beirut: Khayats, 1965.

Zinner, Paul E. *Revolution in Hungary.* New York: Columbia University Press, 1962.

Index

Terror (*Cont.*)
in French Revolution, 15, 210
in Mexican politics, 116-18
in Mexican Revolution, 210
in Russian Revolution (1917), 15, 210
Tewfik Pasha, 161
Third Republic (France), 13, 92
Thomas, David J., 111n.
Thomas, Hugh, 196n.
Thompson, Leonard M., 70n.
Thornton, Thomas P., 30n., 57n.
Tilly, Charles, 87n., 90n.
Tito, 181
Tkachev, P. N., 102
Tojo, Gen. Hideki, 30
Toledano, Lombardo, 115
Toqueville, Alexis de, 41, 45
Touré, Ahmed Sékou, 180
Treason trials, and revolutions, 63
Trotsky, Leon, 15, 49, 68, 82, 88, 102, 149
True Believer, The (Hoffer), 84
Trujillo Molina, Rafael Leonidas, 34
Tshombe, Moise, 72
Tucker, Robert C., 105
Tukhachevskii, Marshal M. N., 16
Tunisia, 214
Turkey, 53, 206, 208, 209, 211
destruction of Caliphate, 142
Kemalist Revolution, 141-44
populism in, 153
revolutionary tradition in, 140-41
revolutionism in, 153
statism in, 153
violence in, 139-40
in World War II, 144
Turkish coup (1960), 22, 29, 144-49, 153
Turkish revolt (1875-1876), 13
Turkish Revolution (1919-1923), 13, 137-56, 206-10
elite role in, 151-52
followers in, 149-52
ideology of, 152-54
impact of, 154-55
leadership of, 143, 149-52
Turks, 139
26th of July Movement (Cuba), 191, 197
Two Treatises of Government (Locke), 10

U

Ulam, Adam B., 35n., 94
U.S.S.R. (*see* Soviet Union)
United Arab Republic (UAR), 174, 179, 180
United Party of the Cuban Socialist Revolution, 191
United States, 42, 70, 81
and Caribbean countries, 39
and Cuba, 184, 187, 193, 194, 201
and Mexican Revolution, 132-33
nonviolence in, 33
U Nu, 47
Uriburu, Gen. José Félix, 60, 78
Urrutia, Manuel, 190, 191
Uruguay, 214

V

Vatikiotis, P. J., 175
Véliz, Claudio, 196n.
Vendée Rebellion, 8, 90
Venezuela, 22n., 214
Venturi, Franco, 102
Vietnam, 57, 62, 69, 104, 106
Vieux Cordelier, Le, 100
Villa, Pancho, 89, 126-29, 133
Villalobos R., Sergio, 87n.
Violence, 3, 19-35
and armed forces, 25-30
as aspect of revolution, 19-22, 56-57
in Cuban politics, 183-86
in Egypt, 160-62
in Mexican politics, 116-18
in Turkey, 139-40
Voltaire, 10

W

Wada, George, 94n.
Wafd Party (Egypt), 161, 163, 165, 166, 169
Ward, Robert E., 148n., 150n.
Washington, George, 79
Weiker, Walter F., 147n., 148
Western Europe, 81
Whitaker, Arthur P., 45n., 57n., 90n.
Wiedner, Donald L., 12n.
Wilkerson, Loree, 199n.
Wilson, Woodrow, 122-23, 133
Wolfe, Bertram D., 106n.